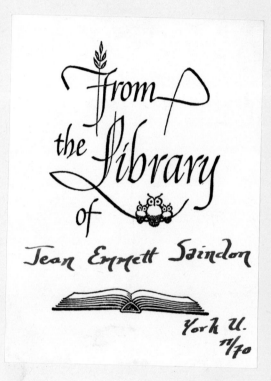

AN ESSAY ON
METAPHYSICS

Oxford University Press, Ely House, London W. 1

GLASGOW NEW YORK TORONTO MELBOURNE WELLINGTON
CAPE TOWN SALISBURY IBADAN NAIROBI LUSAKA ADDIS ABABA
BOMBAY CALCUTTA MADRAS KARACHI LAHORE DACCA
KUALA LUMPUR SINGAPORE HONG KONG TOKYO

AN ESSAY ON
METAPHYSICS

BY

R. G. COLLINGWOOD

OXFORD
AT THE CLARENDON PRESS

FIRST EDITION 1940
REPRINTED LITHOGRAPHICALLY IN GREAT BRITAIN
AT THE UNIVERSITY PRESS, OXFORD
FROM SHEETS OF THE FIRST EDITION
1948, 1957, 1962, 1966, 1969

GENIO

SANCTANDRENSIVM

QVI · HAEC · SCRIPSIT

INTER · EOSDEM · ADLECTVS

V   ❦   S

PREFACE

THIS is not so much a book of metaphysics as a book about metaphysics. What I have chiefly tried to do in it is neither to expound my own metaphysical ideas, nor to criticize the metaphysical ideas of other people; but to explain what metaphysics is, why it is necessary to the well-being and advancement of knowledge, and how it is to be pursued. In the second place I have tried to dispel certain misconceptions about it which have led (and, had they been true, would have led with perfect justice) to the conclusion that metaphysics is a blind alley of thought into which knaves and fools have combined these many centuries past to lure the human intellect to its destruction. In the third place I have offered to the reader's attention a few examples of metaphysics itself, in order to show how metaphysical inquiry will be conducted if the principles laid down in the opening chapters are taken as sound.

These examples occupy nearly half the book; but they are meant to be considered as forming not its main body but a kind of appendix or group of appendices which might be called, as Descartes called a corresponding feature in a book of his own, *specimina philosophandi*. One of them, that on causation, has already been printed in a different shape in the *Proceedings* of the Aristotelian Society for the present year.

There are three debts in connexion with the writing

of this book which I wish to record. First to the University of Oxford for a year's leave of absence on medical grounds from my duties. The duties of a professor may not be very arduous, but they do not encourage a state of mind favourable to the writing of books. Secondly to a wise man of Harley Street (notions about the etiquette of his profession forbid me to name him publicly) who told me that if my leave of absence was to produce the intended result I must use it as an opportunity for writing. Thirdly to Mijnheer C. Koningstein of the Blue Funnel Line, master of the motor vessel *Alcinous*, who rigged me up an open-air study on his own Captain's Bridge where I could work all day without interruption, and thus made it possible for me to write the first draft of the book during a voyage from England to Java under perfect conditions.

R. G. C.

S.S. *Rhesus*, off CAPE ST. VINCENT,
    2 April 1939.

CONTENTS

PART I

METAPHYSICS

I

ARISTOTLE'S METAPHYSICS

IN writing about metaphysics it is only decent, and it is certainly wise, to begin with Aristotle. Metaphysics, as known to all the peoples whose civilization is derived either wholly or to any considerable extent from Christian or Mohammedan sources, is still the science that Aristotle created. Unless we understand its motive in Aristotle's mind and its function in Aristotle's system we are not likely to understand its later history or the obscurities which surround its present position. The first step, therefore, towards clearing these obscurities away is to ask what the name stands for in Aristotle's writings.

The literally correct answer is that it does not stand for anything there, because it does not occur there. It is not Aristotle's name for an Aristotelian science. The word 'metaphysics'[1] represents the Greek phrase τὰ μετὰ τὰ φυσικά, 'the [books] next

---

[1] 'Physics', 'metaphysics', 'ethics', 'politics', and 'economics' are plural in English because they are names of Aristotelian treatises, and a treatise which will go into one modern volume had to be spread over several Greek volumes. But because each of these represents only a single science, these plural substantives govern singular verbs: 'physics is . . .' not 'physics are . . .' We say 'logic', not 'logics', because there is no Aristotelian treatise τὰ λογικά. There is, however, a group of works collectively called τὰ ἀναλυτικά, and from this we have in English 'analytics'. Substantives like 'metaphysic', 'ethic', 'analytic', are solecisms, due to pedantic imitation or ignorant translation of forms which are correct in other languages.

after the *Physics*'; and this phrase was used not by Aristotle himself but by his ancient editors as a title for a certain group of treatises which they placed in that position in the *corpus* of the master's works. As to what those treatises contain, the phrase is entirely non-committal. In its first and most proper sense, therefore, as a title borne by one of Aristotle's works, 'metaphysics' is not the name of a science. It is the name of a book. It corresponds in modern usage not with such titles as *Plane Trigonometry* or *The Origin of Species*, but with such titles as *Collected Works, vol. viii.*

For us, no doubt, the word is no longer merely the name of a book by Aristotle. It is the name of a science. The word 'science', in its original sense, which is still its proper sense not in the English language alone but in the international language of European civilization, means a body of systematic or orderly thinking about a determinate subject-matter. This is the sense and the only sense in which I shall use it. There is also a slang sense of the word, un-objectionable (like all slang) on its lawful occasions, parallel to the slang use of the word 'hall' for a music-hall or the word 'drink' for alcoholic drink, in which it stands for natural science.

Metaphysics is for us the name of a science, and has been for many centuries, because for many centuries it has been found necessary, and still is found necessary, to think in a systematic or orderly fashion about the subjects that Aristotle discussed in the group of treatises collectively known by that name.

Towards the end of the eighteenth century Kant observed that logic had undergone no radical changes since it left the hands of Aristotle. The same observation can be made towards the middle of the twentieth about metaphysics. A great deal of work has been done in metaphysics since Aristotle created it; but this work has never involved a radical reconsideration of the question what metaphysics is. A great deal of grumbling has been done about it, too, and a great many people have declared the whole thing to be a lot of nonsense; but this, too, has never involved a radical reconsideration of what the thing is. On that question Aristotle bequeathed to his successors a pronouncement containing certain obscurities; and from his time to our own these obscurities have never been cleared up. To clear them up is the task of the present essay.

Aristotle calls the science of metaphysics by no less than three different names. Sometimes he calls it First Science, $\pi\rho\dot{\omega}\tau\eta$ $\phi\iota\lambda\sigma\sigma\phi\dot{\iota}\alpha$, $\phi\iota\lambda\sigma\sigma\phi\dot{\iota}\alpha$ being his regular name for science as I have just defined the word. The word 'first' refers to logical priority. First Science is the science whose subject-matter is logically prior to that of every other, the science which is logically presupposed by all other sciences, although in the order of study it comes last. Sometimes he calls it Wisdom, $\sigma\sigma\phi\dot{\iota}\alpha$, with the implication that this is the thing for which $\phi\iota\lambda\sigma\sigma\phi\dot{\iota}\alpha$, science, is the search; this again implying that in addition to their immediate function of studying each its own peculiar subject-matter the sciences have a further function as

leading to a goal outside themselves, namely the discovery of what they logically presuppose. Sometimes
he calls it Theology, θεολογική, or the science which
expounds the nature of God.

By lavishing three different names upon the same
science Aristotle has made it possible for any one who
understands his vocabulary to grasp without further
explanation how he conceived that science's nature.
I will try to show what I mean by offering in the rest
of this chapter a paraphrase of the three names I have
quoted.

'The subject-matter of any science is something
abstract or universal. Abstractness or universality is
subject to degrees. Where a generic universal A is
specified into two sub-forms B and C, as number is
specified into odd and even, A will be more abstract,
more universal, than B or C. In such a case A is the
logical ground of B and C; that is, A by its own
nature gives rise to its own subordinate forms, B and
C. If you understand the nature of number you can
see that it follows from this nature that there must
be odd numbers and even numbers, and that any
number must be either odd or even. This is another
way of saying that number is the logical ground of
oddness and evenness.[1]

'Theoretically, there is or might be a science of any
universal. Practically, one science means what it is

---

[1] The fact that according to Aristotle the generic universal A is
the logical ground of its own specific sub-forms, B and C, may be
expressed by calling the unity of A a 'self-differentiating unity'.
We shall meet this phrase again on pp. 212, 219, 220.

convenient to regard as a single subject of study; so for practical reasons we regard geometry as one science and not a number of sciences, viz. trigonometry or the science of the triangle, cyclometry or the science of the circle, and so forth. But theoretically there are these sciences within the body of what we call geometry; and practically it might some day be found convenient to distinguish them.

'Wherever a generic universal A is specified into sub-forms B and C, and wherever B and C are respectively the subject-matters of two sciences, these two sciences have certain principles in common. These principles form the science whose subject-matter is the universal A. Let A be quantity. There are two kinds of quantity, continuous or measurable and discrete or countable. The special science of continuous quantity is called geometry; the special science of discrete quantity is called arithmetic. For the most part geometry and arithmetic run on different lines, each studying problems peculiar to itself. But there are some principles which they agree in recognizing. These principles, because they figure in both sciences, belong to neither; they belong to a general science of quantity as such, or general mathematics.

'This general science of quantity as such will not be studied by the young mathematician until he has found his way about in the special sciences of geometry and arithmetic. From the learner's point of view it comes after them. But from the logical point of view it comes before them. Its subject-matter is the logical ground of theirs. The propositions it affirms are presupposed by the propositions they affirm. Thus corresponding with the A B C pattern among universals we have an A B C pattern among the sciences that study them. The superordinate science A is always logically prior to the subordinate sciences B and C, but in the order of study it is always posterior to them.

'This A B C pattern among universals is not merely a pattern that crystallizes out among universals here and there. It is present in all universals. All such patterns are part of one single pattern. All universals whatever are to be found somewhere in a system which, according as you look at it, may be called a system of classification or a system of division. Every universal is potentially at least the subject-matter of a science. There is potentially, therefore, a system of sciences corresponding with the system of universals. Within this system any one science will be (i) co-ordinate with another or others whose subject-matter is a universal or universals co-ordinate with its own, as geometry is co-ordinate with arithmetic; (ii) subordinate to another whose subject-matter is a universal superordinate to its own and standing to that as logical ground, as geometry is subordinate to general mathematics; (iii) superordinate to others whose subject-matter is universals subordinate to its own and standing to that as logical consequents, as geometry is superordinate to the special geometries of the triangle and the circle.

'I say this will be true of any one science "within" the system, because it would not be true of the terminal sciences on the fringes of the system. The system does not go on for ever. At the top and bottom it stops. At the base of the system of universals there are universals which are *infimae species*, not giving rise to any further sub-species. At its top there are universals which are *summa genera*, not species of any higher genus. Or rather, strictly speaking, there is only one *summum genus*. The ten "categories" recognized by logic are the ten species of the genus being; they are the γένη τῶν ὄντων, the forms into which being is specified. Thus there is only one pyramid of universals, and at its peak the universal of being.

'The system of sciences will have the same shape. At its bottom will be sciences of all the *infimae species*, and these will be sciences not superordinate to any others. At its top will be a single science, the science of being; being in the abstract or being as such, pure being, τὸ ὄν ἧ ὄν. This will be the First Science in the sense that it is logically presupposed by every other science, although from a learner's point of view it is the Last Science, to be approached only when all the others have been to some degree at least mastered.

'As the Last Science it will be the ultimate goal of the scientist's pilgrimage through the realms of knowledge. The person who studies it will be doing what in all his previous work he was preparing himself to do. Hence if any particular science is described as some particular form or phase of or search for a wisdom which within its own limits it never quite achieves, this First and Last Science must be described not as φιλοσοφία but as σοφία, the Wisdom for which every kind of φιλόσοφος is looking.

'Lastly, since every universal is the immediate logical ground of those immediately subordinate to it, and hence indirectly the ground of the universals which are subordinate to those, the first and last universal, pure being, is directly or indirectly the ground of all other universals, and the First and Last Science is therefore the science of that which stands as ultimate logical ground to everything that is studied by any other science. The ordinary name for that which is the logical ground of everything else is God. The most adequate, explicit, and easily intelligible name for the science which in its relation to other sciences is alternatively called First Science or Wisdom, the name which tells us what it is about, is therefore Theology.'

II

NO SCIENCE OF PURE BEING

In the preceding chapter I have set forth what I take to be Aristotle's programme for a science to be called First Science, Wisdom, or Theology, deducing that programme from those three names. This was the science expounded in the book or books which his editors called the *Metaphysics*; the ancestor of all the subsequent sciences, or attempts at a science, or pseudo-sciences, which have gone under the same name.

This programme is the 'pronouncement' to which I referred as containing certain obscurities which have never been cleared up. There are many things in it about which, however obscure they may be, I shall say nothing. I shall confine my comments to the two following propositions, both contained in it, each of which offers what might be called a definition of metaphysics.

1. Metaphysics is the science of pure being.
2. Metaphysics is the science which deals with the presuppositions underlying ordinary science; where by 'ordinary science' I mean such thinking as is 'scientific' in the sense defined in the preceding chapter, and 'ordinary' in the sense that it is not a constituent part of metaphysics.

In this chapter I shall argue that the first of these two propositions cannot be true because a science of pure being is a contradiction in terms. The second proposition I take to be true, and this book as a whole represents my endeavour to explain its meaning.

In order to focus the issue I will ask the reader to join with me in assuming, simply for the sake of the present argument, that Aristotle was right in the following points, some at least of which are in fact disputable.

(i) That all science is of the universal or abstract; in other words, that its procedure is to ignore the differences between this individual thing and that, and attend only to what they have in common.

(ii) That there is potentially at least a science of every universal, that is, of everything which is common to the individual things we call its instances.

(iii) That there are degrees of universality or abstractness, and that these give rise to a hierarchy of universals and a corresponding hierarchy of sciences; so that whenever a generic universal A is specified into sub-forms B and C there will be hierarchical relations between the superordinate science of A and the subordinate sciences of B and C.

(iv) That A is not only the indispensable presupposition of B and C, but their sufficient logical ground, so that the subject-matter of any superordinate science can be rightly described as generating or creating, in a logical sense, those of the sciences subordinate to it.

Even if these assumptions are made it does not

follow that there must be, or even can be, a science of pure being. Aristotle himself seems half to suggest this. At any rate he was aware that when the process of abstraction is pushed home to the limiting case and arrives at the summit of the pyramid, the thought which has effected this new abstraction and might seem, therefore, to stand upon the threshold of a new science, the science of pure being, stands in a situation not quite like the situations out of which ordinary sciences arise. The situation in which it stands is in certain important ways unprecedented and unique, and it is a debatable question how far and in what sense anything that arises out of it ought to be called a science.

I say that Aristotle was aware of this because he uses language, and carefully chosen language, that expresses it. As I have already explained, the systematic thinking that arises out of any other situation in which the abstractive intellect may find itself he calls φιλοσοφία; but the systematic thinking done in this situation he calls not φιλοσοφία but σοφία. If we translate φιλοσοφία 'science', this implies that the science (so called) of pure being is not a science but something different. What is it? The question may seem a verbal one; but it is not really a verbal one. We are not asking by what name we shall call our systematic thought about pure being. We are asking whether there can be such a thing as systematic thought about pure being, or whether the conditions that would make such thought possible are lacking.

There is no science except where two conditions

are fulfilled. There must be orderly or systematic thinking, and there must be a definite subject-matter to think about. In the 'science of pure being', however admirably the first condition is fulfilled, the second cannot be. In the case of every other science there is a definite subject-matter whose peculiarities differentiate it from the subject-matter of every other science. But the science of pure being would have a subject-matter entirely devoid of peculiarities; a subject-matter, therefore, containing nothing to differentiate it from anything else, or from nothing at all.

The universal of pure being represents the limiting case of the abstractive process. Now even if all science is abstractive, it does not follow that science will still be possible when abstraction has been pushed home to the limiting case. Abstraction means taking out. But science investigates not what is taken out but what is left in. To push abstraction to the limiting case is to take out everything; and when everything is taken out there is nothing for science to investigate. You may call this nothing by what name you like—pure being, or God, or anything else—but it remains nothing, and contains no peculiarities for science to examine.

This is why the science of pure being cannot be called a science in the sense in which an ordinary science is so called.

An ordinary science is the science of some definite subject-matter, having special problems of its own that arise out of the special peculiarities of the subject-matter, and special methods of its own that arise out of the special problems; whereas the 'science of pure being' has a subject-matter which is not a some-thing but a nothing, a subject-matter which has no special peculiarities and therefore gives rise to no special problems and no special methods. This is only a roundabout way of saying that there can be no such science. There is not even a quasi-science of pure being: not even a thing which in certain ways resembles an ordinary science and in certain ways differs from it, such as a collection of statements that are not certain but only probable, connected together in ways that are not convincing but only suggestive. There is not even a pseudo-science of pure being: not even a collection of what seem to be statements but are in fact only the record of guesses, intellectual gropings or emotional reactions that take place within us when we confront an object we do not understand.

This is a more than twice-told tale. Everything I have said in this chapter is implied in what Berkeley said when he delivered his famous onslaught upon 'abstract general ideas'. It is all implied in what Hume said when he endorsed Berkeley's attack as 'one of the most valuable discoveries that has been made of late years in the republic of letters'. It is all im-plied in what Kant said when, in criticism of certain erroneous views as to the nature of metaphysics held in his own day, he argued that 'being is not a predi-cate'. It is all implied in what Hegel said when he expanded that phrase of Kant's into the more explicit statement that pure being is the same as nothing.

I quote these precedents not because I wish to impress the reader with the authority of well-known names, but because I wish to remind him that what has been said in this chapter is nothing new, but has been a commonplace for over two hundred years.

III

METAPHYSICS WITHOUT ONTOLOGY

I PROPOSE to call the science of pure being, when I want a one-word name for it, ontology. As there can be no science nor even a quasi-science or pseudo-science of pure being, I shall not use the name ontology to designate any inquiries that have actually been pursued or any conclusions that have actually been propounded. Ontology will be my name for a mistake which people have made, Aristotle first and foremost, about metaphysics. I do not forget that books have been written under the title of ontology, and have contained a great deal that is true and valuable; but what they have contained is metaphysics, and their ontological title either implies a sense of the word ontology different from that which I have defined or else it represents not their contents but a mistake about their contents.

The distinction is important. If a man while pursuing or expounding a science makes a mistake as to its nature or the nature of its subject-matter, it is quite possible that this mistake will infect all his work with a certain amount of error. But there is no reason why the infection should go so deep as to deprive his work of all scientific value. Suppose, for example, a 'savage' believed that all disease was due to witchcraft. He would represent all his investigations into disease as so many investigations into the varieties of black magic, and all his attempts to cure and prevent disease as so many essays in white magic. Assuming that his belief as to the magical origin of disease is a mistaken belief, everything he said and did in the theory and practice of medicine would be consequently infected with error; but it does not follow that his medical theories must be wholly false or his medical practice wholly futile. It is quite possible that beneath the disguise of a witch-doctor he may be concealing the brain of an acute thinker and the hand of a skilful practitioner. Cases of the same general type are to be found everywhere in the history of science. The geocentric system in astronomy, the physiology of the four humours, the chemistry of phlogiston, may have been errors; but if so they were errors in expounding which astronomers and physiologists and chemists contrived to expound a good deal that was true.

Suppose that Aristotle, instead of using the three different names which he actually does use for what we call metaphysics, had used only one; not any one of these, but a name to be translated ontology; and suppose that this one name had been accepted by all his successors down to the present day. It would still not follow that the investigations pursued and the conclusions expounded under the name of ontology by himself or by any of his successors have been scientifically worthless. If anybody says that metaphysics, as the name of a science, means according to those who expound it simply ontology, and that ontology, according to the view put forward in the preceding chapter, is a chimera; and if he goes on to infer that whatever is expounded under the name of metaphysics is erroneous or nonsensical, all he is doing is to demonstrate that he cannot or will not distinguish between what people are actually doing and what they think they are doing. This may be mere stupidity on his part; but it may also, like many sophistical arguments, involve a certain dis-ingenuousness.

He might, for instance, argue thus. 'Metaphysics is the name given to the non-existent science of a non-existent subject-matter. Now I will not deny that a book professing to be a metaphysical treatise may contain valuable truths; but so far as what it contains is true it is not metaphysics, and so far as it is metaphysics it is not true; therefore everything in the book is either irrelevant or untrue, so nothing in it is worth reading.'

This is not a genuine argument: it is a sophistical excuse for refusing to read the book. It is sophistical because it implies that any account which a thinker gives of his own scientific work must, unless he is so bad a thinker as to deserve universal neglect, be both accurate and adequate; so that if some such account is appended to his book in the shape of a title you can tell from the title whether the book is worth reading. But you cannot. From title to contents *non valet consequentia*. The only way to find out whether a book is worth reading is to read it.

However, this case does not arise. Aristotle did not describe his own metaphysical investigations in terms implying that he regarded metaphysics as merely synonymous with ontology. In order to satisfy himself that something is left of Aristotle's project for a science of metaphysics when ontology has been dismissed as a chimera, the reader need not do anything so laborious as trying to find out what Aristotle actually said in the books called metaphysical. From Aristotle's metaphysical programme, as I sketched it in the first chapter, I have extracted two propositions about the nature of metaphysics: that it is the science of pure being, and that it studies presuppositions. I have shown that there cannot be a science, nor even a quasi-science or pseudo-science, of pure being. Perhaps the other formula will prove more rewarding.

IV

ON PRESUPPOSING

WHENEVER anybody states a thought in words, there are a great many more thoughts in his mind than are expressed in his statement. Among these there are some which stand in a peculiar relation to the thought he has stated: they are not merely its context, they are its presuppositions.

I write these words sitting on the deck of a ship. I lift my eyes and see a piece of string—a line, I must call it at sea—stretched more or less horizontally above me. I find myself thinking 'that is a clothes-line', meaning that it was put there to hang washing on. When I decide that it was put there for that purpose I am presupposing that it was put there for some purpose. Only if that presupposition is made does the question arise, what purpose? If that presupposition were not made, if for example I had thought the line came there by accident, that question would not have arisen, and the situation in which I think 'that is a clothes-line' would not have occurred.

The priority affirmed in the word presupposition is logical priority. It is not a priority in time, whether that time belong to the history of the clothes-line or to the history of my thoughts about it. When I say that its being for some purpose is a presupposition of its being for that purpose, I do not mean that first the line was for some purpose, that it first had a kind of general or indeterminate purposiveness, and that then, when it was rigged as a clothes-line, it exchanged this general or indeterminate purposiveness for a particular or determinate one by beginning to serve the purpose of hanging up washing to dry. I am not now asking whether anything like this really happened or not when the line was put up; I am only saying that, even if it did happen, it is not what I was referring to when I used the word 'presupposition'.

Nor did I mean that my thoughts about the clothes-line moved from 'that line is meant for something' to 'that line is meant to hang washing on'. They might have moved in that way, and if I had been thinking about the line in an orderly or scientific manner I should have seen to it that they did move in that way; but as a matter of fact they did not. The thought 'that is a clothes-line' came plump into my mind, so far as I am aware, all at once and unheralded. Only by a kind of analysis, when I reflect upon it, do I · come to see that this was a presupposition I was making, however little I was aware of it at the time.

Here lies the difference between the desultory and casual thinking of our unscientific consciousness and the orderly and systematic thinking we call science. In unscientific thinking our thoughts are coagulated into knots and tangles; we fish up a thought out of our minds like an anchor foul of its own cable, hanging upside-down and draped in seaweed with shell-fish sticking to it, and dump the whole thing on deck quite pleased with ourselves for having got it up at all. Thinking scientifically means disentangling all this mess, and reducing a knot of thoughts in which everything sticks together anyhow to a system or series of thoughts in which thinking the thoughts is at the same time thinking the connexions between them.

Logicians have paid a great deal of attention to some kinds of connexion between thoughts, but to other kinds not so much. The theory of presupposition they have tended to neglect; and this is perhaps why the theory of metaphysics, which depends on it, has been allowed to remain in an unsatisfactory condition. I will try to state so much of this theory as seems necessary for my present purpose. For the sake of reference later on, I will state it in a formal manner, in numbered propositions, with definitions of such terms as are used in senses they do not bear in ordinary English usage, or of terms whose meaning in ordinary usage depends on the propositions I am expounding. In expounding these propositions I shall not be trying to convince the reader of anything, but only to remind him of what he already knows perfectly well.

PROP. 1. *Every statement that anybody ever makes is made in answer to a question.*

When I speak of statements I do not mean only statements made out loud to somebody else; I include statements made by somebody to himself in the course of solitary thinking. Similarly when I speak of questions I do not mean only questions asked him by somebody else; I include questions asked him by himself.

The reader's familiarity with the truth expressed

in this proposition is proportional to his familiarity with the experience of thinking scientifically. In proportion as a man is thinking scientifically when he makes a statement, he knows that his statement is the answer to a question and knows what that question is. In proportion as he is thinking unscientifically he does not know these things. In our least scientific moments we hardly know that the thoughts we fish up out of our minds are answers to questions at all, let alone what questions these are. It is only by analysing the thought which I expressed by saying 'this is a clothes-line' that I realize it to have been an answer to the question 'what is that thing for?' and come to see that I must have been asking myself that question although at the time I did not know I was asking it.

Note. A question is logically prior to its own answer. When thinking is scientifically ordered, this logical priority is accompanied by a temporal priority: one formulates the question first, and only when it is formulated begins trying to answer it. This is a special kind of temporal priority, in which the event or activity that is prior does not stop when that which is posterior begins. The act of asking the question begins and takes a definite shape as the asking of a determinate question before the act of answering it begins; but it continues for the whole duration of this latter. Unless the person who answered a question were still going on asking it while he formulated the answer, he would have 'lost interest in the subject', and the 'answer' would not have been an answer at all. It would have been a meaningless form of words. By being answered a question does not cease to be a question. It only ceases to be an unanswered question.

DEF. 1. *Let that which is stated (i.e. that which can be true or false) be called a proposition, and let stating it be called propounding it.*

Note. This is an arbitrary use of the words. In English usage a question or supposition is, equally with a statement, said to be 'propounded', and the word 'proposition' is not exclusively used for that which is stated. I adopt it here, warning the reader that it is jargon, because it is customary among logicians.

PROP. 2. *Every question involves a presupposition.*

It may be doubted whether any question that was ever asked involved one presupposition and no more. Ordinarily a question involves large numbers of them. But a distinction should be made between what a question involves directly and what it involves indirectly. Directly or immediately, any given question involves one presupposition and only one, namely that from which it directly and immediately 'arises' (see Def. 2). This immediate presupposition, however, has in turn other presuppositions, which are thus indirectly presupposed by the original question.

Unless this immediate presupposition were made, the question to which it is logically immediately prior could not be logically asked. Verbally, no doubt, it might be asked. There is no verbal impossibility in the way of asking a man whom you suppose to be an indulgent husband whether he has stopped beating his wife. But there is a logical impossibility; for that question arises from the presupposition that he has been in the habit of beating her. If he is not supposed to have been in that habit, the question whether he has stopped 'does not arise'.

DEF. 2. *To say that a question 'does not arise' is the ordinary English way of saying that it involves a presupposition which is not in fact being made.*

A question that 'does not arise' is thus a nonsense question: not intrinsically nonsensical, but nonsensical in relation to its context, and specifically to its presuppositions. A person who asks another a question which 'does not arise' is talking nonsense and inviting the other to talk nonsense in the same vein.

As one can ask questions without knowing it, and *a fortiori* without knowing what questions one is asking, so one can make presuppositions without knowing it, and *a fortiori* without knowing what presuppositions one is making. When I ask 'What is that thing for?' I need not be aware that I am presupposing that it is 'for' something. It is only in proportion as I am thinking scientifically that I take trouble to make myself aware of this. For example, when I am trying to decipher a worn and damaged inscription I know very well that before I begin answering the question 'What does that mark mean?' I must first assure myself that the mark is not accidental but is part of the inscription; that is to say, I must first answer the question 'Does it mean anything?' An affirmative answer, i.e. the statement 'That mark means something', causes the question to arise, 'What does it mean?'

DEF. 3. *The fact that something causes a certain question to arise I call the 'logical efficacy' of that thing.*

The question 'What does that mark mean?' would equally have been caused to arise if I had not stated but only 'assumed' or 'supposed for the sake of argument' that it means something; and this is what, like any other epigraphist, I do when I find myself unable to give a definite answer to the question whether a certain mark is part of the inscription or not. The logical efficacy of the supposition that the mark means something is identical with the logical efficacy of the proposition that it means something.

DEF. 4. *To assume is to suppose by an act of free choice.*

A person who 'makes an assumption' is making a supposition about which he is aware that he might if he chose make not that but another. All assumptions are suppositions, but all suppositions are not assumptions; for some are made altogether unawares, and others, though the persons who make them may be conscious of making them, are made without any consciousness of the possibility, if it is a possibility, that others might have been made instead. When correctly used, the word 'assumption' is always used with this implication of free choice, as when it is said 'let us assume $x = 10$'. Sometimes it is in correctly used of malice prepense, by way of an insult; as when a man says to another with whom he is arguing, 'you are assuming that no one will work except for payment', where the point is that no one but a fool would make that assumption, though it is a supposition that might easily be made unawares. Similarly a man who wishes to be insulting may ask 'What do you mean by treading on my toe?' knowing perfectly well that the treader meant nothing by it, because he did not do it on purpose.

PROP. 3. *The logical efficacy of a supposition does not depend upon the truth of what is supposed, or even on its being thought true, but only on its being supposed.*

The point has already been made clear in discussing the previous proposition. It is a matter of common knowledge in the conduct of scientific thinking; where it is possible and often profitable to argue from suppositions which we know to be false, or which we believe to be false, or concerning which we have neither knowledge nor belief as to whether they are false or true. These doubts or negations in no way affect the validity of the argument.

The point is no less familiar in the conduct of practical affairs than it is in the conduct of scientific thinking. A man (or at any rate an intelligent man) does not regard himself as insulted if some one who has paid him a sum of money asks him for a receipt, or if the family of a lady whom he is about to marry proposes that a marriage settlement should be drawn up. He knows that the request or proposal is based on the assumption that he is capable, or will one day become capable, of acting dishonourably; but though he knows people assume this he does not necessarily think they believe it. He finds no difficulty in distinguishing between their supposing him a rascal and their believing him one, and he does not regard the former as evidence of the latter.

PROP. 4. *A presupposition is either relative or absolute.*

In this context the word 'presupposition' refers not to the act of presupposing but to that which is presupposed.

DEF. 5. *By a relative presupposition I mean one which stands relatively to one question as its presupposition and relatively to another question as its answer.*

Thus, if I do a piece of surveying in the course of which I take some hundreds of measurements with my old 66-foot tape, every time I ask any question in the form 'What is the distance between these two points?' I presuppose that the answer as given by a reading on my tape will be the right answer: that is, I presuppose that my tape is within a certain percentage of the length which it professes to be. But this is only a relative presupposition. A tape by a reputable maker is not likely to have been made grossly inaccurate in the first instance; but it is quite likely to have stretched during years of service in all weathers; and a sensible man will check it from time to time against something not liable to that accident, for example a surveyor's chain. The accuracy of the tape, which while I am using it is a presupposition of the questions I ask, is one of the two possible answers, the affirmative answer, to the question I ask while I am thus checking it.

A man may use a measuring-tape without its ever occurring to him that the question of its accuracy might be raised. In that case his assumption of its accuracy remains unquestioned, and one might suppose that this fact removed it from the sphere of relative presuppositions as above defined. But this would be a mistake. That a certain conclusion follows from certain premisses is not disproved by the fact that some one who states the premisses fails to see that the conclusion follows. Similarly, that certain presuppositions are questionable is not disproved by the fact that some one who makes them fails to see that they are questionable. The business of logical inquiries, like that on which we are now engaged, is to study high-grade or scientific thinking: their conclusions are not impaired by the fact that low-grade or unscientific thinking also exists.

To question a presupposition is to demand that it should be 'verified'; that is, to demand that a question should be asked to which the affirmative answer would be that presupposition itself, now in the form of a proposition. To verify the presupposition that my measuring-tape is accurate is to ask a question admitting of the alternative answers 'the tape is accurate', 'the tape is not accurate'. Hence to speak of verifying a presupposition involves supposing that it is a relative presupposition.

Def. 6. *An absolute presupposition is one which stands, relatively to all questions to which it is related, as a presupposition, never as an answer.*

Thus if you were talking to a pathologist about a certain disease and asked him 'What is the cause of the event E which you say sometimes happens in this disease?' he will reply 'The cause of E is C'; and if he were in a communicative mood he might go on to say 'That was established by So-and-so, in a piece of research that is now regarded as classical.' You might go on to ask: 'I suppose before So-and-so found out what the cause of E was, he was quite sure it had a cause?' The answer would be 'Quite sure, of course.' If you now say 'Why?' he will probably answer 'Because everything that happens has a cause.' If you are importunate enough to ask 'But how do you know that everything that happens has a cause?' he will probably blow up right in your face, because you have put your finger on one of his absolute presuppositions, and people are apt to be ticklish in their absolute presuppositions. But if he keeps his temper and gives you a civil and candid answer, it will be to the following effect. 'That is a thing we take for granted in my job. We don't question it. We don't try to verify it. It isn't a thing anybody has discovered, like microbes or the circulation of the blood. It is a thing we just take for granted.'

He is telling you that it is an absolute presupposition of the science he pursues; and I have made him a pathologist because this absolute presupposition about all events having causes, which a hundred years ago was made in every branch of natural science, has now ceased to be made in some branches, but medicine is one of those in which it is still made.

Absolute presuppositions are not verifiable. This does not mean that we should like to verify them but are not able to; it means that the idea of verification is an idea which does not apply to them, because, as I have already said, to speak of verifying a presupposition involves supposing that it is a relative presupposition. If anybody says 'Then they can't be of much use in science', the answer is that their use in science is their logical efficacy, and that the logical efficacy of a supposition does not depend on its being verifiable, because it does not depend on its being true: it depends only on its being supposed (prop. 3).

PROP. 5. *Absolute presuppositions are not propositions.*

This is because they are never answers to questions (def. 6); whereas a proposition (def. 1) is that which is stated, and whatever is stated (prop. 1) is stated in answer to a question. The point I am trying to make clear goes beyond what I have just been saying, viz. that the logical efficacy of an absolute presupposition is independent of its being true: it is that the distinction between truth and falsehood does not apply to absolute presuppositions at all, that distinction being (see def. 1) peculiar to propositions.

Putting the same point differently: absolute presuppositions are never (see def. 1) propounded. I do not mean that they sometimes go unpropounded, like the so-called 'propositions' of the fashionable modern logic, which are called propositions even when nobody in fact propounds them, and would on that account be more accurately called 'proponibles'; I mean that they are never propounded at all. To be propounded is not their business; their business is to be presupposed. The scientist's business is not to propound them but only to presuppose them. The metaphysician's business, as we shall see, is not to propound them but to propound the proposition that this or that one of them is presupposed.

Hence any question involving the presupposition that an absolute presupposition is a proposition, such as the questions 'Is it true?' 'What evidence is there for it?' 'How can it be demonstrated?' 'What right have we to presuppose it if it can't?', is a nonsense question.

Hence, too, it is nonsense to say, as some modern logicians do say, that supposing is one of various 'attitudes' which we can take up towards a proposition, where a proposition means something which can be either true or false. This is merely a device for imposing on unwary readers the dogma, of which more will be said hereafter, that all presuppositions are relative, or that there are no absolute presuppositions.

V

THE SCIENCE OF ABSOLUTE
PRESUPPOSITIONS

In low-grade or unscientific thinking we hardly know that we are making any presuppositions at all. Because of their tangled condition, the thoughts which come up out of the bottom of our minds present a deceptive appearance of 'immediacy'. I find myself thinking 'That is a clothes-line', and if I merely reflect on this thought without analysing it I decide that what has happened is this: I have been confronted with something which in itself, quite apart from what anybody may think about it, just is a clothes-line; and being a clever fellow I have just 'apprehended' that clothes-line, or 'intuited' it, for what it really is, a clothes-line. And if I never think at all except in this quite casual and unscientific way, I shall always be content to believe this is all that knowledge can ever be: the simple 'intuition' or 'apprehension' of things confronting us which absolutely and in themselves just are what we 'intuite' or 'apprehend' them as being.

This theory of knowledge is called 'realism'; and 'realism' is based upon the grandest foundation a philosophy can have, namely human stupidity. Any one, at any moment, without taking the smallest trouble, can put himself in a position where first-hand experience will prove to him that a 'realistic' theory of knowledge is true. All he need do is to let his mind drift until he is thinking in so casual and haphazard a way that he is hardly thinking at all; and at that moment he will find himself automatically doing exactly what the 'realists' tell us that we all do whenever we think.

There would be no objection to 'realism', let me observe in passing, if this were all it professed to be: a study of the ways in which anchors get foul, the twists in their cables and the odds and ends that are found sticking to them, when mariners are negligent and the bottom is bad. All this is very interesting. Moreover, in calm weather and at neap tides an anchor in that condition may actually hold the ship. 'Realists' point triumphantly to cases in which, thinking almost at zero-level of efficiency, we say 'That is a clothes-line', 'What I am looking at is my hand', 'The bookcase is farther away than the table', and are right. The only harm is that people sometimes suppose this 'realism' to be doing over again, and doing it better, what people like Descartes and Kant have done in their so-called theories of knowledge; not realizing that even the best account of unscientific knowledge can never supersede even the worst account of scientific knowledge, and that a whole library of books about foul anchors will not replace one page of Descartes or Kant, who knew well enough that anchors get foul, but cared about making them hang the right way up, so that even in a tideway or a gale the ship would be safe.

To return. In the lowest type of low-grade thinking we are wholly unaware that every thought we find ourselves thinking is the answer to a question. We are wholly unaware that the question arises from a presupposition. This low-grade thinking, therefore, will never give rise to metaphysics; and this is why 'theories of knowledge' which accept instances of low-grade thought as adequate examples of what thought is can never understand why there should be metaphysics, or what metaphysics is about.

If man has succeeded in dominating the natural forces within him and around him, and in giving both to himself and to his environment a unique character, the character of being a self-made inhabitant of a world called civilization which he has made for himself to live in, the original nature both of himself and of his surroundings serving only as the raw material of his craft; if man has done this, it is because in addition to low-grade thinking he is capable of high-grade or scientific thinking.

High-grade thinking means thinking energetically instead of idly: thinking hard instead of allowing your mind to drift.

The higher types of animal organism are higher because instead of being content to function placidly at a low level of intensity they have found out how to store energy against an occasion when it will be needed, and when such occasion arises to meet it by an expenditure of energy that lifts their mechanical effectiveness high above its average level and overwhelms the obstacle as if by a tidal wave.

What the higher animals have learned to do with their bodies is what man has learned to do with his

mind. To call him the only animal that has learned
how to think hard would probably be untrue; but it
is certainly true that he is the only animal who has
learned this lesson so thoroughly as to transform the
whole structure of his life by its means, as the structure of life in the higher animals has been transformed
by their learning how to store chemical energy and
release it at need. Everything that we call specifically
human is due to man's power of thinking hard.

Mere increase of effort, intellectual or any other,
does little to increase its effectiveness unless the in-
creased effort is well directed. Without such direction the additional effort is always in great part, and
sometimes completely, wasted. High-grade thinking,
therefore, depends on two things: increase of mental
effort, and skill in the direction of that effort.

Increase of mental effort brings about not only a
difference of degree in the intensity of thinking but
also a difference of kind in its quality. At the lowest
level of intensity, as we have seen, one is conscious
only of 'intuiting' or 'apprehending' what presents
itself to one's mind. To say that it presents itself to
one's mind is only a way of saying that one thinks
about it without noticeable effort. When one becomes aware of effort, one becomes aware of a mental
hunger that is no longer satisfied by what swims into
one's mouth. One wants what is not there and will
not come of itself. One swims about hunting for it.
This ranging of the mind in search of its prey is called
asking questions. To ask questions, knowing that
you are asking them, is the first stage in high-grade

thinking: the first thing that distinguishes the human mind from the sea-anemone mind of the 'realist' theory of knowledge.

The second stage is not merely to hunt one's prey but to hunt it cunningly. To hunt it at all is to ask questions; to hunt it cunningly is to ask questions with skill, or scientifically.

Here again there are two stages. The first is disentangling, the second is arranging. When a question first comes into one's mind it is generally (I speak for myself, and perhaps I am not here very different from other people) a confused mass of different questions, all of which, because all must be answered before I can catch my dinner, and because I am hungry, I ask at once. But they cannot all be answered at once. Before they can be answered they must be distinguished, and the nest of questions resolved into a list of questions where each item is one question and only one.

The logic-books furnish a well-known example. 'Have you left off beating your wife yet?' is there given as the stock instance of the 'fallacy of many questions', the logical vice of asking what, logically, are many questions in a form of words which, grammatically, has the form of a single question. A skilful thinker, practised in disentangling such knots, will quickly resolve it into four:

1. Have you a wife?
2. Were you ever in the habit of beating her?
3. Do you intend to manage in future without doing so?
4. Have you begun carrying out that intention?

After disentangling comes arranging. The reason why questions have to be arranged is because one of them may be contingent upon a certain answer being given to another. The question whether you ever beat your wife does not arise unless an affirmative answer has been given to the question whether you ever had one. Scientific or 'orderly' thinking, as I pointed out at the beginning of Chapter IV, is orderly in the sense that it deals with things in their logical order, putting what is presupposed before what presupposes it. I have already given an example by not only resolving into four questions the grammatically single question 'Have you left off beating your wife yet?' but arranging these four in their logical order, that is, arranging them so that each arises when, and only when, an affirmative answer has been given to the one next before it.

The power of causing a question to arise I have called logical efficacy; and in Chapter IV, prop. 3, I have said that the logical efficacy of a supposition does not depend upon the truth of what is supposed, or even upon its being thought true, but only on its being supposed. In a case like the present, therefore, the process of thought from question to question does not depend on each question's being answered truly, but only on its being answered: and not upon the questioner's thinking the answers true, but only on his accepting the answers given him, or 'assuming them for the sake of argument'.

This work of disentangling and arranging questions, which in the preceding chapter I have called analysis, may be alternatively described as the work of detecting presuppositions. The question whether a man has left off beating his wife yet presupposes that he has formed the intention of leaving off. That presupposes that he used to beat her. That presupposes that he has one. All these are relative presuppositions: each of them stands now as the presupposition to a question, now as the answer to one. Each is both a presupposition and a proposition.

But there are absolute presuppositions. And no one can call a presupposition relative until he has asked whether it is relative or absolute. Not, that is, if he is thinking scientifically. The question 'What does this presuppose?' itself presupposes an affirmative answer to the question 'Does it presuppose anything?'; and to ask that question is to contemplate the possibility of the thing's being an absolute presupposition, and to claim that you would know it for one if it was one. The analysis which detects absolute presuppositions I call metaphysical analysis; but as regards procedure and the qualifications necessary to carry it out there is no difference whatever between metaphysical analysis and analysis pure and simple as I have been hitherto describing it. In either case the question is being constantly asked, 'Is this presupposition relative or absolute?' and the *modus operandi* is the same, whichever answer is given.

As regards its *modus operandi*, then, all analysis is metaphysical analysis; and, since analysis is what gives its scientific character to science, science and metaphysics are inextricably united, and stand or fall together. The birth of science, in other words the establishment of orderly thinking, is also the birth of metaphysics. As long as either lives the other lives; if either dies the other must die with it.

In saying this I am assuming that metaphysics is the science of absolute presuppositions. I am assuming it because it is what I find in Aristotle, who invented metaphysics; or rather, because it is what I find left in Aristotle's account of what metaphysics is, when something else which I have shown to be nonsensical has been removed. The reader may say, 'Whether you assume it or not is your own affair; it is of no interest to me until you prove it'. But if he says this I do not know, and I doubt whether he himself knows, what he is asking for. The only thing, so far as I can see, which a sensible man would ask for in these terms would be an examination of some admittedly metaphysical problems and discussions, and a demonstration that these are concerned with absolute presuppositions. This I propose to give in Part III of the present essay. If I do not proceed to it at once, the reason is that I prefer, before considering whether it is true that metaphysics is the science of absolute presuppositions, to consider what it means.

People do not need to analyse their thoughts very deeply in order to find out that there are a good many things they take for granted without asking whether they are true; but this expression generally means not that they have decided on consideration that it would be nonsensical to ask whether these things are true, but that they have asked this in a half-hearted way, and have been satisfied with answers that would not have satisfied a resolute and unprejudiced inquirer. In such cases the analysis has not been pushed home with sufficient firmness to settle the question whether the things are being taken relatively for granted or absolutely for granted: whether they are suppositions whose verification is being deferred to a more appropriate occasion or procrastinated out of idleness or faintness of heart, or suppositions which in principle neither admit nor require verification.

It might seem that the question should be an easy one to answer, because presupposing is a thing people do in their minds, and the distinction between presupposing relatively and presupposing absolutely is a distinction between two ways of doing it, so that a man need only be ordinarily intelligent and ordinarily truthful, one might think, to give an accurate answer to the question which of them he is doing.

But things are not quite so simple as that. To begin with, people may have a motive for deceiving themselves and each other. Where certain things which may happen in people's minds are conventionally regarded with disapproval, the lengths to which people in whose minds they actually do happen will go, in order to persuade themselves and others that they do not happen, are most remarkable. In modern Europe absolute presuppositions are unfashionable. The smart thing to do is to deny their existence. Even people who regard this as a silly fashion may very well be so far influenced by it as to weaken at the critical moment when every available ounce of determination is needed in order to decide whether a given presupposition is absolute or relative; and may allow a kind of mass-suggestion to decide them in favour of its being relative.

In the second place candour and veracity of themselves, and even combined with intelligence, can do very little towards answering the question, because the question is not one that can be settled by introspection. Introspection can do no more than bring into the focus of consciousness something of which we are already aware. But in our less scientific moments, when knowledge appears to us in the guise of mere apprehension, intuiting that which simply confronts us, we are not even aware that whatever we state to ourselves or others is stated in answer to a question, still less that every such question rests on presuppositions, and least of all that among these presuppositions some are absolute presuppositions. In this kind of thinking, absolute presuppositions are certainly at work; but they are doing their work in darkness, the light of consciousness never falling on them. It is only by analysis that any one can ever come to know either that he is making any absolute presuppositions at all or what absolute presuppositions he is making.

Such analysis may in certain cases proceed in the following manner. If the inquirer can find a person to experiment upon who is well trained in a certain type of scientific work, intelligent and earnest in his devotion to it, and unaccustomed to metaphysics, let him probe into various presuppositions that his 'subject' has been taught to make in the course of his scientific education, and invite him to justify each or alternatively to abandon it. If the 'inquirer' is skilful and the 'subject' the right kind of man, these invitations will be contemplated with equanimity, and even with interest, so long as relative presuppositions are concerned. But when an absolute presupposition is touched, the invitation will be rejected, even with a certain degree of violence.

The rejection is a symptom that the 'subject', co-operating with the work of analysis, has come to see that the presupposition he is being asked to justify or abandon is an absolute presupposition; and the violence with which it is expressed is a symptom that he feels the importance of this absolute presupposition for the kind of work to which he is devoted. This is what in the preceding chapter I called being 'ticklish in one's absolute presuppositions'; and the reader will see that this ticklishness is a sign of intellectual health combined with a low degree of analytical skill. A man who is ticklish in that way is a man who knows, 'instinctively' as they say, that absolute presuppositions do not need justification. In my own experience I have found that when natural scientists express hatred of 'metaphysics' they are usually expressing this dislike of having their absolute presuppositions touched. I respect it, and admire them for it; though I do not expect scientists who give way to it to rise very high in the scientific world.

This is a precarious method, because the qualifications it demands in the 'subject' are too delicate. As soon as the 'subject' understands what is going on he will lose the ticklishness on which his value depends, because it is conditional on a kind of virginity in the reflective faculties. Perhaps there was a kind of justice in the allegation that Socrates, the great master of this method, 'corrupted the young men', where the word translated 'corrupt' was the same word which, when used of a girl, meant 'seduce'. The only altogether satisfactory method is for the analyst to experiment on himself; because this is the only case in which familiarity with the experiments will make the subject more valuable, instead of less valuable, to the inquirer. But it demands great resolution, and the temptation to cheat is stronger than one would expect.

The purpose of the experiments is to find out what absolute presuppositions are as a matter of fact made on a certain occasion or on occasions of a certain kind. The process, simply *qua* analysis, is identical with the analysis of ordinary science. In either case presuppositions are brought to light, and about each one the question is raised and settled whether it is relative or absolute. But after this the two processes diverge. In ordinary science the relative presuppositions are put into the basket, and later on the question is raised when and how they shall be justified. The absolute presuppositions are thrown back. In metaphysics it is the relative presuppositions that are thrown back, and the absolute presuppositions that are put into the basket; not in order to justify them, because to talk of justifying them is to talk nonsense (Chap. IV, prop. 5); but in order to have them scientifically described.

Aristotle's identification of metaphysics with theology may serve as a reminder that no human being can contemplate these two alternative procedures with quite the same feelings. You may call it superstition or what you will, but hard names make no difference to the fact that there is something a little uncanny about absolute presuppositions. They give people more than a touch of the feeling which Rudolf Otto called numinous terror. This mattered less at a period of history when people had their well-established methods (magic, we call them) of dissipating the terror and enabling themselves to face the things that inspired it. Ours is an age when people pride themselves on having abolished magic and pretend that they have no superstitions. But they have as many as ever. The difference is that they have lost the art, which must always be a magical art, of conquering them. So it is a special characteristic of modern European civilization that metaphysics is habitually frowned upon and the existence of absolute presuppositions denied. This habit is neurotic. It is an attempt to overcome a superstitious dread by denying that there is any cause for it. If this neurosis ever achieves its ostensible object, the eradication of metaphysics from the European mind, the eradication of science and civilization will be accomplished at the same time. If a sufficient number of Europeans want to destroy science and thus accomplish the suicide of civilization, nothing I can do will stop them; but at present, in England, they have not the power to prevent me from warning those who neither share nor suspect their design.

To sum up. Metaphysics is the attempt to find out what absolute presuppositions have been made by this or that person or group of persons, on this or that occasion or group of occasions, in the course of this or that piece of thinking. Arising out of this, it will consider (for example) whether absolute presuppositions are made singly or in groups, and if the latter, how the groups are organized; whether different absolute presuppositions are made by different individuals or races or nations or classes; or on occasions when different things are being thought about; or whether the same have been made *semper*, *ubique*, *ab omnibus*. And so on.

There will also be something which I call pseudo-metaphysics. This will be a kind of thought in which questions are asked about what are in fact absolute presuppositions, but arising from the erroneous belief that they are relative presuppositions, and therefore, in their capacity as propositions, susceptible of truth and falsehood. Pseudo-metaphysics will ask such questions as this, where AP stands for any absolute presupposition: Is AP true? Upon what evidence is AP accepted? How can we demonstrate AP? What right have we to presuppose it if we can't?

Answers to questions like these are neither metaphysical truths nor metaphysical errors. They are nonsense: the kind of nonsense which comes of thinking that (as the logicians say) supposing is one of the attitudes we can take up towards a proposition, so that what is absolutely supposed must be either true or false. That kind of nonsense I call pseudo-metaphysics.

Note to Chapter V.—I have hinted above (p. 45) and said explicitly below (pp. 49 seqq.) that absolute presuppositions change. A friend thinks readers may credit me with the opinion that such changes are merely 'changes of fashion', and asks me to explain what, otherwise, I believe them to be.

A 'change of fashion' is a superficial change, symptomatic perhaps of deeper and more important changes, but not itself deep or important. A man adopts it merely because other men do so, or because advertisers, salesmen, &c., suggest it to him. My friend's formula 'if we like to start new dodges, we may' describes very well the somewhat frivolous type of consciousness with which we adopt or originate these superficial changes. But an absolute presupposition is not a 'dodge', and people who 'start' a new one do not start it because they 'like' to start it. People are not ordinarily aware of their absolute presuppositions (p. 43), and are not, therefore, thus aware of changes in them; such a change, therefore, cannot be a matter of choice. Nor is there anything superficial or frivolous about it. It is the most radical change a man can undergo, and entails the abandonment of all his most firmly established habits and standards for thought and action.

Why, asks my friend, do such changes happen? Briefly, because the absolute presuppositions of any given society, at any given phase of its history, form a structure which is subject to 'strains' (pp. 74, 76) of greater or less intensity, which are 'taken up' (p. 74) in various ways, but never annihilated. If the strains are too great, the structure collapses and is replaced by another, which will be a modification of the old with the destructive strain removed; a modification not consciously devised but created by a process of unconscious thought.

VI

METAPHYSICS AN HISTORICAL SCIENCE

TOWARDS the end of the last chapter I gave some examples of metaphysical questions. The reader may have noticed that they all had in common not only the fact of being about absolute presuppositions, but also the fact of being historical questions: questions as to what absolute presuppositions have been made on certain occasions. This was not an accident. All metaphysical questions are historical questions, and all metaphysical propositions are historical propositions. Every metaphysical question either is simply the question what absolute presuppositions were made on a certain occasion, or is capable of being resolved into a number of such questions together with a further question or further questions arising out of these.

This is the central point of the present essay. I will try therefore to put it, even at the risk of repeating myself, as clearly as I can. For this purpose I will go back to the example of causation, and remind the reader of three familiar facts.

(*a*) In Newtonian physics it is presupposed that some events (in the physical world; a qualification which hereinafter the reader will please understand when required) have causes and others not. Events not due to the operation of causes are supposed to be due to the operation of laws. Thus if a body moves freely along a straight line $p_1, p_2, p_3, p_4 \ldots$ its passing

the point p_3 at a certain time, calculable in advance
from previous observation of its velocity, is an event
which is not according to Newton the effect of any
cause whatever. It is an event which takes place not
owing to a cause, but according to a law. But if it
had changed its direction at p_0, having collided there
with another body, that change of direction would
have been an event taking place owing to the action
of a cause (see Note on p. 57).

(b) In the nineteenth century we find a different
presupposition being made by the general body of
scientists: namely that all events have causes. About
the history and interpretation of this I shall have
more to say in the concluding chapters. Here I will
anticipate only so far as to say that I do not know any
explicit statement of it earlier than Kant; and accordingly I shall refer to the physics based upon it as the
Kantian physics. The peculiarity of Kantian physics
is that it uses the notion of cause and the notion of
law, one might almost say, interchangeably: it regards
all laws of nature as laws according to which causes
in nature operate, and all causes in nature as operating
according to law.

(c) In modern physics the notion of cause has
disappeared. Nothing happens owing to causes;
everything happens according to laws. Cases of
impact, for example, are no longer regarded as cases
in which the Laws of Motion are rendered inopera-
tive by interference with one body on the part of
another; they are regarded as cases of 'free' motion
(that is, motion not interfered with) under peculiar

geometrical conditions, a line of some other kind being substituted for the straight line of Newton's First Law.

It might seem, but wrongly, as I shall try to show, that the metaphysician is here confronted by a rather embarrassing problem. It might seem that there are three schools of thought in physics, Newtonian, Kantian, and Einsteinian, let us call them, which stand committed respectively to the three following metaphysical propositions:

(i) Some events have causes.
(ii) All events have causes.
(iii) No events have causes.

It might seem that these three propositions are so related that one of them must be true and the other two false; and that the metaphysician's duty is to say which of them is true: an important duty, because when we know which of the three propositions is true we shall know which of these three schools of physicists is on the right lines, and we shall know that the others are doomed from the start to a career of illusion and error owing to faults in their metaphysical foundations.

I call it an embarrassing problem for the metaphysician because I assume him to be a conscientious man. If he is an irresponsible and dogmatic person it will not embarrass him at all. He will pronounce loudly and confidently in favour of one alternative, whichever he fancies, expressing the fact that he fancies it by calling it 'self-evident' or the like, and will pour scorn on any one who hesitates to agree with him; and this will give him a good deal of satisfaction. But if he is a conscientious man, who thinks that the right way of dealing with problems is to solve them, the problem will embarrass him because there is no way in which he or for that matter any one else can solve it. This is because it is what at the end of the preceding chapter I called a pseudo-metaphysical problem: a problem in the form 'Is AP true?' What I have now to explain is that the reason why it is not a metaphysical problem is that it is not an historical problem.

The sentences numbered (i), (ii), (iii), above, express absolute presuppositions made respectively in three different schools of physical science. Each is important, and fundamentally important, to the science that makes it, because it determines the entire structure of that science by determining the questions that arise in it, and therefore determining the possible answers. Thus every detail in these respective sciences depends on what absolute presuppositions they respectively make. But this does not mean that it depends on these presuppositions' being thought true, or that the truth of the conclusions arrived at depends on the presuppositions' being in fact true. For the logical efficacy of a supposition does not depend on its being true, nor even on its being thought true, but only on its being supposed (see Chap. IV, prop. 3). It is a mistake, therefore, to fancy that by investigating the truth of their absolute presuppositions a metaphysician could show that one school of science was fundamentally right and another

fundamentally wrong. The 'embarrassing problem'
does not arise.

A reader may reply: 'I see that you have proved
metaphysics to be perfectly useless for the purpose
for which it is generally thought useful, namely assist-
ing the progress of science by showing which presuppositions, and therefore which schools of scientific
thought, are justified in the light of metaphysical
criticism and which are not. But whereas I draw
from this conclusion the inference that metaphysics
is a futile occupation and had better be stopped, you
seem to be inferring that metaphysics is not, for
example, the attempt to decide whether it is true or
false that all events have causes, but an attempt to do
something different. This seems to me perverse.'

There is no need to repeat the grounds upon which
I am assuming metaphysics to be the science of absolute presuppositions, because the point at issue
between myself and the reader I have just quoted
lies in the interpretation we put upon the phrase
'science of absolute presuppositions'. He thinks that
there are two things you can do with absolute presuppositions: you can presuppose them, which is
what the ordinary scientist does with them; or you
can criticize them in order to find out whether they
are true or false, which is what the metaphysician
does with them, though actually it is of no use. I
deny this, because the second thing (the thing which
my reader calls metaphysics and I pseudo-metaphysics) is one which simply cannot be done, whether
usefully or uselessly. To inquire into the truth of a

presupposition is to assume that it is not an absolute presupposition but a relative presupposition. Such a phrase as 'inquiry into the truth of an absolute presupposition' is nonsense (p. 33).

But I agree with my hypothetical reader that there are two things you can do with absolute presuppositions, and I agree that one of them is what the ordinary scientist does, and the other what the metaphysician does. You can presuppose them, which is what the ordinary scientist does; or you can find out what they are, which is what the metaphysician does. When I speak of finding out what they are I do not mean finding out what it is to be an absolute presupposition, which is work for a logician; I mean finding out what absolute presuppositions are in fact made. When I say that this is what metaphysicians do I mean that this is what I find them doing when I read their works from Aristotle onwards. I shall give a few examples in Part III.

Let us return to my three numbered sentences. The business of an ordinary scientist relatively to these three sentences is to presuppose in his scientific work:

(AP i) if he is a Newtonian, that some events have causes;

(AP ii) if he is a Kantian, that all events have causes;

(AP iii) if he is an Einsteinian, that no events have causes.

The business of a metaphysician is to find out:

(M i) that Newtonian scientists presuppose that some events have causes;

(M ii) that Kantian scientists presuppose that all events have causes;

(M iii) that Einsteinian scientists presuppose that no events have causes.

I have marked these last three propositions with an M, by way of indicating that they are metaphysical propositions. These three are true metaphysical propositions; their contradictories would be false metaphysical propositions. It will be clear that the true metaphysical propositions are true historical propositions and the false metaphysical propositions false historical propositions. It is the proper business of a metaphysician to answer the question what absolute presuppositions are or were made by Newtonians, Kantians, Einsteinians, and so forth. These are historical questions.

The historical nature of the metaphysician's inquiries is at once evident when the propositions he makes it his business to state are stated as they are above in the examples (M i), (M ii), (M iii). What makes it evident is that the wording of each statement includes the formula 'so-and-so presupposes (or presupposed) that . . .'. Since the presupposition alleged to be made is an absolute presupposition, and since the question whether it is made is not a personal one but one concerning the peculiarities of a certain phase of scientific thought, the formula would be more accurately rendered: '*in such and such a phase of scientific thought it is (or was) absolutely presupposed that . . .*'. This formula I call the 'metaphysical rubric'.

In a long discussion about the absolute presuppositions of any one phase of thought it would not only be intolerably wearisome to introduce every sentence expressing one such presupposition by prefixing to it the metaphysical rubric; it would also be an insult to the reader; and in such cases, therefore, it is omitted on the assumption that the reader is intelligent enough and enough accustomed to this kind of literature to put it in for himself.

This is common form. History has its own rubric, namely 'the evidence at our disposal obliges us to conclude that' such and such an event happened. What I call scissors-and-paste history has the rubric 'we are told that' such and such an event happened. There is also a rubric for use in narrating legends, which in some kinds of legendary literature is here and there explicitly inserted: 'the story says that . . .', or 'now the story goes on to say that . . .'. Where the reader is assumed to know the ropes these rubrics are left out.

There may be an alternative reason for leaving them out: namely because the writer himself does not see that they are required. It is only when a man's historical consciousness has reached a certain point of maturity that he realizes how very different have been the ways in which different sets of people have thought. When a man first begins looking into absolute presuppositions it is likely that he will begin by looking into those which are made in his own time by his own countrymen, or at any rate by persons belonging to some group of which he is a member.

This, of course, is already an historical inquiry. But various prejudices current at various times which I will not here enumerate have tended to deceive such inquirers into thinking that the conclusions they have reached will hold good far beyond the limits of that group and that time. They may even imagine that an absolute presupposition discovered within these limits can be more or less safely ascribed to all human beings everywhere and always. In that case, mistaking the characteristics of a certain historical milieu for characteristics of mankind at large, they will leave out the metaphysical rubric on purpose, and present a piece of purely historical research as if it were a research into the universal nature of understanding. But their mistaking it for something else does not alter the fact that it is history.

Note to pp. 49–50.—The reader must not object: 'In Newton "free" motion is a hypothetical limiting case, a type of event that never actually happens, though it would happen if all interferences were removed, which they never are; the events which happen uncaused are events which never actually happen; all events which actually happen are caused; and the contradiction between "Newtonian" and "Kantian" science is removed.'

For in Newton 'free' motion is not a limiting or hypothetical case. In the *Principia*, a motion that is subject to interference is analysed into two 'momenta', the 'free' motion and the motion due to the interfering cause (see the Corollaries to the Third Law). In the world of actual events Newton certainly thought that 'free' motion occurred only in such combinations; but this is a very different thing from saying it never occurs at all. If he had said this second thing he would have built the whole fabric of the *Principia* on a breach of his own rule 'hypotheses non fingo'.

VII

THE REFORM OF METAPHYSICS

METAPHYSICS has always been an historical science; but metaphysicians have not always been fully aware of the fact. This was not altogether their fault, because it is only within the last half-century that the aims and methods of history have defined themselves with the same sort of precision that those of natural science achieved round about the year 1600. Until that happened people did not understand that history is a kind of thinking whereby absolutely cogent inferences about the past are drawn from interpretation of the evidence it has left behind. Or rather, the people who understood this were rare even among historians, and the occasions on which they understood it were exceptional. The ordinary belief was that history is a repeating of statements about the past which are found ready-made in the writings or on the lips of persons whom, because the historian believes what they tell him, he calls his authorities. This repetition of ready-made statements which the historian is allowed within limits to decorate with comments of his own devising I call scissors-and-paste history: a phrase in which the word 'history' means 'history improperly so called'.

Some readers of this book will reject my statement that metaphysics is an historical science because, being half a century out of date in their notions as to what history is, they fancy it to be an affair of scissors and paste. I hasten to assure them of my sympathy. I should never dream of suggesting that metaphysics was a scissors-and-paste affair. For it does not proceed by the scissors-and-paste method of accepting testimony; as I explained in Chapter V, it proceeds according to a method called metaphysical analysis, by which the metaphysician discovers what absolute presuppositions have been made in a certain piece of scientific work by using the records of that work as evidence. It is because people until lately regarded history as a scissors-and-paste affair that they could not realize the historical character of metaphysics.

But history to-day is no longer a scissors-and-paste affair. Instead of repeating statements accepted on the testimony of authorities, the historian of to-day makes his own statements on his own authority according to what he finds the evidence in his possession to prove when he analyses it with a certain question in his mind. And I know perfectly well that people who understand the nature of historical thought, as historical thought exists to-day among even the rank and file of quite ordinary historians, will not need to be convinced that metaphysics is an historical science. They will need only to understand the statement in order to see at once that it is true.

Dissatisfaction with the state of metaphysics has been endemic among philosophers ever since at least the time of Kant. It has been partly the fault of metaphysicians and partly the fault of those who have been dissatisfied. I will not say whose fault I think has been the greater. My business is to show how the dissatisfaction can be removed.

It can be removed by taking seriously the proposition that metaphysics is an historical science. Let it be understood both by metaphysicians and by their critics that metaphysics is the science of absolute presuppositions. Let the distinction between metaphysics and pseudo-metaphysics be firmly grasped. Let it be understood that the business of metaphysics is to find out what absolute presuppositions have actually been made by various persons at various times in doing various pieces of scientific thinking. Let it be understood that if a certain absolute presupposition has been made on one occasion by one person this fact makes it probable that the same presupposition has been made by other persons having in general what may be called the same cultural equipment as himself: the same outfit of social and political habits, the same religion, the same sort of education, and so forth; but correspondingly improbable that it has been made by persons whose cultural equipment was noticeably different. At the same time let it be understood that probabilities are not history, which demands proof; and that the only way to prove that somebody has made or has not made a certain absolute presupposition is to analyse the records of his thought and find out.

When this is done the peculiar perplexities and obscurities that have always been felt to surround the work of the metaphysician will disappear. At the same time the scope of metaphysical inquiry will be greatly enlarged. New and interesting problems will arise, not hitherto envisaged because the possibilities of metaphysical thinking have been as imperfectly understood as its methods. I will make a few observations on each of these two heads.

1. *Perplexities removed.*

(*a*) As to subject. What is metaphysics about? Ever since the time of Aristotle this has been a perplexing question. I have shown that the perplexity goes back to Aristotle himself. Aristotle knew well enough that the science he was creating was a science of absolute presuppositions, and the text of his *Metaphysics* bears abundant witness to the firmness with which he kept this in mind and the perspicacity with which he realized its implications; but Aristotle is also responsible for having initiated the barren search after a science of pure being, and for the suggestion that a science of pure being and a science of absolute presuppositions were one and the same. This perplexity has never been overcome. The history of metaphysics since Aristotle shows that at no point have people become quite clear in their minds as to what metaphysics was about. With this perplexity has gone another, as to how the metaphysician should train himself for his work. In the Middle Ages it was supposed that his preliminary training should consist chiefly of logic; in the seventeenth century, of physics; in the nineteenth, of psychology.

These questions can now be answered. Metaphysics is about a certain class of historical facts, namely absolute presuppositions. Its subject-matter is as clearly defined as if it had been, for example, the history of mathematics or metallurgy. Because the metaphysician is a special kind of historian, his training should consist first in a general historical education; secondly in special attention to the history of science; and finally in concentrating on problems of the following type: Here is a document providing evidence about the history of science; what light does it throw on the question what absolute presuppositions have been made?

(b) As to method. The perplexity as to what metaphysics is about has naturally bred perplexity as to how it should proceed. The ghost of Aristotle's science of pure being has always haunted it with the suggestion that some part at least of its proper method consists in groping blindly for what is not in fact there. If its object is inaccessible the search for that object can only consist in doing something futile; and although no metaphysician has ever taken this inference quite seriously, it cannot be denied that most of them have been to some extent daunted by it into half thinking that their proper place is among the shades, and that a little flitting, a little gibbering, are among the duties of their profession.

This again is now cleared up. The problems of metaphysics are historical problems; its methods are historical methods. We must have no more nonsense about its being meritorious to inhabit a fog. A metaphysician is a man who has to get at facts. He must be quite clear in his mind what facts he wants to get at and by means of what evidence he proposes to get at them. We live in the twentieth century; there is no excuse for us if we do not know what the methods of history are.

Another perplexity as to method, or perhaps only the same one over again, arises from the recognition that metaphysics investigates presuppositions. Surely, it is argued, a science that investigates presuppositions must avoid making presuppositions in the course of its own work; for how can you detect a presupposition in your neighbour's eye if you have a whole faggot of them in your own? So the idea got about that metaphysics must be a science with no presuppositions whatever, a science spun out of nothing by the thinker's brain.

This is the greatest nonsense. If metaphysics is a science at all it is an attempt to think systematically, that is, by answering questions intelligently disposed in order. The answer to any question presupposes whatever the question presupposes. And because all science begins with a question (for a question is logically prior to its own answer) all science begins with a presupposition. Metaphysics, therefore, either has presuppositions or is no science. The attempt at a metaphysics devoid of presuppositions can only result in a metaphysics that is no science, a tangle of confused thoughts whose confusion is taken for a merit. Not only has metaphysics quite definite presuppositions, but every one knows what some of them are, for as metaphysics is an historical science it shares the presuppositions of all history; and every one, nowadays, has some acquaintance with the principles of historical thought.

(*c*) As to form, two different perplexities may be instanced. First, should a metaphysician aim at completeness? Is there a certain repertory of problems which are 'the' problems of metaphysics; and is it the duty of a metaphysician who takes his work seriously to tackle the whole set?

I call this a perplexity because a great many metaphysicians, as any one can see from their writings, have been troubled by it: conscious of an attraction always drawing them towards the idea that there is what I have called a repertory of metaphysical problems and that the proper way of going about their business is to solve the whole lot systematically, and yet conscious that when they come closer to grips with this idea it fails to fulfil its promises, for either their problems will not make up into a really systematic form, or the desire to make them up into such a form fails to survive a closer acquaintance with the problems themselves. All science undoubtedly is systematic; and metaphysics, if metaphysics is to be a science, will be systematic too; but does this imply that metaphysical thinking should aim at system-building? Thus doubts arise, as with the other problems I have enumerated; and these in practice lead for the most part to compromises that satisfy nobody: repertories of problems which are not quite closed, systems that are not quite systematic, and a general air of pretence to do what hardly anybody firmly believes to be worth doing.

These doubts can now be resolved. Metaphysics aware of itself as an historical science will be systematic in the sense in which all historical thought is systematic and in no other. Its systematic character will be exhibited in the clear-cut and orderly manner in which it states problems and marshals and interprets evidence for their solution. But the idea that these problems form a closed repertory, or even a repertory with the door ajar, is the purest illusion. So, therefore, is the corresponding idea that the metaphysician's business is to 'cover the ground' of this repertory, to deal with all the problems, and thus to build a system. *Nil actum reputans si quid superesset agendum*, Kant quoted, stuck fast in the grip of this illusion. The historian's work is never finished; every historical subject, like the course of historical events itself, is open at the end, and however hard you work at it the end always remains open. People who are said to 'make history' solve the problems they find confronting them, but create others to be solved, if not by themselves, by their survivors. People who write it, if they write it well, solve problems too; but every problem solved gives rise to a new problem.

A second perplexity as to form arises from the question whether the various problems of metaphysics are so related that a correct solution of one would lead to the correct solution of others: whether, in technical language, there are relations of implication or entailment between their various solutions. This is the question often asked in the shape of the question whether metaphysics is a 'deductive' science.

The answer is, unhesitatingly, No. Let us suppose that the metaphysician is trying to analyse out one single set of absolute presuppositions, namely those of ordinary science in his own society and his own time. I speak of a set of absolute presuppositions, because if metaphysics is an historical science the things which it studies, namely absolute presuppositions, are historical facts; and any one who is reasonably well acquainted with historical work knows that there is no such thing as an historical fact which is not at the same time a complex of historical facts. Such a complex of historical facts I call a 'constellation'. If every historical fact is a constellation, the answer to the question 'What is it that such and such a person was absolutely presupposing in such and such a piece of thinking?' can never be given by reference to one single absolute presupposition, it must always be given by reference to a constellation of them.

What is the logical relation, then, between the presuppositions making up this constellation? The constellation, complex though it is, is still a single fact. The different presuppositions composing it are all made at once, in one and the same piece of thinking. They are not like a set of carpenter's tools, of which the carpenter uses one at a time; they are like a suit of clothes, of which every part is worn simultaneously with all the rest. This is to say that, since they are all suppositions, each must be *consupponible* with all the others; that is, it must be logically possible for a person who supposes any one of them to suppose concurrently all the rest.

It need not, however, be anything more than this. It need not be a relation of such a kind that a person supposing any one of them is logically committed to supposing all or indeed any of the others. Metaphysicians have often thought it was; but that is because they thought of metaphysics as a kind of quasi-mathematics, and did not realize that it was a kind of history.

I say that the relation between the constituents in a single constellation of absolute presuppositions need not be of this kind; but actually it cannot be. For if any one of these constituents logically necessitated any other, the first would be a presupposition of the second, and therefore the second would not be an absolute presupposition. Taken together, the constellation forms a single historical fact; but any constituent within it taken separately is also a single historical fact, discoverable by the metaphysician only in the way in which any historian discovers any historical fact, by the interpretation of evidence. If a given person in a given piece of thinking makes the absolute presuppositions AP_1, AP_2, AP_3, AP_4 . . ., each of these is a genuinely independent presupposition which can no more be deduced from the rest than waistcoat can be deduced from trousers or from trousers and coat together. Metaphysics, aware of itself as an historical science, will abandon once for all the hope of being a 'deductive' or quasi-mathematical science.

It follows that the literary form of a treatise in which a metaphysician sets out to enumerate and discuss the absolute presuppositions of thought in his own time cannot be the form of a continuous argument, leading from point to point by way of quasi-mathematical demonstration, as in the *Ethics* of Spinoza. It must be the form of a *catalogue raisonné*, as in the fourth book of Aristotle's *Metaphysics* or in the *Quaestiones* of a medieval metaphysician.

(*d*) As to the effect which a metaphysician hopes to produce on the minds of his readers, there is a foolish idea that his business is to found a 'school', if he is a great enough man, and if not, to bring recruits into the 'school' to which he himself belongs, the school of Platonists, Aristotelians, Thomists, Scotists, Cartesians, Hobbists, Spinozists, Leibnitians, Berkeleians, Humians, Kantians, Hegelians, or whatever it may be. This once more I call a perplexity because a great many people can see, when they think, how foolish it is and yet cannot entirely rid themselves of it. They find themselves on the whole agreeing with A's doctrines rather than B's; why not say so?

Metaphysics, aware of itself as an historical science, will abolish in one clean sweep not only the idea of 'schools' but the idea of 'doctrines'. It will realize that what are misdescribed as A's 'metaphysical doctrines' are nothing more than the results of A's attempt to discover what absolute presuppositions are made by scientists in his own time. Thus it is not a 'metaphysical doctrine' or 'metaphysical theory' of Spinoza's that Nature is the same as God. If you understand the metaphysical rubric when you read what he says about this you will see that what he is doing is to state an historical fact about the religious foundation of seventeenth-century natural science. When I accept what Spinoza says on this subject I am no more going Spinozist in a war of metaphysical sects than I am going Tacitean in a war of historical sects when I accept Tacitus's statement that Agricola conquered southern and central Scotland. What I am doing in either case is to say: 'Here is a statement as to certain facts made by a contemporary writer. The evidence at my disposal proves that it is true.'

Sometimes a metaphysician will make a mistake and say that an absolute presupposition is made which in fact is not made. It is still being said to-day, for example, in spite of a public and altogether right protest made several years ago by Earl Russell,[1] that 'all events have causes'. His protest was altogether right because the point he made was the point that mattered: that the idea of causation is not presupposed in modern physics. In such cases it would be *suggestio falsi* to call the mistake a 'metaphysical doctrine' of the persons who make it. It is not a doctrine, it is a blunder.

Sometimes we find a metaphysician of the past correctly describing an absolute presupposition made in his own times which is still being made to-day; sometimes one which is to-day obsolete. No one who understands that metaphysics is an historical science will be so silly as to say in the first case that his

[1] 'On the Notion of Cause'. *Proc. Arist. Soc.*, 1911–12; reprinted in *Mysticism and Logic*, 1918.

'doctrine' or 'theory' is true, and in the second that it is false.

All this stuff about schools, doctrines, theories, agreement and disagreement, useful though it certainly is for amusing the minds of would-be metaphysicians who cannot get ahead with their work because they do not know how, has nothing to do with metaphysics. It belongs to the apparatus of pseudo-metaphysics.

2. *Scope enlarged.*

Metaphysicians up to now, so far as they have evaded the perplexities mentioned above and have attended to their own proper business, the study of absolute presuppositions, have been working no doubt at history; but their unawareness that history was what they were working at has narrowed the scope of their work. It has prevented them from studying the absolute presuppositions that have been made in the so-called past, because that would be history, and has confined their attention to those made in the so-called present, because that is not history but metaphysics. I say the 'so-called' present and past because the 'present' referred to in that antithesis is not really a present, it is a past, but a relatively recent past. The 'so-called present' means the more recent past, the 'so-called past' means the remoter past.

Metaphysics not aware of itself as an historical science; accordingly, has been in the habit of confining its attention to the absolute presuppositions made in that recent past which is loosely called the present. Aristotle describes us the absolute presuppositions of Greek science in the fourth century B.C.; St. Thomas those of European science in the central Middle Ages; Spinoza those of European science in the seventeenth century, or rather those of them which he thinks relevant to his special purpose. This habit of attending only to the recent past cannot survive the discovery that metaphysics is an historical science. That discovery enlarges the scope of metaphysical study by opening to it no longer the merest antechamber of the past, but the past in its entirety.

(a) The first consequence of this enlargement is that the metaphysician, instead of being confined in his studies to one single constellation of absolute presuppositions, has before him an indefinite number of them. He has as many worlds to conquer as any conqueror can want. He can study the presuppositions of European science at any phase in its history for which he has evidence. He can study the presuppositions of Arabic science, of Indian science, of Chinese science; again in all their phases, so far as he can find evidence for them. He can study the presuppositions of the science practised by 'primitive' and 'prehistoric' peoples. All these are his proper work; not an historical background for his work, but his work itself.

If he is a lazy or a stupid man, he may find this enlargement embarrassing; but no one is asking him to eat all the thistles in his field, only the kind he likes best, and so many of them as he has a stomach for. The ordinary metaphysician will treat this field very much as any ordinary historian treats any historical field. He will recognize that it is inexhaustible and will decide for reasons of one sort or another what part of it he will make peculiarly his own. In this part he will do genuine, first-hand historical work. In the parts that impinge on it he will be content to know the first-hand work that others have done, without doing any himself. In remoter parts he will be content to look at second-hand work: compilations and text-books and what are called, *a non lucendo*, 'histories'; and where the penumbra shades off into complete darkness he may even sink so low as to consult the encyclopaedia.

(*b*) When he has some knowledge about several different constellations of absolute presuppositions, he can set to work comparing them. This is not a high class of historical work, but it has its uses. For one thing it will convince the metaphysician, if it is honestly done, that there are no 'eternal' or 'crucial' or 'central' problems in metaphysics. It will rid him of the parish-pump idea that the metaphysical problems of his own generation or, more likely, the one next before his own are the problems that all metaphysicians have been worrying about ever since the world began. For another thing it will give him a hint of the way in which different sets of absolute presuppositions correspond not only with differences in the structure of what is generally called scientific thought but with differences in the entire fabric of civilization.

(*c*) But all this is still a very superficial kind of

historical study, based as it is on the false assumption
that an historical 'phase'—a civilization, a phase of
scientific thought, a set of absolute presuppositions—
is a static thing, whose relations with others can be
adequately studied by comparing them and noting
resemblances and differences. The essential thing
about historical 'phases' is that each of them gives
place to another; not because one is violently destroyed by alien forces impinging on its fabric from
without by war or from within by revolution, but
because each of them while it lives is working at
turning itself into the next. To trace the process by
which one historical phase turns into the next is the
business of every historian who concerns himself with
that phase. The metaphysician's business, therefore,
when he has identified several different constellations
of absolute presuppositions, is not only to study their
likenesses and unlikenesses but also to find out on
what occasions and by what processes one of them
has turned into another.

This is the only legitimate (that is, historical) way
in which he, or anybody else, can answer the question
'Why did such and such people at such and such a
time make such and such absolute presuppositions?'
Like all questions in metaphysics, this is either a
nonsense question or an historical question. It is a
nonsense question if the answer it expects is one
which identifies the cause of the historical fact in
question with something outside history, like the geographical or climatic environment of that fact or the
psycho-physical characteristics of the human beings

concerned in it. It is a significant question if it expects an answer in the form: 'Because they or the predecessors from whom they inherited their civilization had previously made such and such a different set of absolute presuppositions, and because such and such a process of change converted the one set into the other.' If any one is dissatisfied with this kind of answer his dissatisfaction shows that the question, as he was asking it, was a nonsense question.

(*d*) The dynamics of history is not yet completely understood when it is grasped that each phase is converted into the next by a process of change. The relation between phase and process is more intimate than that. One phase changes into another because the first phase was in unstable equilibrium and had in itself the seeds of change, and indeed of that change. Its fabric was not at rest; it was always under strain. If the world of history is a world in which *tout passe, tout lasse, tout casse*, the analysis of the internal strains to which a given constellation of historical facts is subjected, and of the means by which it 'takes up' these strains, or prevents them from breaking it in pieces, is not the least part of an historian's work.

Thus if Gibbon seems out of date to a modern student of the Roman Empire it is not because Gibbon knew fewer facts than the modern student knows; it is because Gibbon was not sensitive enough to the internal strains of what he wrote about. He begins by depicting the Antonine period as a Golden Age, that is, an age containing no internal strains whatever; and from the non-historical or anti-historical tone of its opening his narrative never quite recovers. If Hegel's influence on nineteenth-century historiography was on the whole an influence for good, it was because historical study for him was first and foremost a study of internal strains, and this is why he opened the way to such brilliant feats as that analysis of internal strains in nineteenth-century economic society which entitles Karl Marx to the name of a great historian. If Oswald Spengler, who was so much talked about a few years ago, is to-day deservedly forgotten, it is because whenever he set himself to describe a constellation of historical facts (what he called a 'culture') he deliberately ironed all the strains out of it and presented a picture in which every detail fitted into every other as placidly as the pieces of a jig-saw puzzle lying at rest on a table.

Where there is no strain there is no history. A civilization does not work out its own details by a kind of static logic in which every detail exemplifies in its own way one and the same formula. It works itself out by a dynamic logic in which different and at first sight incompatible formulae somehow contrive a precarious coexistence; one dominant here, another there; the recessive formula never ceasing to operate, but functioning as a kind of minority report which, though the superficial historian may ignore it, serves to a more acute eye as evidence of tendencies actually existing which may have been dominant in the past and may be dominant in the future. And even an historian whose eye is not acute enough to detect this recessive element may have feelings sensitive enough to savour the peculiar quality which its presence imparts to the whole. The historian in his study can perhaps afford to neglect these strains, because he does not really care about being a good historian; but the man of action cannot afford to neglect them. His life may depend on his ability to see where they are and to judge their strength. It was not by gunpowder alone that Cortez destroyed Montezuma; it was by using gunpowder to reinforce the strains which already tended to break up Montezuma's power.

The same characteristic will certainly be found in any constellation of absolute presuppositions; and a metaphysician who comes to his subject from a general grounding in history will know that he must look for it. He will expect the various presuppositions he is studying to be consupponible only under pressure, the constellation being subject to certain strains and kept together by dint of a certain compromise or mutual toleration having behind it a motive like that which causes parties to unite in the face of an enemy. This is why the conception of metaphysics as a 'deductive' science is not only an error but a pernicious error, one with which a reformed metaphysics will have no truce. The ambition of 'deductive' metaphysics is to present a constellation of absolute presuppositions as a strainless structure like a body of propositions in mathematics. That is all right in mathematics because mathematical propositions are not historical propositions. But it is all wrong in metaphysics. A reformed metaphysics will conceive any given constellation of absolute propositions as having in its structure not the simplicity and calm that characterize the subject-matter of mathematics but the intricacy and restlessness that characterize the subject-matter, say, of legal or constitutional history.

This is the answer to the somewhat threadbare question 'How can metaphysics become a science?' The answer is: 'By becoming more completely and more consciously what in fact it has always been, an historical science.' The reform of metaphysics, long looked for and urgently needed, can be brought about by nothing more abstruse or difficult than its adoption of principles and methods which are now common form among historians. And the extent to which metaphysics has already been a science in the past is governed by the extent to which it has already been history.

By this reform metaphysics will find a complete and conclusive answer to the various criticisms which at various times have been brought against it, so far as those criticisms have been justified by defects in its own practice. And so far as they have not been justified it may help people to clear them out of their minds.

PART II

ANTI-METAPHYSICS

VIII

WHAT ANTI-METAPHYSICS IS

In the first part of this essay I have tried to show that the business of metaphysics is to study absolute presuppositions; that this is an historical study; and that metaphysics can set its house in order by living up to its proper character as an historical science.

In the second part I pass from metaphysics to anti-metaphysics, by which I mean a kind of thought that regards metaphysics as a delusion and an impediment to the progress of knowledge, and demands its abolition.

The possibility of science and the possibility of metaphysics are bound up together, as I have explained in Chapter V. It is therefore absurd to maintain that the interests of knowledge could be served by the abolition of metaphysics. But absurdities exist, and anti-metaphysics among them; and in this chapter I propose to ask under what conditions this happens: not under what conditions it conceivably might happen, because I do not see that to ask this question would serve any purpose which for my own part I am conscious of entertaining, but under what conditions it actually does happen. For anti-metaphysics is and has been for some time past a thing that actually exists; and everything I shall say in this chapter will be concerned with conditions actually existing, now or in the past, which are generating it or have generated it.

Among these conditions I shall not include faults in the programme and practice of metaphysics as conceived by those who profess to practise it. Such faults must certainly be expected to generate dissatisfaction, and dissatisfaction may lead to antagonism; but so far as antagonism to metaphysics is or has been due to these causes, it has already been dealt with by implication in the preceding chapter. The causes I shall deal with in this chapter and those that follow it will, therefore, be causes which would not be wholly removed by the reform of metaphysics already described.

There are three sets of conditions, all relevant to the situation now existing, under which anti-metaphysics of three different kinds would be generated.

1. *Progressive Anti-Metaphysics.* Professional metaphysicians (by which I mean not persons who are paid for being metaphysicians, but persons who profess to be metaphysicians, i.e. who claim for their own work the name of metaphysics because they regard it as a study of absolute presuppositions) may fail to do the kind of work which is required of them by the advance of ordinary or non-metaphysical thought because their metaphysical analysis has become out of date, i.e. presupposes that ordinary thought still stands in a situation in which it once stood, but in which it stands no longer. In that case natural scientists (to take one type of example) may come to think of metaphysics as a kind of thought which is essentially obscurantist and thus an impediment to the progress of their own work.

2. *Reactionary Anti-Metaphysics*. The opposite case may arise. The necessary contact between metaphysical and 'ordinary' thinking may be lost because metaphysical analysis has outrun its partner. Persons engaged in some kind of 'ordinary' thought may wish to pursue it in a way which gives them a bad metaphysical conscience, e.g. by treating presuppositions as absolute which the best contemporary thought treats as relative, or which the best metaphysical analysis has pronounced to be relative. For such persons metaphysical thinking is as much to be dreaded as an audit is dreaded by a man given to embezzlement; and this dread they express by calling metaphysics a subversive or revolutionary kind of thought and demanding its abolition as a measure of safety; or alternatively, if the way in which they wish to pursue their own thinking is an obsolete one, by proscribing all metaphysics except the metaphysics which was up to date when that method was up to date.

3. *Irrationalist Anti-Metaphysics*. A more complex case would be that in which a movement was going forward for the abolition of science itself, in order to bring into existence a form of human life in which all the determining factors should be emotional. An 'irrationalist' movement of this kind would aim at the ultimate abolition of systematic and orderly thinking in every shape; but, working (as in the modern world it must work) within a civilization that had for many centuries set a high value on such thinking, it would be obliged to conceal this ultimate aim and work

under a disguise calculated not to arouse alarm. For this purpose it might very well make use of an already existing anti-metaphysical movement of type 1 or 2, or (still better) a confused mixture of both.

Further consideration of this third case will be deferred until Chapter XIII. The rest of the present chapter will be devoted to cases 1 and 2.

1. *Progressive Anti-Metaphysics.*

Professional students of metaphysics are not the only persons who are interested in the work of discovering and defining absolute presuppositions. I have already pointed out that metaphysical analysis, the discovery that certain presuppositions actually made are absolute presuppositions, is an integral part or an indispensable condition, you can put it whichever way you like, of all scientific work. This does not make scientific work an impossible or even a terribly difficult thing; because metaphysical analysis is not difficult when you know what you are trying to do. It is only confusion as to what he is about that makes the metaphysician's work harder than that of other scientists.

If a certain kind of work is not really necessary, and if the people who profess to be doing it are not succeeding, it can be left undone. But if it is really necessary, somebody else will have to take it in hand; presumably the persons whose interests demand that it should be done. In the interests of science it is absolutely necessary that the work of metaphysics should be done: done not in the sense of being carried to completion, for it is a work which in the nature of it can never be complete, but done as required, piece by piece, when the need arises.

The full meaning of this statement will become clear only when the term science is regarded as covering (a) not natural science alone but orderly and systematic thinking on every subject, (b) not orderly and systematic 'theoretical' thinking alone but orderly and systematic 'practical' thinking as well, such thinking as we refer to when we speak of a man thinking out a way of making a table or organizing a secretarial staff or defeating an enemy. It is important for every one without exception who either thinks scientifically in this widest sense, or profits by the fruits of other people's scientific thinking, that the work of metaphysics should be done, and well done.

If a case arises when, for the sake of progress in any scientific inquiry, there is need for a certain piece of analysis to determine whether a certain presupposition newly brought to light is a relative one or an absolute one; and if it appears that professional metaphysicians have not already done this piece of analysis and are not willing to do it now, or, if willing, are not able to do it well, then persons who do not profess to be metaphysicians, but are concerned for the progress of scientific inquiry in this actual case, have to undertake it for themselves. If this happens repeatedly, the result will be a crop of amateur metaphysics: metaphysical work done by persons who do not regard themselves as qualified to do it, but find they have to do it because a metaphysical problem has arisen out of their own special work to which the professional metaphysicians do not seem to be attending, and unless this problem is solved their own special work cannot go forward.

The necessity for amateur metaphysics will arise more often according as ordinary scientific work goes more busily forward (not in the sense of merely working out the consequences of discoveries already made, but in the sense of making new discoveries; a distinction to which I shall return in the second part of this chapter), and according as metaphysicians fail to keep in touch with this advance, either through mere indolence and ignorance, or on principle because they think that metaphysics has to do with 'eternal' or traditional problems, which in practice means the problems of the last generation,[1] not the problems of this generation.

If anybody wishes to judge for himself the extent to which amateur metaphysics has flourished in the soil of recent European thought, let him take a few score of large-scale works on various branches of natural science, history, law, economics, and so forth, preferably works which are regarded as original and important contributions to knowledge, and examine them, especially their introductory chapters, for meta-

[1] The problems which exercised the great classical metaphysicians? No. The metaphysicians who believe in eternal problems are bad historians, or they would not believe in eternal problems. Being bad historians they do not know what the problems of the great classical metaphysicians were. They read into them the problems of their own time, or rather of a time just before their own. Cf. Chapter XV.

physical propositions. They should be large-scale works because in small-scale works material of this kind tends to be crowded out.

A person who acquaints himself in this way with a sample of amateur metaphysics will be struck not only by the fact that a far larger quantity of it exists than he had supposed, but by a curious tone in the expression of it, which will soon become familiar to him. He will find the amateur metaphysician well aware that there are professional metaphysicians and that if they did their work properly he would not have to be doing it for himself. So his exposition of this work not seldom betrays a tone of resentment against the persons who ought to be doing it: a resentment due to the fact that their neglect of their own work has forced him to do something for which he feels that he is not qualified and in which he accordingly fears that he is making a fool of himself.

But there is a further complication. He regards the persons against whom he feels this resentment as having a prescriptive right to the name of metaphysicians, and the work which they do, as opposed to the work which by neglecting it they force him to do instead of themselves, as having a prescriptive right to the name of metaphysics. His resentment extends itself, therefore, to these names, and makes it hard for him to say either to others or to himself (what is actually the truth) 'Now I am going to turn metaphysician for a few pages', or 'This is metaphysics', because he has already conceded these names to what he is dissatisfied with. This resentment makes him think of his own metaphysical work not as a contribution to metaphysics but as an exposure of metaphysics; not as a piece of help given by himself to metaphysicians in the pursuit of their own proper business, but as an attack on them and their business too.

Thus, not for any logical reason, but simply because of the emotions arising from the uneasy consciousness of their own amateur status, amateur metaphysicians become anti-metaphysicians, and amateur metaphysics becomes anti-metaphysics.

I will try to sum up what I have said.

Progressive anti-metaphysics is:

  (i) *metaphysics*

  (ii) *undertaken by a man who does not consider it his proper job*

  (iii) *because the interests of his proper job demand it and because the professionals have neglected it.*

  (iv) *The amateur resents being forced by this neglect into a job he does not regard as his own;*

  (v) *this resentment makes him feel himself as the professional metaphysicians' enemy, and his work as an attack on their work.*

  (vi) *But he concedes to them and their work the titles of metaphysicians and metaphysics;*

  (vii) *hence his resentment makes him regard his metaphysical work as anti-metaphysics.*

Scientifically considered, it is not anti-metaphysics. It is metaphysics, sometimes good and sometimes bad, which has acquired the emotional quality of anti-metaphysics by being seen through a haze of resentment against metaphysicians. Not only is this resentment often justified, but the metaphysics which it disguises as anti-metaphysics is often good metaphysics; so that the metaphysicians against whom the resentment is directed may often be found taking lessons, and sometimes useful ones, from their self-appointed enemies.

Criticism of such an anti-metaphysical position, therefore, leaves its real motive untouched. What makes anti-metaphysicians is the thing which modern psychologists if they belong to Freud's sect call an Oedipus complex, and if they belong to Adler's an inferiority complex. This is more likely to be exacerbated than alleviated by criticism; the more so because criticism cannot help showing that the anti-metaphysician is the thing he hates, a metaphysician. But criticism is worth doing; for it will help to show any one not already blinded by passion the scientific structure of the anti-metaphysical arguments; which after all profess to be scientific arguments, and are sometimes adopted as their own for other motives by persons who do not themselves feel the resentment which, for a true-blue anti-metaphysician, is the motive for embracing them.

An example of this progressive anti-metaphysics is Newton's warning against 'metaphysical hypotheses' in 'experimental philosophy.'[1] Newton did not mean to warn his readers against his own meta-

---

[1] 'Hypotheses, seu Metaphysicae, seu Physicae, seu Qualitatum Occultarum, seu Mechanicae, in *Philosophia Experimentali* locum non habent' (*Scholium Generale, Principia* ad fin.).

physics. He meant to warn them against the meta-physics of professional metaphysicians, in order to forestall the criticisms such people were likely to bring against his own metaphysics, which was an integral part of his own physics. We have seen a similar situa-tion in our own time, when another new movement in physics, the most important since Newton, has found itself obliged, as Newton was obliged, to put forward new metaphysical propositions as part and parcel of its own work; and has consequently found, as Newton found, that the scientific validity of that work in its entirety was denied by professional metaphysicians whose ideas had become fixed in a mould belonging to a past age.

But the modern anti-metaphysical movement is not simply a reaffirmation of Newton's warning. It is derived partly from the same motives that underlay that warning; but partly from very different motives which assimilate it to case 2.

2. *Reactionary Anti-Metaphysics.*

In certain circumstances a kind of anti-metaphysics might come into existence through causes in one sense identical with those of case 1, namely a loss of effective contact between professional metaphysicians and a certain class of non-metaphysical thinkers, combined with all the other factors enumerated above, but with this difference: that for 'neglect' must be read 'opposition'; and for 'resentment', 'fear'.

Suppose that professional metaphysicians, instead

of working too slowly to keep pace with the advance of ordinary scientific thought, had been working too fast. Suppose that in consequence professional metaphysics had been dealing with problems at which a certain branch of 'ordinary' thought had not yet arrived. There would then be the same disharmony between metaphysics and this branch of 'ordinary' thought, and the same tendency for persons representing the latter to engage in amateur metaphysics; but with the difference that amateur metaphysics would now be taking up what as compared with professional metaphysics must be called a reactionary instead of a progressive attitude. The amateur metaphysician would be dissociating himself from the contemporary advance of metaphysical knowledge, and attaching himself to some past phase in the history of metaphysics.

There are two points to be noticed about such an attachment.

(*a*) It converts metaphysical issues into pseudo-metaphysical issues. For suppose the past phase to be represented by the metaphysical work of a man called X, and let his work be called *x*. Let Y be the man who now, in opposition to the tendencies of thought in his own time, embraces *x* as his own 'doctrine', claims that X was 'right', and professes himself an 'Xist'. We know (above, Chapter VII, 1 (*d*)) that this state of things is characteristic of pseudo-metaphysics. X's work is being considered in abstraction from the historical context to which alone it was relevant *qua* metaphysics. What X was doing was to discover by analysis the absolute presuppositions of thought in his own time. What Y is doing is to accept X's answer to this (metaphysical) question as an answer to a different (pseudo-metaphysical) question, namely the question whether those presuppositions, or the admittedly different presuppositions of thought in Y's time, are true.

(*b*) It is based not on hostility to metaphysics as such (for, as I have shown, it actually rests on metaphysical thinking, viz. thinking about the presuppositions of thought in Y's time) nor yet on hostility to pseudo-metaphysics (for pseudo-metaphysics is what it actually advocates; which is odd, considering that it professes hostility to metaphysics and at the same time defines metaphysics as pseudo-metaphysics); but on hostility to ordinary science as practised in its own time. For it is primarily an attack on contemporary metaphysics understood as pseudo-metaphysics, i.e. understood as if the presuppositions it records were propositions which it stated: an attack on the ground that these 'propositions' are false or meaningless. But these 'propositions' are in fact presuppositions which the modern metaphysician has detected somewhere in modern science; in calling them false or meaningless, therefore, the reactionary anti-metaphysician is describing as false or nonsensical the science that makes them. The reactionary anti-metaphysician is only secondarily a reactionary in metaphysics. Primarily he is a reactionary in ordinary science.

It will be useful to give some brief account of the

reasons for which, and the way in which, reactionary anti-metaphysics became a living force in the nineteenth century.

After the revolutionary movements of the eighteenth century the early nineteenth saw in science as well as in politics a counter-revolution. The aim of this counter-revolution was not so much to undo the work of the eighteenth century as to consolidate its results. In order that they should be consolidated it was thought, rightly or wrongly, that the revolutionary spirit which had created them must be held in check. Further revolutions must be deferred until the fruits of the already accomplished revolution had been allowed to ripen. The consequent desire to put a brake on further discussion of fundamental principles and confine the work of thought to something more 'constructive', that is, to the development of eighteenth-century ideas, become the dominant motive of European thought from the end of the Napoleonic wars until within twenty or thirty years of the nineteenth century's close.

The nineteenth century conceived itself as peculiarly an age of progress; but as regards fundamentals, for those two generations at least, it was predominantly an age of reaction. Its official doctrine was that as regards fundamentals the work had been done in the eighteenth century; all that was left to do was to apply this work to detail and profit increasingly by the application. I will give two examples. James Watt had laid down the principles of the reciprocating steam-engine as early as 1769; between 1820 and

1880, and indeed even later, engineers who were interested in prime movers did practically nothing except make bigger and more powerful steam-engines on the lines determined by Watt. Only after 1900 did Daimler's petrol engine and Parson's steam turbine break the virtual monopoly of the reciprocating steam-engine for propelling traffic on land and sea respectively. John Locke had worked out the theory of the English parliamentary system before the end of the seventeenth century. That theory, with certain modifications introduced in the eighteenth century, became the official doctrine of European politics in the nineteenth, when parliamentary constitutions on Locke's model were manufactured with as much regularity and as much self-satisfaction as steam-engines on the model of Watt.

Late in the nineteenth century, when this state of things began breaking up, every one who had a vested interest in its maintenance tried, naturally enough, to arrest its decay. In the realm of 'thought', in the customary narrower sense of that word, there were in especial two new developments to be opposed. There was a new physics, very different from that of Newton, which together with a new 'non-Euclidean' geometry was to produce what we now know as the physics of relativity. There was a new history, cutting itself loose from the age-old method of scissors and paste, which was to revolutionize the accepted view of the human world (and therefore of the political world) at least as completely as the new physics was to revolutionize the accepted view of 'nature'. The spirit of nineteenth-century thought, fighting for its life against these new tendencies, expressed itself in two war-cries, each for a time very celebrated in Germany, the country of their birth: 'Back to Kant' and 'No More Metaphysics'.

Kant was to the nineteenth-century 'sciences', especially in Germany, what Locke was to nineteenth-century politics, especially in England. It was Kant, as I shall explain in Chapters XXII—XXVIII, who laid down the lines on which natural science was content to travel throughout the central part of the nineteenth century. The new physics and the new geometry involved a definite breach with the Kantian system. This breach had been foreseen, and some of its consequences actually worked out, by Hegel, who had been boycotted for that reason throughout the central part of the nineteenth century, and only began to be studied again when people began to be dissatisfied with the principles accepted during that period. So the battle-cry of 'Back to Kant' expressed in philosophical terms the attempt of nineteenth-century scientific orthodoxy to muster in its own support all the forces which could be conjured into reactionary activity by appeal to the name of a great and honoured philosopher whose doctrines, understood in a pseudo-metaphysical sense, gave no support to the movements that threatened it.

The cry of 'No More Metaphysics' expressed, as ambiguously as the situation required, the aspirations of an anti-metaphysics which, like all others, was not really anti-metaphysical. When it said metaphysics it meant pseudo-metaphysics; and it did not demand the abolition of pseudo-metaphysics, it only demanded the maintenance of a pseudo-metaphysical *status quo*. It represented the typical nineteenth-century conviction that all questions about fundamentals had been settled and must on no account be reopened. This is what people mean by calling the nineteenth century 'dogmatic', 'superficial', 'hypocritical', or the like. The 'science' which was to be protected by this cry of 'No More Metaphysics' was being in effect described as a reactionary science, one which could only be imperilled by a critical inquiry into its foundations. Behind that cry there lay a feeling that the constellation of absolute presuppositions made by this reactionary science was exposed to strains which could only be 'taken up' by keeping them in darkness. If people became aware that in certain contexts they were in the habit of treating this or that presupposition as an absolute one, they would be unable to go on doing it.

The history of the steam-engine may serve as a parable of the time. As James Watt had created it, it was still, down to the end of the century, enjoying a practical monopoly for all purposes where a prime mover·was required. Kipling's marine engineer of the eighteen-nineties was only repeating the contemporary commonplaces about progress when he called a high-pressure cylinder 'the noblest outcome of human ingenuity'. Yet the degree of thermodynamical efficiency of which it was capable was startlingly low. According to the standard text-book of those days[1] 'the highest efficiency now attainable is a little over 7 per cent. with the marine steam engine, and is generally less—say nearer 5 or 6 per cent.'. The noblest outcome of human ingenuity was a heat-engine that wasted between 92·9 and 95 per cent. of the coal it consumed.

That capitalists chose to throw away roughly £94 out of every £100 they spent on keeping their machinery in motion, for sheer inability to invent a more efficient prime mover, is sufficiently remarkable. But let the reader translate these figures into terms of lives lost in coal-mines; for every 6 men killed that ships or the like should travel, 94 killed to honour the divine shades of Watt: and then let him wonder, if he can, why in that humanitarian age there were people who blasphemed against what was called 'the religion of science'.

The Lockian system in politics had a similar history. That system is based on private property, and therefore logically presupposes a 'state of nature' in which property is already a factor. In the course of the eighteenth century it became evident that the Lockian system presupposed something else, namely the thing which is nowadays called nationality; where nationality, like property, is conceived not as a product of political activity in the past (in which case it would have been for political history a relative presupposition) but as a 'natural' basis, an absolute presupposition, of all political activity whatever. It was in

[1] *The Marine Steam-Engine*, by R. Sennett and H. J. Oram, ed. 3, 1898, p. 21.

1775 that 'the principle of nationality first asserted itself in the modern world as a dynamic political force'.[1] The things that were done in the nineteenth century in the name of nationality, the things that are still done to-day, at what expense in life and wealth I shall not try to estimate, are done for the sake of an eighteenth-century 'metaphysical' idea.

The immaturity of historical technique in the eighteenth century found its characteristic expression in the doctrine that historical events were the effects of causes in the world of nature: causes physiological, psychological, climatic, geographical, and so forth. Nature seemed to the eighteenth-century historian an absolute presupposition of all historical thinking. The rapid development of historical thought in the nineteenth century dispelled this illusion. It became evident that when eighteenth-century historians spoke of nature as the cause of historical events what they ought to have said, and would have said if their grasp on historical method had been firmer, was that man's historical activities were conditioned not by nature itself but by what he was able to make of nature. And since what man makes of nature depends on man's own historical achievements, such as the arts of agriculture and navigation, the so-called conditioning of history by nature is in reality a conditioning of history by itself. Nationality for the modern historian is a relative presupposition; it cannot be an absolute one. Nationality can make history only because

---

[1] I quote from Professor A. J. Toynbee in *Foreign Affairs*, vol. xvii, p. 316 (New York, 1939).

history has made nationality and is constantly destroying and remaking it. In the latter part of the nineteenth century this had become a commonplace to every historian. But it was a piece of metaphysics; and people who wanted to go on practising the political arts of the eighteenth century could shelter themselves behind the cry of 'No More Metaphysics' in order to kill and destroy with a good conscience as the obsolete metaphysics of the eighteenth century bade them.

Here it is the politician who represents reactionary anti-metaphysics; it is the historian who, in the course of his ordinary historical thinking, has worked out the metaphysics against which the politician is trying to defend himself. Whether the historian is to be regarded as agreeing on the points here at issue with the professional metaphysicians of his own time, or whether in relation to them he is to be classified as an amateur metaphysician, is a question of little importance in the present context.

To sum up:

Reactionary anti-metaphysics is

   (i) *pseudo-metaphysics passing under the name of metaphysics*

  (ii) *undertaken by a man who does not consider it his proper job*

 (iii) *because he wishes to do that job on reactionary principles consistent with obsolete pseudo-metaphysical doctrines but inconsistent with the results arrived at by contemporary metaphysicians, professional or amateur.*

   (iv) *He fears this inconsistency as a source of danger to his own work, and*

   (v) *consequently feels himself as the enemy of these metaphysicians and their work.*

  (vi) *But he concedes to them and their work the titles of metaphysicians and metaphysics;*

 (vii) *hence his fear makes him regard his own (pseudo-)metaphysics as anti-metaphysics.*

IX

PSYCHOLOGY AS ANTI-METAPHYSICS

If the business of metaphysics is to reveal the absolute presuppositions that are involved in any given piece of thinking, the general class of study to which metaphysics belongs is clearly the study of thought. Metaphysics is in fact one branch of the science of thought. If this proposition were laid down in the hearing of almost any psychologist he would draw his own conclusions and perhaps express them in some such words as the following. I give the gist of a discourse to which I have often listened.

'If I understand you rightly you are maintaining that nobody ever thinks without making presuppositions; and that of these some are what you call absolute presuppositions, which are never questioned, never verified, and never even stated, although they play an indispensable part in determining the lines along which we think. This, you say, is none the less true for the fact that in a general way we do not know that they exist at all, still less what they are. You are maintaining that there is or ought to be a science which by some kind of analytic process finds out what on any given occasion these absolute presuppositions are; whether they are constant or whether they vary according to the different kinds of people who are thinking and the different kinds of things they are thinking about; and so forth. To

H

this actual or possible science you give the name of metaphysics.

'Very good. If you choose to employ the word metaphysics in that way I shall not try to prevent you, although I will remark that your idea of what meta-physicians are doing is a very eccentric one. The point is this. The work which you assign to meta-physics actually belongs to psychology. The inquiry you are desiderating is one which is being actively and profitably pursued by psychologists all over the world. You seem to be unaware of this; not a very creditable state of things for a person who professes to be a student of thought, but a natural consequence of the fact that you live in a University where it is bad form to recognize the existence of anything less than two thousand years old.

'Psychology is the science which tells us how we think. In its earlier days when introspective methods were the only ones at its disposal it could only tell us how we think in so far as we do our thinking con-sciously; but modern analytic methods have enabled it to probe into the deepest recesses of the uncon-scious, and to reveal the existence and the dynamic power of thought-processes which, because the people in whom they occur are wholly unaware of them, have never before been studied. To these processes, by your own admission, belongs the subject-matter of what you call metaphysics. Metaphysics itself, again by your own admission, has always been a fumbling, confused, unscientific sort of business. The inference is plain. For one so ignorant of psychology you have done very well to guess (I will not say to discover, because what you have done has not been done by scientific methods and has, therefore, no scientific value) that what you call absolute presuppositions exist. Burn your metaphysical books; leave the study of these things in the hands of the psychologists; and all will be well.'

If psychology is really the science which tells us how we think, it is beyond doubt that what I have called metaphysics falls within its province. And there I would gladly leave it if once I could satisfy myself that this phrase, even if not a complete account of psychology, is a correct one so far as it goes. But on this point I ask to be fully satisfied. The work of metaphysics is too important, too intimately bound up with the welfare of science and civilization (for civilization is only our name for systematic and orderly thinking about what are called 'practical' questions), to be handed over to any claimant on the strength of his own unsupported assertion that he is its rightful owner.

That is why I do not propose to place metaphysics in the hands of the psychologists until I have examined their claim that psychology is the science that teaches us how we think. The history of science contains many records of pseudo-sciences, and of pseudo-scientific elements in sciences not wholly delusive. In their time the pseudo-sciences have often made more noise than the genuine sciences. The few who protested against their pretensions have generally been howled down by a confederacy of those who wished to deceive and those who wished to be deceived. But it is an absolute condition of scientific vitality that the protest, however ineffectual, should be made.

'But how are you going to examine the credentials of psychology? If the practitioners of a science claim that it gives genuine knowledge about its subject-matter, who is to tell them that they are wrong? They are the persons who study it scientifically, and they are the only persons who are qualified to criticize whatever passes for a scientific study of it. Other people no doubt have a kind of rough-and-ready, unscientific knowledge of it; but if unscientific thought is permitted to pass judgement on scientific thought, the progress of science is at an end.'

I accept the principle here appealed to. But I do not accept the professed application of it. For even if psychology is the science which tells us how we think, it is not the only science which tells us how we think. Plenty of other people beside the psychologists have been studying thought, and studying it in an orderly and systematic way, for a long time: metaphysicians, logicians, and others whom I will not enumerate. And it is useless to reply that since by my own admission both metaphysics (as I have said with some elaborateness) and logic (as I have more than hinted) stand in need of reform, the testimony of metaphysicians and logicians against psychology is invalid. There are plenty of psychologists who have spoken quite as candidly about the defects of current psychology as I have spoken about the defects of current metaphysics. I have not admitted, and could never conscientiously admit, that metaphysics in the past has got nowhere. It has got quite far enough, and so has logic, to justify those who profess it in examining the claims of a science that proposes to put them out of business.

X

PSYCHOLOGY AS THE SCIENCE
OF FEELING

PSYCHOLOGY under that name has been recognized as a distinct science from the sixteenth century, when the word was used by Melanchthon, Goclenius, and others as a new name to designate what was in effect a new science. There already existed an old-established group of sciences which made it their business to study thought, where thought stands as the general name for a number of different activities (questioning, supposing, and stating or propounding as these words were used in Chapter IV) which together make up the complex activity of knowing. These activities, considered sometimes as emanating from and sometimes as constituting an entity traditionally known as intellect, reason, or mind, had been regarded ever since the days of ancient Greek thought as having two different modes of functioning, one theoretical and the other practical. Theoretical thinking meant trying to think out the truth about something. Practical thinking meant trying to think out what to do in a given situation.

Greek thinkers, and the same is true of medieval and even Renaissance thinkers down to the time of which I am speaking, did not regard 'trying', or aiming at a definite end, as something peculiar to mind. They did not believe, as many people believed in the seventeenth century and later, that bodies merely functioned mechanically, driven *a tergo* by the operation of efficient causes, while minds were drawn onwards from in front, as it were, by the attraction of ends to be realized. The Greeks, followed by medieval and Renaissance thinkers, regarded the human body and its kindred the bodies of other animals and of vegetables as no less teleological in their behaviour than the human mind. They thought of physiological functioning as a complex of efforts directed to the self-preservation of a given organism and the reproduction of its species. What they regarded as peculiar to mind was not having ends but being aware of this and having opinions, in some cases knowledge, as to what its own ends were.

If a mind is something which has opinions as to what it is trying to do, its possession of these opinions will in certain ways complicate its behaviour. An organism unconsciously seeking its own preservation will simply on any given occasion either score another success or score for the first and last time a failure. A mind aiming at the discovery of a truth or the planning of a course of conduct will not only score a success or a failure, it will also think of itself as scoring a success or a failure; and since a thought may be either true or false its thought on this subject will not necessarily coincide with the facts. Any piece of thinking, theoretical or practical, includes as an integral part of itself the thought of a standard or criterion by reference to which it is judged a successful or unsuccessful piece of thinking. Unlike any kind of bodily or physiological functioning, thought is a self-criticizing activity. The body passes no judgement upon itself. Judgement is passed upon it by its environment, which continues to support it and promote its well-being when it pursues its ends successfully and injures or destroys it when it pursues them otherwise. The mind judges itself, though not always justly. Not content with the simple pursuit of its ends, it also pursues the further end of discovering for itself whether it has pursued them successfully.

The sciences of body and mind respectively must take this difference into account. Each must take notice so far as it can of all the essential features in its subject-matter. The science of body must describe the physiological functions of which bodily activity is composed and try to discover upon what ends they are directed. The science of mind, in addition to doing this, must describe the self-judging function which is part and parcel of all thinking and try to discover the criteria upon which its judgements are based.

This demand was recognized by the Greeks; and in their attempts at a science of thought they tried to satisfy it. They constructed a science of theoretical thought called logic and a science of practical thought called ethics. In each case they paid great attention to the task of defining the criteria by reference to which theoretical and practical thought respectively judge of their own success. In view of this attention to the idea of a criterion or standard of judgement, in Latin *norma*, these sciences have been traditionally called normative sciences. But the word 'normative' may prove misleading. It conveys by its form the suggestion that the standard or criterion to which it refers is a criterion belonging to the practitioner of the science thus described, and used by him to judge whether the thinking which he studies has been well or ill done; as if it were for the logician to decide whether a non-logician's thoughts are true or false and his arguments valid or invalid, and for the student of ethics to pass judgement on the actions of other people as having succeeded or failed in their purpose. This suggestion is incorrect. The characteristic of thought in virtue of which a science of thought is called normative consists not in the possibility that one man's thoughts may be judged successful or unsuccessful by another, real though that possibility is; but in the necessity that in every act of thought the thinker himself should judge the success of his own act. To avoid that misleading suggestion I propose to substitute for the traditional epithet 'normative' the more accurate term 'criteriological'.

The sixteenth-century proposal for a new science to be called psychology did not arise from any dissatisfaction with logic and ethics as sciences of thought. It arose from the recognition (characteristic of the sixteenth century) that what we call feeling is not a kind of thinking, not a self-critical activity, and therefore not the possible subject-matter of a criteriological science. Greek and medieval thinkers had generally taken it for granted that feeling is a cognitive activity; that when we feel cold or see a red colour or hear a shrill sound we are coming to know in the various ways corresponding to the various natures of the object known that there is something cold or red or shrill in the world about us. In the sixteenth century it was for the first time both clearly and generally recognized that this was not the case: that in feeling a coldness or seeing a redness or hearing a shrillness we were not cognizing an object but simply having a feeling, due no doubt to things in our environment but not itself constituting knowledge of these things. The proof of this was that the activity of feeling or sensation contained no element of self-criticism. The business of thinking includes the discovery and correction of its own errors. That is no part of the business of seeing, hearing, touching, smelling, tasting, and experiencing the emotions associated with them.

These activities were thus not activities of the 'mind', if that word refers to the self-critical activities called thinking. But neither were they activities of the 'body'. To use a Greek word (for the Greeks had already made important contributions to this science of feeling) they were activities of the 'psyche', and no better word could have been devised for the study of them than psychology. Thus psychology was put on the map of the sciences, to march on the one hand with physiology and on the other with logic and ethics; a science of feeling, designed to fill a gap between the existing science of bodily function and the existing sciences of mind, in no way competing with any of them.

The distinction between an 'empirical' science of feeling and a 'criteriological' science or sciences of thought (where 'empirical' means 'non-criteriological'), although the people who first made it believed that bodies both organic and inorganic behaved teleologically, had no connexion with that belief, and was therefore unaffected by its partial or even complete abandonment, the mechanization of physics or even of physiology as well.

XI

PSYCHOLOGY AS THE PSEUDO-SCIENCE OF THOUGHT

WE have now to consider first how and when, and secondly with what degree of success, psychology decided to abandon its status as a mere science of feeling and to capture for itself the business formerly done by the sciences of thought.

The critical period was the eighteenth century. Modern sentimentalism has created for itself a fancy picture of the eighteenth century as an age of good taste, easy living, and gentlemanly refinement. For some it may have been that; but for others it was an age of fanatical revolt; a Voltairian age of *écrasez l'infâme*, a Rousseauesque age of nostalgia for the forest, a Humian age of reason as the slave of the passions, a Wordsworthian age whose prophets told their disciples to close up the barren leaves of science and of art; and over all its gentlemanly refinement lay the shadow of the guillotine.

The intellectual task of the eighteenth century was the liquidation of Europe's debt to Greece. The Middle Ages were a time during which Aristotle had been increasingly to every European the 'master of those who know'. The anti-Aristotelianism of the sixteenth century had gone along with a Platonic revival and a deepening sense of indebtedness to the ancient world. At last, by the end of the seventeenth century, the European mind felt itself able to stand alone, and thereafter began to develop and express this feeling by singling out for ridicule, criticism, and repudiation all the lessons it was conscious of having learned from the Greeks.

The religious innovations of the eighteenth century were in essence an attack not upon Christianity but upon Christian doctrines and Christian institutions so far as these, being inherited from the Middle Ages and the Renaissance, expressed a mentality moulded by Greek influence. Its scientific innovations were in essence an attack upon just those sciences in which the legacy of Greece was most evident. Biology was one focus of this attack, because biology was at that time the last refuge of teleological natural science. Biology was the science of the organism; and the organism was, one might almost say by definition, the embodiment of that typically Greek idea, the idea of purposive action. Hence the characteristic biology of the eighteenth century became a material-istic or mechanistic biology whose key position was the doctrine that organisms are nothing but com-plexes of material particles and operate solely accord-ing to mechanical principles. If that doctrine could be vindicated biology would fall into line with New-tonian physics and rid itself of everything it owed to the tradition of Aristotle.

In the theory of knowledge the same revolt was at work. Here it took the form of maintaining that intellectual activities, or operations of thought, were nothing but aggregations and complexes of feelings and thus special cases of sensation and emotion.

Theoretical reason or knowledge was only a pattern of sensations; practical reason or will, only a pattern of appetites. Just as the aim of materialistic biology was to wipe out the old biology with its guiding notion of purposive function, so the aim of what I will call 'materialistic epistemology' was to wipe out the old sciences of thought, logic and ethics, with their criteriological methods and their guiding notions of truth and error, good and evil. Just as materialistic biology hoped to study organisms by substituting for the old biological methods the modern methods of Newtonian physics, so materialistic epistemology hoped to study the processes of thought, theoretical and practical, by substituting for the old methods of logic and ethics the modern methods of psychology, the science of feeling.

This programme, as the more acute and painstaking thinkers of the eighteenth century especially in its later years were not slow to realize, was foredoomed to failure. It might very well be true that a revolt against the old logic and ethics had been desirable and had proved beneficial; for it might very well be true that people who professed those sciences had misunderstood their normative character, and had claimed a right of censorship over the thoughts and actions of other people; and for the sake of scientific progress such tyranny might very well have to be overthrown. When it is a case of overthrowing tyranny one should not be squeamish about the choice of weapons. But the tyrannicide's dagger is not the best instrument for governing the people it has liberated. Epistemological materialism, in attacking the criteriological science of logic (for brevity's sake I shall henceforth say nothing about ethics) and offering to replace it by psychology, deliberately proceeded on the assumption that thought did not possess that power of self-criticism which had in the past been rightly regarded as distinguishing it from feeling. If any one who thinks has before his mind a criterion, the double notion of truth and falsehood, by reference to which he judges his thought, any science of thought which repudiates the character of a criteriological science becomes thereby a pseudo-science of thought.

This was what happened when the proposal was made to substitute a psychological science of thought for a logical. Misunderstandings apart, the only difference of principle between a logical and a psychological science of thought is that a logic of thought faces the fact that thought is self-critical and consequently attempts to give some account of the criteria used in this self-criticism, while a psychological science does not. It was, and is, mere bluff to protest that psychology, being a science and therefore having no aim but the discovery of truth, approaches the study of thought with a determination to get at the truth, the whole truth, and nothing but the truth about the subject with which it deals. No science has an aim so vague as this. A science which had no more definite idea than this as to what it was getting at would never get anywhere. Psychology has always approached the study of thought with a perfectly clear and conscious determination to ignore one whole department of the truth, namely to ignore the self-critical function of thought and the criteria which that function implied. From this determination it cannot depart. It stands committed to it, not in its character as science, but in its character as psychology, a science which ever since the sixteenth century has been working out with a good deal of success methods appropriate to the study of feeling.

The nineteenth century saw a great boom in epistemological materialism. Many people who were interested in the advancement of natural science still had the same old motive for embracing it, because they still found their way blocked by the obstacles their ancestors had encountered in the eighteenth century: academic and ecclesiastical authority, combined with misunderstanding as to the true function of the criteriological sciences. It is characteristic of many important nineteenth-century movements, as I remarked in Chapter VIII, that they were reactionary in fundamentals: they had no new ideas of their own but simply took over some idea which had been left them ready made by the eighteenth century. The development of psychology in the nineteenth century is an example of this. Its fundamental fallacy had already been exposed; but its adherents allowed themselves to pretend either that those who had exposed it did not know what they were talking about or that psychology as it now existed was a new and different thing. Before the nineteenth century had gone very far it was being said on all hands that psychology was the science of thought, and that by its work the false pretensions of that out-of-date pseudo-science, logic, had been exploded and the study of thought placed upon a scientific basis.

But these claims, throughout the nineteenth century and right down to the present day, have always continued to be based on the principles of epistemological materialism. Hence, when we are told that psychology is the science which tells us how we think, we must never forget that the word 'think' is being used in a rather special sense. It has lost all suggestion of self-criticism. It has lost all suggestion of an attempt to think truly and avoid thinking falsely. In fact, since this is at bottom what distinguishes thinking from feeling, the word 'think' here simply means feel.

Nothing could be easier than to show that, however remarkable have been the triumphs of psychology when it has attended to its proper business, the study of feeling, its claim to have thrown light on the processes of thinking is incapable of surviving any critical inspection of the work done by psychologists when they deal with such matters as the nature and function in human life of religion or art; the aims and prospects, hopes and fears, of what is called civilization; or the intellectual structure of institutions which, because they are found in civilizations other than that to which the writer belongs, are called savage. These are matters with which any genuinely scientific study of human thought would find itself competent to deal; and it would be perfectly fair and highly instructive to judge the soundness of modern psychology regarded as a science of thought by its success in propounding, for the problems they present, convincing and helpful and agreed solutions.

But just because it has so completely failed to do this the critical method I have defined would require more space for its convincing development than the present book can afford. It would not take long to expose the tissue of errors and confusions that underlies, for example, Freud's *Totem and Taboo*;[1] but when that had been done, many readers would pass it off with a shrug, saying either 'I am not a Freudian', or 'This is only skirmishing, and does not touch Freud's real position'; and perhaps none of these would see that by such answers they were conceding my point. To plead that one is not a Freudian is to say that the question whether Freud is right or wrong is not a scientific question but a question of party loyalties. To plead that a criticism of *Totem and Taboo* does not touch Freud's real position is to say that his views on religion, magic, and civilization are not grounded in his work as a scientist but are the mere opinions of a man whose reputation as a scientist has won for them a consideration they do not deserve.

What I propose to do, therefore, is to examine

---

[1] I name *Totem and Taboo* partly because Freud is by common consent the greatest psychologist of the last half-century, and partly because I have already published a small sample of the criticism mentioned in the text, on pp. 62–4 and p. 77, note, of *The Principles of Art* (1938).

three characteristic passages from books intended by their authors and treated by their readers as text-books, the authors being accredited teachers of psychology and the passages characteristic of what their pupils are expected to learn. The reader will understand that what I shall discuss is only an exceedingly small part of the evidence upon which I rely when I say that psychology, in its capacity as the science which tells us how we think, is a pseudo-science. From this small sample, however, there emerges not that conclusion only, but the further suspicion that the authors I shall quote are more or less conscious of this. The passages not only prove that their authors are neglecting the established canons of scientific thought, but suggest that they are more or less consciously defying them. They are not trying to think scientifically in the sense in which people who pursue other sciences are trying to think scientifically. They are trying to do something else.

It seems to me that there is a certain connexion between these two conclusions. Psychology cannot be a science of thought, because the methods it has developed in its history as a science of feeling preclude it from dealing with the problems of criteriology. It has nothing to say about truth and falsehood. If a science of feeling has nothing to say about truth and falsehood, nobody need worry. To discuss these things is not its business, it is the business of the science of thought. But if a science of thought has nothing to say about truth and falsehood the omission becomes important. It can only mean that according to this science the distinction between truth and falsehood does not exist. And this is what psychology as the science of thought does, implicitly at any rate, teach: that the distinction between truth and falsehood is part of that antiquated lumber which has at last, thanks to its own success in superseding a logical science of thought by a psychological, been thrown on the dust-heap.

Since the drawing of a distinction between truth and falsehood belongs to the very essence of thinking, a 'science of thought' which does not discuss the function by which thought distinguishes these things, and neglects to give a scientific account of the distinction itself, is doing something more than merely renouncing by its actions any claim which it may make in words to be considered a science of thought. It is actually teaching that there is no difference between the pursuit of truth, or science, and the pursuit of falsehood, or sophistry; no difference between scientific teaching or the inculcation of truth and pseudo-scientific teaching or the inculcation of falsehood. A science of thought which maintains that truth is a meaningless word (and any science of thought maintains this by implication if it neglects its own proper duty of trying to settle what the word means) is maintaining that science is a meaningless word; and consequently that in spite of all claims to the contrary it is itself not a science at all, whether of thought or of anything else. And so we reach the conclusion, surprising perhaps but not to be escaped, that when psychology claims to be the science which teaches us how we think it is covertly describing itself as no science at all.

By merely working out the logic of its own position (a thing which need not be consciously done in order to be done effectively) psychology as the science of thought must sooner or later bring itself into a state in which it cares nothing for scientific method or scientific accuracy; in which it has ceased to wear even a pseudo-science's customary sheep's clothing of traditional scientific dress, but exhibits quite cynically the fact that it does not even propose to argue on the points about which it pretends to argue, does not even try to avoid contradicting itself as to what its so-called investigations prove, and does not even profess to vindicate its claims by showing that it can discover things nobody knew before.

XII

A PSEUDO-SCIENCE REFUTES ITSELF

AMONG the characteristic features of a pseudo-science are the following. (1) Red herrings, or the pretence of discussing a topic belonging to the field with which it professes to deal, while in fact discussing a different topic not belonging to that field. (2) Self-contradiction, or the betrayal of its inability to establish any genuine results by asserting concurrently as genuine fruits of scientific research two propositions which cancel one another out. (3) Plagiarism, or presenting as discoveries of its own what are in fact matters of common knowledge. I shall confine myself to these three heads, and give only one example of each.

1. *Example of Red Herrings.* I take a standard textbook, Professor W. McDougall's *Outline of Psychology*, and open it at p. 193. The chapter title is 'Habit and Intelligence in Animals'; the section heading, 'The Method of Trial and Error'. The question under discussion is how 'animals' (the author means non-human animals) learn. One way in which things are learnt is by 'trial and error'; and this is the process of which we are to be offered a psychological account.

Before looking at it let us observe that the author does not propose to use the familiar phrase 'trial and error' in a new and esoteric sense, for he offers no definition of it. Evidently he means us to accept the phrase for what it actually is, a common expression in everyday use, and to understand him as meaning by it what in everyday use it actually means. Let us consider, then, what as so used it does mean.

(i) Generically it refers not merely to a way in which we learn something but to a method by which we set ourselves to find something out through a process of deliberate experimentation.

(ii) Specifically it refers to a method by which we 'try' one thing at a time, and if this does not work reject it as an 'error', and try again.

This method involves five stages:

(*a*) Framing a certain hypothesis.

(*b*) Asking whether it is true or false.

(*c*) Performing an action deliberately designed to test it, in the twofold conviction that the action will have one result if it is true and another result if it is false, and that we shall be able to tell which result it has had.

(*d*) If the action had the second result, inferring that the hypothesis was an 'error'.

(*e*) Beginning again with a different hypothesis.

A little attention to facts will convince the reader that all this is meant when we describe a man as learning by trial and error what key fits a certain lock, or what switch controls a certain light, or what photographic exposure is correct for a certain subject.

Professor McDougall writes: 'Much human, as well as animal, learning proceeds in this way, and many experimental studies of such animal learning have been made.' He exemplifies this by quoting

E. L. Thorndike's famous experiments on cats. I repeat Professor McDougall's own summary.

> Thorndike confined young cats in cages . . . [whose] door was fastened . . . by a catch or button which could easily be turned by the animal. In each instance the cat was placed in the cage in a condition of 'utter hunger'; and food was placed outside the bars of the cage, beyond reach of the cat's paw. The result . . . was that each animal scratched and clawed about the front of his cage for some time, until, in the course of these random movements, he turned the button, escaped, and secured food. Each animal was put through the process again and again; and in the main the result was that he gradually shortened the period of 'random' movement, until after many repetitions he learned to go straightway to the button, turn it, and so escape.

In the facts here reported there is no shred of evidence, I will not say that the method of trial and error has been employed, but even that any single one of the five stages which go to compose it has occurred.

(a) There is no evidence even suggesting, far less proving, that the cat began by forming an hypothesis as to the right way of getting out.

(b) There is no evidence suggesting that, even if it has formed such an hypothesis, the cat has asked itself whether that hypothesis is true.

(c) There is no evidence suggesting that, even if it has asked itself this question, the cat deliberately acts in a way by which it has planned to discover the answer.

(d) There is no evidence suggesting that when a

certain movement has failed to secure its escape the cat decides to abandon the original hypothesis.

(*e*) There is no evidence suggesting that, even if this does happen, the cat then starts over again with a fresh hypothesis.

On the other hand, the evidence is not entirely neutral as to what is going on in the cat's mind. It suggests that the cat is not 'thinking' on any 'method' whatever, but is behaving like a man who has lost his head under some such influence as that of panic fear, and is therefore not capable of using 'the method of trial and error', or indeed any other method.

In the passage quoted, moreover, there is no evidence suggesting that the author was under any misapprehension as to what the evidence suggested about the cat's state of mind. On the contrary, the words quoted show quite clearly that he did not for a moment believe that anything was going on which even remotely resembled any kind of deliberate experimentation, let alone that kind of deliberate experimentation which is called 'trial and error'. When the cat's movements are described as 'random' movements of 'scratching and clawing about the front of his cage', it is being emphatically said that nothing at all like deliberate experimentation was going on.

The famous experiments thus throw no light whatever on the method of trial and error, and Professor McDougall knows that they throw no light on it. But that phrase has been used as a section heading, because it is the name of a process of thought, and psychology has got to keep up the pretence of telling us how we think.

The way in which Professor McDougall discusses them shows that he wishes to suggest that there is no difference between scientifically testing an hypothesis and acting under such an influence as that of panic fear. Briefly, the answer he is giving to the question 'How do we think?', as that question arises in the special case of trial and error, is 'we do not think at all. What is called thinking is a random scratching and clawing about.'

2. *Example of Self-Contradiction.* For this I will quote Professor C. Spearman's famous book *The Nature of 'Intelligence' and the Principles of Cognition.* The author has stated in this book with obvious care a large number of psychological 'laws' which, he claims, have been established by himself through minute and highly scientific experiments. In the ninth chapter he enumerates one group of such laws which he calls 'Quantitative Principles'. The second of these (p. 132) is called 'the principle of retentivity', and runs thus: '*the occurrence of any cognitive event produces a tendency for it to occur afterwards*'. The third, two pages later, is called 'the principle of fatigue', and runs thus: '*the occurrence of any cognitive event produces a tendency opposed to its occurring afterwards*'. Here, within two pages, one and the same cause is credited with the production of precisely opposite effects: not merely incompatible effects, but contrary ones.

If any one having a general acquaintance with the

principles of scientific research read a book in which at one page a physicist had said 'the occurrence of a rise of temperature in a rod of metal produces a tendency for it to expand', and two pages later 'the occurrence of a rise of temperature in a rod of metal produces a tendency for it to contract', his first idea would certainly be that the physicist's pen had slipped. If that hypothesis failed he would infer that the physicist, however many experiments he had tried, had not tried any which told him anything about the effect of temperature on metals. He would probably go on to remark that it was evidently no good looking to the author for any guidance whatever on any scientific subject, because a person capable of contradicting himself with so little apparent distress lacked one of the elementary qualifications without which nobody could ever become a scientist at all. He might further conclude that if in the face of a performance like this the author could hold down the job of professor of physics in a great university and earn the admiration of his fellow physicists, physics must be a pretty thorough fraud; a conscious and confessed fraud, one that had become so cynical as to abandon even the pretence of offering a consistent statement on a point under discussion.

These comments would not depend on the fact, for fact it is, that physics is an aristocrat of the sciences, whose nobility obliges it to conform with an exceptionally high standard of logical integrity. Meteorology has comparatively small pretension to exactitude; but if a meteorologist found that owing to haste in composition he had written on one page 'Low-pressure systems tend to revolve counter-clock-wise' and, two pages later, 'Low-pressure systems tend to revolve clockwise', he would blush for his carelessness and insert the qualifications 'in the nor-thern hemisphere' and 'in the southern hemisphere' respectively. If he discovered the contradiction too late for these insertions fear of professional disgrace if no higher motive would, I imagine, induce him to suppress the whole edition of his book.

Yet Professor Spearman's self-contradiction does not read like an inadvertency. The wording and the italics suggest that it is deliberate. Whether it is deliberate or not it is fatal to the claims of the 'science' he professes to expound; for its very occurrence is proof that the methods he so proudly advocates are no defence against the most elementary kind of scientific disaster. This is no reflection on Professor Spearman's personal character or on his personal qualifications for scientific work. All I am suggesting is that he is a man in a false position; a man committed, unfortunately for himself, to maintaining the false dogma that psychology is the science which tells us how we think. Error, too, has its martyrs.

3. *Example of Plagiarism.* For this I will quote Professor Spearman again, at pp. 229–30.

Thus, then, the mental event asserted, more speculatively than evidentially, by such a long array of writers—the πάθημα of Plato, the 'impressions' of Hume and most associationists —receives finally an experimental corroboration.

In other words: something which the author claims

to have discovered (never mind what it is) by the methods of inquiry to which he attaches so much importance, not merely is, but is by himself expressly said to be, something that a long array of writers has been saying for well over two thousand years.

Ah, but, says he, these earlier writers asserted it only speculatively: I assert it evidentially. But what do these long words mean? Do they mean that when Plato spoke of παθήματα ἐν τῇ ψυχῇ he was only guessing, and that now for the first time, thanks to Professor Spearman's own researches, we are entitled to say that Plato guessed right? If so the inference is that so far as this case is concerned Professor Spearman's researches are useless. If they had obliged us to say that Plato's guess was wrong, they would at least have done something. But as for the preceding 2,000 years and more every one had believed Plato's guess to be right, and as the Professor allows us to do that still, his researches have left the subject exactly where they found it.

And this is not surprising. If the methods used by psychology in its investigation of intellectual processes can establish no results whatever (and this is implied in the admission that they may establish two opposite answers to one and the same question) it follows that whatever positive doctrine is advanced by its votaries must have come not from these methods but from elsewhere; perhaps out of their own prejudices, perhaps out of the propositions advanced by the old-fashioned sciences it is their express aim to supersede. Their attempt to confer a new value on these borrowed propositions by claiming to have at last confirmed them by experimental methods is untrue in fact because these methods are powerless to confirm anything, as is shown by their faculty of yielding self-contradictory results; and would be fatal, if it were true, to the claims of the new science; because in so far as a new science can only offer new reasons (however bad) for believing what has long been taught by its despised predecessor the boasted innovation in method leads to no new discoveries and is scientifically valueless.

If any professed scientist had argued at any time between 1600 and 1900 in the way in which we find these distinguished psychologists arguing in the passages I have quoted, both of which were published in 1923, it could only have been through some momentary lapse from what in his normal working life he recognized as the principles of scientific method. But the passages I have quoted do not represent momentary lapses. Their authors realize pretty clearly what they are doing. And they are not isolated exceptions. Of the vast psychological literature professedly concerned with intellectual processes which pours incessantly from the press, they are entirely typical both in their complete scientific futility and in the fact that their authors recognize this futility and make only the most perfunctory and half-hearted attempts to conceal it from their readers.

In this respect the pseudo-science of psychology, the psychology which professes to be the heir of logic and the first genuinely scientific science of thought, is not quite on all fours with old pseudo-sciences like alchemy or astrology. For these at any rate kept up a pretence of being scientific. With the psychology of thought the pretence is dropped almost as soon as it is made. No psychologist, as I am very well aware, will think the worse either of Professor McDougall or of Professor Spearman if he reads what I have written about them and recognizes its truth. Over and over again when reading what psychologists have written or when conversing with them, in which occupations I have spent a good deal of time during the last ten years, I have got the impression that their real aim has nothing to do with their loudly professed allegiance to the traditional principles of European science. I may be wrong, but the suspicion has been repeatedly borne in upon me that they are doing something definite, and doing it with almost perfect unanimity and a considerable degree of success.

How far they or any of them really understand what they are doing I cannot say. Whatever it is, it has no real resemblance to the work of constructing a science; though the claim that it is the work of constructing a science is a claim which is accepted as substantially true by a large proportion of the public: in fact by most people except those whose interests, by bringing them into constant and effective touch with the work of human thought, theoretical and practical, have rendered them proof against egregious falsehoods about it. I refer to such persons as historians, scholars, artists and art-critics, lawyers, politicians, whose open scorn of psychology is notorious and a cause of some indignation to the psychologists themselves, when it ought rather to be a cause of anxious self-examination.

XIII

THE PROPAGANDA OF IRRATIONALISM

As to what it is that the psychologists are doing I have my suspicions; and I will try to explain what they are. I can best do this by asking the reader to follow me in making certain assumptions.

Let us suppose a civilization whose most characteristic features had for many centuries been based upon the predominance, among those who shared it, of the belief that truth was the most important thing in the world, and that consequently scientific thinking, systematic, orderly thinking, theoretical and practical alike, pursued with all the energy at his command and with all the skill and care at his disposal, was the most valuable thing man could do. In such a civilization every feature would be marked with some peculiar characteristic derived from this prevailing habit of mind and not to be expected in a civilization differently based.

To take a few examples. Religion would be predominantly a worship of truth in which the god is truth itself, the worshipper a seeker after truth, and the god's presence to the worshipper a gift of mental light. Philosophy would be predominantly an exposition not merely of the nature of thought, action, &c., but of scientific thought and orderly (principled, thought-out) action, with special attention to method and to the problem of establishing standards by which on reflection truth can be distinguished from falsehood.

Politics would be predominantly the attempt to build up a common life by the methods of reason (free discussion, public criticism) and subject to the sanction of reason (i.e. the ultimate test being whether the common life aimed at is a reasonable one, fit for men who, no matter what differences divide them, agree to think in an orderly way). Education would be predominantly a method for inducing habits of orderly and systematic thinking. Social structure would be predominantly of such a kind as to place in the most honourable and commanding position those who were intellectually the *élite* of the people, the priest-kings of the god of truth, men of science and learning on the one hand, men of affairs on the other. Economic life would come into line with the prevailing habit of mind by converting customary methods of production, distribution, transport, &c., into 'scientific' ones; that is, by applying the notion of orderly and systematic thinking to economic matters no less than to any others. These half-dozen instances should suffice.

Now let us suppose that such a civilization had been in existence for a long time, during which the application of its fundamental principles had reached a somewhat elaborate development. Suppose, for example, that the rationalization of economic life had reached such a point that its populations could not be kept alive at all, or protected from starvation and disease, let alone kept in the degree of comfort to which they had become accustomed, except by the ceaseless exertion of innumerable scientists. And sup-

pose that now within this same civilization a movement grew up hostile to these fundamental principles.
I will not speak of a conspiracy to destroy civilization; not because I shrink from a notion so reminis-
cent of a detective novel, but because what I am
thinking of is something less conscious, less deliberate,
less dependent upon the sinister activities of any mere
gang, than a conspiracy: something more like an
epidemic disease: a kind of epidemic withering of
belief in the importance of truth and in the obliga-
tion to think and act in a systematic and methodical
way. Such an irrationalist epidemic infecting religion
would turn it from a worship of truth to a worship
of emotion and a cultivation of certain emotional
states. Infecting education it would aim at inducing
the young to abandon the habit of orderly thinking,
or to avoid forming such a habit by offering to their
imitation examples of unscientific thinking and holding up the ideals of science to contempt by precept and
example. Infecting politics it would substitute for
the ideal of orderly thinking in that field the ideal
of tangled, immediate, emotional thinking; for the
idea of a political thinker as political leader the idea
of a leader focusing and personifying the mass-
emotions of his community; for the ideal of intelligent agreement with a leader's thought the idea of
an emotional communion with him; and for the idea
of a minority persuaded to conform the idea of un-
patriotic persons (persons not sharing that communion) induced to conform by emotional means,
namely by terror.

Next let us suppose that the tissues of the civilization invaded by this irrationalist disease are to a considerable extent resisting it. The result will be that the infection can progress only by concealing its true character behind a mask of conformity to the spirit of the civilization it is attacking. The success of the attack will be conditional on the victims' suspicions not being aroused. Thus in educational institutions an explicit proposal to abandon the practice of orderly and systematic thinking would only bring those who made it into disrepute, and discredit them with the very persons they were trying to infect. But so long as nothing like a panic was created, liberties could be taken which would quickly have proved fatal among persons whose faith in scientific thought had not already been weakened. Let a sufficient number of men whose intellectual respectability is vouched for by their academic position pay sufficient lip-service to the ideals of scientific method, and they will be allowed to teach by example whatever kind of anti-science they like, even if this involves a hardly disguised breach with all the accepted canons of scientific method.

The ease with which this can be done will be much greater if it is done in an academic society where scientific specialization is so taken for granted that no one dare criticize the work of a man in another faculty. In that case all that is necessary to ensure immunity for the irrationalist agents is that they should put forward their propaganda under the pretence that it is itself a special science, which therefore other scientists will understand that they must not criticize. Thus irrationalism will avail itself of the privileges accorded to science by a rationalist civilization in order to undermine the entire fabric of that civilization.

The reader is lastly to suppose, if he will, that the situation I have described is the one in which, together with the rest of the world, he now stands. I do not wish him necessarily to confine this to a matter of mere supposition; I will confess that to myself it is more than a supposition, it is a fact, and I think the reader might be well advised to consider it in the same way. If he wishes to do something on his own account towards considering whether it is a fact or not, he should ask himself the following questions among others.

1. Has the prevailing religion of our civilization in the past been a worship not of sectional or tribal ends but of a truth which has been regarded as in principle the same for all human beings?

And has there been a tendency of late years, even in theological circles, to ignore and vilify the traditional theology of this religion and to regard religion as an affair of the emotions? Has this tendency anywhere gone so far as to substitute for the worship of universal truth and goodness the worship of a sectional or tribal god personifying the mass-emotions of a particular people? If so, where have these tendencies been most evidently at work?

2. Has the traditional philosophy of our civilization in the past expounded ideals of rational thinking

and rational acting, the orderly or systematic 'theoretical' thinking which is called science, and the
various kinds of orderly or systematic 'practical'
thinking which are called forming and carrying out
a policy or acting like a man of principle, in other
words wisdom or virtue?

And has there been a tendency of late years to
belittle the notion of scientific thought, either by
magnifying emotion at the expense of intellect, or
by expounding an ideal of disorderly or unsystematic
thinking, called 'intuition' or the like, as something
preferable to the methodical or progressive (if you
want to sneer, you say 'plodding') labour of reason?
Has there been a tendency towards belittling rules,
principles, policies, in the field of action, and towards
developing a kind of ethical intuitionism or a kind of
ethical emotionalism?

3. Has the political tradition of our civilization
been based on the idea of a political life lived according to a plan whose chief recommendation has been
its claim to reasonableness? Have political leaders
been chosen in the past for their supposed intelligence, far-sightedness, grasp on principles, and skill
in devising means to ends that accorded with these
principles? Have their followers been persons whose
intellect, inferior to theirs in power, nevertheless
agreed with it as one intellect does agree with another,
by thinking in the same way? Have the methods by
which leaders carried their points against opponents
and secured their hold over their followers been the
methods of reason; that is, public discussion of princi-

ples, public statement of facts, and public debate as
to the relation between principles and policies, between ends and means?

And has there been a tendency of late years to
become impatient with the work of politically educat-
ing an entire people; to choose leaders not for their
intellectual powers but for their ability to excite mass-
emotions; to induce in followers not an ability to
think about political problems, but certain emotions
which in persons untrained to think will explode into
action with no questions asked as to where such
action will lead; and to suppress discussion and information in favour of what is called propaganda,
that is, statements made not because they are true
but because they generate these emotions or spark
them into action? And have these changes gone so
far that even the characteristic facial expression of
a political leader has changed from the expression
of a thinker (the mathematician-thinker's face of a
Napoleon, the humanist-thinker's face of a Glad-
stone) to the expression of a hypnotist, with scowling
forehead and glaring eye?

All I am asking the reader to do is to suppose, for
the time being, that the answer to all these questions
is in the affirmative and the evidence for an irrationalist epidemic sweeping over at least a large part of
Europe, therefore, prima facie convincing. Let us
think what would follow.

Civilizations sometimes perish because they are
forcibly broken up by the armed attack of enemies
without or revolutionaries within; but never from

this cause alone. Such attacks never succeed unless the thing that is attacked is weakened by doubt as to whether the end which it sets before itself, the form of life which it tries to realize, is worth achieving. On the other hand, this doubt is quite capable of destroying a civilization without any help whatever. If the people who share a civilization are no longer on the whole convinced that the form of life which it tries to realize is worth realizing, nothing can save it. If European civilization is a civilization based on the belief that truth is the most precious thing in the world and that pursuing it is the whole duty of man, an irrationalist epidemic if it ran through Europe unchecked would in a relatively short time destroy everything that goes by the name of European civilization.

Consider one consequence alone: that affecting economic life. For a little while the emotional pressure which is the life-blood of an irrationalist society, acting positively in the shape of loyalty or negatively in the shape of terror, would compel a number of technicians to retain their hold on the results of scientific inquiry with sufficient firmness to enable them to tend and repair, possibly even to improve, the mechanical and other plant on which the populations of European and Europeanized countries depend by now for their very existence. But this would not last long. When scientific workers, instead of living as the honoured intellectual *élite* of a society that worships truth, lived as the helots of a society that despised the spirit of their work though depending upon its fruits, neither loyalty nor terror would enable them to carry that work on. Loyalty would make them incapable of worshipping a god whom their society had renounced. Terror would make them incapable of thinking systematically.

Science is a plant of slow growth. It will not grow (and for a plant the end of growth is the end of life) except where the scientist as the priest of truth is not only supported but revered as a priest-king by a people that shares his faith. When scientists are no longer kings, there will be (to adapt a famous saying of Plato's) no end to the evils undergone by the society that has dethroned them until it perishes physically for sheer lack of sustenance.

The hypothesis we are considering is that among ourselves the progress of such an irrationalist epidemic, though rapid, is still opposed by certain obstacles. One of these is the conviction among professional thinkers that scientific thinking, as orderly and systematic as they know how to make it, is one of the things which for them make life worth living. And this is why the present condition of psychology is a matter of such importance. As the science of feeling, psychology is not only a science of respectable antiquity; it is a science with great triumphs to its credit, some of long standing, others lately achieved, others even yet incomplete, and (one may hope) others to come in the future. I do not wish any reader of these pages to form an impression, or even a suspicion, that I value these achievements at a low rate. The study by psychologists of sensation and emotion, whether in the laboratory or in the consulting-room or in what other conditions soever they think it capable of being pursued, is a most important kind of research and a thing which every friend of science will encourage by every means at his command.

My suspicions are not about this; they are about the status of psychology as the pseudo-science of thought which claims to usurp the field of logic and ethics in all their various branches, including political science, aesthetics, economics, and whatever other criteriological sciences there may be, and finally of metaphysics. In these fields I find it to be a fact that psychological inquiries have proved absolutely incapable of adding anything to our knowledge. I find it to be a fact that they are conducted in open defiance of the recognized canons of scientific procedure. I find it to be a fact that their devotees and advocates are not abashed by all this. They regard the calling of attention to it as a symptom of an obsolete mentality and a thing to be treated with obloquy and contempt, not as a criticism which they must meet by reforming their work or else by abandoning it. I do not think it possible to suppress, or conscientious to conceal, a suspicion that the true explanation of these facts may be that psychology in its capacity as the pseudo-science of thought, teaching by precept that what is called thought is only feeling, and by example that what is called science is nothing more, is no mere addition to the long list of pseudo-sciences; it is an attempt to discredit the very idea of science. It is the propaganda of irrationalism.

XIV

POSITIVISTIC METAPHYSICS

FROM the psychological attack upon metaphysics I turn to the positivistic. Positivism is the name of a philosophy greatly favoured in the nineteenth century whose motives were a good deal like those of eighteenth-century materialism. Its central doctrine was that the only valid method of attaining knowledge is the method used in the natural sciences, and hence that no kind of knowledge is genuine unless it either is natural science or resembles natural science in method. These considerations made it a question of great importance to others than natural scientists what the method of natural science actually was; and it was the attempt to answer this question that led John Stuart Mill, the founder and leader of positivism in its English form, whose personal interests lay not in natural science but in the science of man, to overhaul the traditional logic with far-reaching results.

The positivists were too much interested in the validity of scientific thought to join hands with psychology in its attack on logic. They could tolerate no theory of thought that ignored the problems of criteriology. As champions of scientific thinking against unscientific thinking they were not impressed by the mere fact that a process of thought had occurred; they wanted to know whether it had or had not satisfied the scientific criterion of validity.

In defining this criterion, however, they were a little too easily satisfied. They regarded the process of scientific inquiry as falling into two stages. First facts were ascertained; then they were classified. The ascertaining of facts was work for the senses; the business of thought was to classify them. A concept or notion was thus the same thing as a class of facts; and since facts were by definition observable (where to observe meant to ascertain by the use of the senses) a concept or notion was valid only if the facts of which it was a class were observable facts, which they could be known to be only on condition that they were observed. An 'hypothesis'—that important feature of all modern science—could thus be defined as an expectation of observing facts of a certain kind under certain conditions. A scientific 'law' could be defined as the proposition that under conditions of a certain kind facts of a certain kind were uniformly observable. Any 'hypothesis' or 'law' which could not be defined in terms like these would be written off as a pseudo-hypothesis or pseudo-law, just as a 'notion' which turned out not to be a class of observable facts would be written off as a pseudo-notion.

In suggesting that this is too naïve a theory of scientific method I have especially in mind two shortcomings. In the first place it was not very acute in the positivists to think that the 'facts' of which a scientist speaks are observed by the mere action of our senses. The science of psychology had been founded centuries ago on the recognition that by means of our senses we never observe any facts at all, we only undergo feelings. Here positivism ignored the whole history of modern thought and reverted in a single jump to a long-exploded error of the Middle Ages. It was one example of a medievalist tendency which crops out not infrequently among the manifestations of the positivist mind.

This is not to suggest that the positivists were wrong to insist as they did on the importance of facts, and in particular upon their importance in the economy of natural science. What they failed to see was that 'fact' is a term belonging to the vocabulary of historical thought. Properly speaking a 'fact' is a thing of the kind which it is the business of historians to ascertain. The word is sometimes used in another sense, as if it were merely a synonym for 'truth'; there are people who will not shrink from calling it a fact that twice two is four; but no such misuse of the word is implied when facts are spoken of in the vocabulary of natural science. Here facts are always and notoriously historical facts. It is a fact for the astronomer that at a certain time on a certain day a certain observer saw a transit of Venus taking place. If it is of any interest for this observer or any one else to know subsequently that the transit took place then, the only way in which he can know it is by knowing the historical fact that it was observed; and historical facts are not apprehensible to our senses. Positivism thus implied, but did not attempt to furnish, a theory of historical knowledge as a foundation for its theory of natural science. Failing that, it

was bankrupt from the start. It had staked its sol-
vency on assets it did not possess.

In the second place it was rash of the positivists to
maintain that every notion is a class of observable (if
you like, historical) facts. This amounted to saying,
what in fact positivists have always tried more or less
consistently to say, that scientific thought has no
presuppositions. For if the function of thought is to
classify observed facts, there must be facts available
for classification before thought can begin to operate.
And once facts are available there is no need to presuppose anything. You just set to work and classify
them. This would be a tenable position if the work
of observing facts were done by the senses without
any assistance from the intellect. But as this is not
the case, as what the positivists called 'observing'
facts is really historical thinking, which is a complex
process involving numerous presuppositions, it is far
from tenable.

The positivists inherited in a somewhat attenuated
form the eighteenth-century programme of waging
war against the Greek elements still to be found in
modern thought. They pursued this programme not
by continuing the attack on logic (as we have seen,
they knew better than to do that) but by attacking
metaphysics. The ground of their attack was not an
objection to its method but an objection to its subject-
matter. If they had recognized that all thinking involves absolute presuppositions, they would have been
eager to find out what, on this or that kind of occasion,
was being thus presupposed. But owing to their too

hasty analysis of scientific thought they failed to recognize the logical function of suppositions in general, and never discovered that there were such things as absolute presuppositions at all. What are in fact suppositions they consistently misunderstood as propositions. What is in fact a presupposition they misunderstood as a general proposition about matters of fact, advanced upon credit and awaiting verification. This would do at a pinch as an account of relative presuppositions, in whose case verification is a word that has meaning; though it is not an accurate account even of these, because (see Chap. IV, prop. 3) their logical efficacy depends merely upon their being supposed; consequently, from the point of view of a person interested simply in their logical efficacy, that is, interested in the logic of scientific method, they are not generalizations about matters of fact and do not await verification. As an account of absolute presuppositions, which never in any context stand as propositions, and are therefore neither in need of verification nor susceptible of it, the description of them as generalizations is nothing but nonsensical. Towards absolute presuppositions, therefore, as such and on principle, the positivist's attitude could only be a flat *non possumus*. There could not be such things, because if there were they would be, *qua* presuppositions, propositions advanced on credit and awaiting verification; but, *qua* absolute, propositions of such a kind that they could never be verified by any conceivable observation or series of observations; and it is a principle of positivism that

there can be no such propositions: therefore, &c.
And in the most modern form of positivism this
ancient error is still perpetuated in the doctrine that
supposing, and therefore presupposing, is one of the
various attitudes, as they are called, which one can
take up towards a proposition.

But this *non possumus* was not quite so final as it
might seem. Actually, it left the positivist free to say
either of two things (both, of course, false) about any
absolute presupposition. (1) He might if he liked
describe it as a generalization about matters of fact;
a pretty sweeping one perhaps, but in principle that
and nothing more; and consequently maintain that
by observing facts one could hope to verify it. And
indeed, he might continue, it must have been arrived
at by observing facts; for here it was; so it must have
been arrived at; and there was no other way in which
that could have happened. Heads I win. (2) He
might say that it was obviously not a thing of the
kind which could have been arrived at by observing
facts, for it was not a record of observations; and
that, since there was no other way in which it could
have been arrived at, it had not been arrived at;
consequently, although it looked like a significant
statement, it could not be one; it was just a piece of
nonsense. Tails you lose.

Any positivist stands logically committed to the
principle that metaphysics is impossible. But at the
same time he is quite at liberty to indulge both in
metaphysics and in pseudo-metaphysics to his heart's
content, so long as he protests that what he is doing

is just ordinary scientific thinking, as scientific thinking is understood by himself; that is, so long as he
finds himself disposed for what I call the 'heads I
win' attitude of pretending that a given absolute presupposition is a generalization from observed facts.

Thus the positivists, ostensibly the inveterate
enemies of all metaphysics whatever, were in practice
exponents of a certain metaphysical method. This
was to take absolute presuppositions which, by dint
of perfectly sound metaphysical analysis, they detected as implied in the methods of natural science,
and then, turning into pseudo-metaphysicians, play
'heads I win' with them, in order to justify them on
positivistic principles, that is, to exhibit them as
generalizations from observed facts. Their reason
for playing 'heads I win' with them, when 'tails I
lose' would have been at least equally legitimate,
arose from the fact that, having constituted themselves philosophical patrons of natural science, they
thought themselves bound to justify any presuppositions which natural science thought fit to make.

As an example of this I will refer to John Stuart
Mill's discussion of what he calls the uniformity of
nature: the 'fact', as he calls it, 'that the universe is
governed by general laws'.[1] Mill understood that
when a natural scientist tries to discover the law
according to which a given event E happens, the
question he is asking presupposes that the event E
happens according to some law. The scientist is convinced that E happens according to some law before

[1] *Logic*, Book III, ch. iii (ed. 1, vol. i, pp. 371 seqq.).

he finds out, if he ever does find out, what this law is; indeed he is convinced of this before he knows that E exists at all. The conviction, therefore, does not result from any observations he may have made of E itself. Yet analysis of his thought shows beyond doubt that he has such a conviction; and that it is a conviction not concerning E alone, but concerning all events whatever. The scientist is convinced that E happens according to law because he is convinced that all events happen according to laws. How does he come by this conviction?

What Mill has done is first to carry out a perfectly valid piece of metaphysical analysis (though not a very original one) resulting in the discovery of the historical fact that natural scientists in his own time were convinced that all events happen according to law, and then to throw away the fruits of this discovery by misunderstanding the nature of the thing he has discovered. The thing he has discovered is in fact an absolute presupposition, and the only significant meaning which can attach to the question how scientists came by this presupposition would be: 'out of what other constellation of absolute presuppositions, by what process of change, did the constellation containing this absolute presupposition come into being?' But this is not what Mill means. Like the typical positivist that he is, he confuses suppositions with propositions,[1] and consequently thinks

---

[1] The *locus classicus* for this confusion on Mill's part is his analysis of an hypothetical proposition, which he regards as a compound proposition asserting a relation between two propositions;

that a person who argues from an absolute presupposition stands or falls by that presupposition's
being true. So 'How does he come by it?' means
'How does he know it is true?'; which, as we know,
is a pseudo-metaphysical question.

Mill's attempt to answer this pseudo-metaphysical
question is so admirable that it almost raises pseudo-
metaphysics to the rank of a science. Granted that
'all events happen according to law' is not a supposition but a proposition, and that it lies at the
foundations of natural science, it must be true (for
otherwise the positivistic faith in natural science
would be mistaken), and the natural scientist who
argues from it must know that it is true. Now it is a
generalization; and according to the positivistic theory
of knowledge generalizations come to be known by
means of induction. Any proposition in the form
'All A's are B' is the fruit of an induction based on
the known facts A_1 is B, A_2 is B, A_3 is B, and so on.
'Every event happens according to some law' must,
therefore, be the fruit of an induction based on the
facts that E_1 happens according to some law, so
does E_2, so does E_3, and so on. But it is only by
induction, Mill holds, that laws are discovered. We
know that E_1 happens according to some law only
because we have found out by induction what its

by which analysis the proposition 'If it rains I shall stay indoors'
becomes 'It will rain and so I shall stay indoors'. In his own
words ' "if A is B, C is D" is found to be an abbreviation of the
following: "the *proposition* C is D is a legitimate inference from
the *proposition* A is B".' (*Logic*, Book I, ch. iv, § 3; ed. 1, vol. i,
p. 111; my italics.)

law is. The generalization that every event happens according to some law, Mill concludes, is the fruit of an induction of the second order, based on numerous cases in which inductions of the first order have revealed to us the laws of particular events.[1]

The circle in Mill's argument leaps to the eye. Throughout these numerous first-order inductions we were presupposing that every event happens according to law. Only because of that presupposition did the question arise, What was the law of the particular event we were at the moment investigating? We were therefore already committed to the principle that every event had a law, before we could arrive at a single one of the facts on the strength of which we constructed the second-order induction that led to the 'discovery' of that principle. But if we had not 'discovered' it until the second-order induction was complete we had no right to presuppose it as a foundation to our first-order inductions.

This is perfectly true; but it is not a valid criticism of Mill. Mill, like a true positivist, did not possess the idea of an absolute presupposition. He thought that what he called the uniformity of nature was an empirical proposition, a generalization about matters of fact. Now it is quite possible for certain processes

---

[1] In his own words: 'the proposition that the course of nature is uniform is the fundamental principle, or general axiom, of Induction. It would yet be a great error to offer this large generalization as any explanation of the inductive process. On the contrary, I hold it to be itself an instance of induction, and induction by no means of the most obvious kind.' *Logic*, ed. cit. i. 372.

of thought to go forward on the assumption that a statement of fact which they all presuppose is accurate, and for the question whether it is accurate to be postponed until they are finished. For example a surveyor might make a map without knowing the length of his chain. He could make his map on the assumption that the chain was 66 feet long. When he had finished his work he could check this assumption and insert a corrected scale on his map. The analogy, of course, breaks down; because unless the natural scientists of Mill's day had been absolutely presupposing that all events had laws they would have treated every proposition in the form 'L is the law of E' as provisional and contingent upon ultimate verification of the proposition 'events have laws'. And this they did not do. But this is only another way of saying that the analogy breaks down because it is not an empirical proposition that the course of nature is uniform, i.e. that events have (or happen according to, or as Mill says are governed by) laws. If it had been an empirical proposition, as Mill thought it was, Mill's idea of verifying it by means of a second-order induction would have been sound.

'Metaphysics', said Bradley,[1] 'is the finding of bad reasons for what we believe upon instinct.' If I understand this epigram correctly, it is an accurate description of what Mill was doing when he attempted to justify inductively the belief that the course of nature is uniform. What Bradley seems to be saying is this: 'Why we believe things of that kind I do not

[1] *Appearance and Reality*, preface; ed. 1930, p. xii.

know. Let us give this ignorance a name by saying that we believe them upon instinct; meaning that, at any rate, it is not because we see reason to believe them. Metaphysics is the attempt to find reasons for these beliefs. Experience shows that the reasons thus found are always bad ones.' Bradley is popularly regarded as an opponent of Mill; but he was never so much that as a disillusioned and rather cynical follower. He constantly subjected Mill to sharp criticism; but his aim in this criticism was not to annihilate Mill's doctrines, it was to amend them into a form in which he could find them acceptable. You can see the same attitude towards Mill in, for example, the ethical and political works of T. H. Green. Bradley's epigram represents the state of mind of one who has begun by accepting the first principle of positivistic metaphysics, the principle that all the presuppositions we can detect underlying our thought must be justified, and justified by an appeal to observed facts; has gone on to recognize that in practice this justification regularly fails; but has not yet taken the step of inferring that the game is not worth the candle, still less of asking whether the game is really metaphysics at all. It is in fact, of course, pseudometaphysics.

XV

A POSITIVISTIC MISINTERPRETATION OF PLATO

THIS chapter is a digression. It may be regarded as a note appended to the last paragraph of the preceding; and a reader who is anxious about following the thread of the argument had better leave it out.

Although Aristotle must be called the inventor of metaphysics, it stands to reason that in this as in other respects he was working on material prepared for him by his predecessors, and especially by Plato. It is not in my opinion possible to reconstruct from Plato's works anything that can be misdescribed as Plato's own system of metaphysics:[1] still less anything that can be misdescribed as a Socratic metaphysical system of which Plato has constituted himself the Boswell. But it is impossible to read Plato attentively without realizing that both he, and the Socrates to whom (as some ingenious and learned scholars would have us think) he played Boswell, had gone far both in metaphysics itself and in reflection as to what metaphysics is.

[1] Readers who recollect what I have said towards the end of the first part of Chapter VII will perhaps forgive me for reminding others that I there denied the existence of anything that can properly be called 'X's metaphysical system', and said that what goes by that name is X's answer to his own question 'What absolute presuppositions are made by ordinary scientific thought in my time, in the society in which I live?' I think Aristotle tried to answer that question in writings which have come down to us; but not Plato.

In a famous passage of the *Republic* (509 D, seqq.) he makes Socrates distinguish between two methods of thinking, one called mathematical and the other called dialectical. The mathematical method is described as one which takes its stand on ὑποθέσεις, 'hypotheses', and argues from them. The dialectical method is described as 'removing hypotheses', τὰς ὑποθέσεις ἀναιροῦσα (533 C). If 'hypotheses' are presuppositions (and there is no doubt, I think, that they are), 'removing hypotheses' can only mean cancelling presuppositions, that is, ceasing to presuppose them.

This is only a question of translating the Greek. The word ὑποτιθέναι means quite literally 'sup-position', the placing one thing under another, where the logical relation indicated by ὑπό ('under', that is, 'by way of foundation') is the relation which we call, following Aristotle, logical priority. The word ἀναιρεῖν means 'to remove' or 'take away'; it is simply the opposite of the τιθέναι in ὑποτιθέναι. The literal translations of τιθέναι and ἀναιρεῖν, *ponere* and *tollere*, are the regular words in logician's Latin for asserting and denying. Hence ὑπόθεσιν ἀναιρεῖν means, as clearly as Greek can mean it, 'removing' or un-supposing a supposition.

It is not difficult to see what 'Socrates' is talking about. In mathematics—I take my example from the kind of mathematics which people were supposed to know by the time they began studying philosophy under Plato—you begin a job of thinking by doing something that is enjoined in the words 'Let ABC be a triangle, and let the angle ABC be a right angle'. Then you try to show that the square on AC is equal to the sum of the squares on AB and BC. What you do at the start, what you were told to do in the words 'Let ABC', &c., is making, or positing, or setting up, a supposition which relatively to the rest of your thinking in this particular job is a presupposition or 'hypothesis'. Being consciously made, and by a person who might have made a different one if he had chosen, it is not only a supposition but an assumption. Throughout your subsequent work on this particular job you have got to stand by that assumption. It has been 'posited', or put, and you must see that it stays put.

How do conditions differ in dialectic? Dialectic is Plato's name for the kind of thinking which is going on in the *Republic* itself, and that will do very well for an example. The general question is: What is justice? The question is first tackled under the presupposition that justice can be subsumed under the notion of craft or skill, τέχνη. In its first form this presupposition emanates from Polemarchus, who thinks that justice is a special kind of craft or skill. We work out the consequences of that, and find them nonsensical because the implications of the supposition that certain actions proceed from some special kind of skill contradict the implications of the supposition that they proceed from justice. So we come to the second form of the same presupposition, Thrasymachus's form, according to which it is injustice that is a special kind of skill—the art of getting on in the world—whereas justice is a negative term, a name for the lack of that skill. Here too the consequences are found to be nonsensical; and the inference is, first, that justice is not a name for lack of skill in the art of getting on, and secondly that since justice cannot be defined either as a craft or as the lack of a craft it cannot be subsumed under the notion of craft at all.

This shows what 'removing hypotheses' means. It means causing the non-supposal of what had been supposed. What had been supposed need not have been assumed; the supposing of it, that is, need not have been conscious and deliberate. Polemarchus did not know that he was supposing justice to be a τέχνη until Socrates by his superior analytical skill showed him that he was doing so. The dialectician may have to bring 'hypotheses' to light before he can remove them.

In bringing 'hypotheses' to light the dialectician resembles the metaphysician. But in 'removing' them he is doing something which it is certainly not the metaphysician's business to do. Accordingly, if a reader of Plato gets it into his head that the dialectician is a metaphysician, he will boggle at the perfectly clear and obvious translation of ὑποθέσεις ἀναιρεῖν by 'removing hypotheses'. And if in addition to this he embraces the positivistic error as to what metaphysics is, and still wants to make sense of Plato's words, he will have a motive, more or less powerful, for making Plato into a metaphysical positivist by substituting for the phrase 'removing hypotheses' some phrase signifying something very different, confirming hypotheses; not merely continuing to suppose them or asking others to suppose them, but showing reason why they should be thought true.

This has actually happened. Such an interpretation of the passage was put forward in the latter part of the nineteenth century by an entire school of commentators in Oxford. Jowett and Campbell, in their edition of the *Republic* published in 1894 after Jowett's death, comment on the passage as follows: 'The hypotheses are done away with; that is, when seen in their relation to the good they cease to be hypotheses' (vol. ii, p. 347). Bosanquet, in his *Companion to Plato's Republic* (1895), p. 300, comments: 'the hypotheses are destroyed *as hypotheses* [his italics], to be incorporated in the body of science in a modified form as assured principles'. Nettleship, in his *Philosophical Remains* (posthumously published in 1897, but incorporating lectures on the *Republic* given 1885-8; vol. ii, p. 253) comments: 'The truths they [mathematicians] start from await the confirmation of being shown to be elements in an interconnected whole.'

This attempt to explain the phrase 'removing hypotheses' as meaning not removing them but confirming them by removing from them their hypothetical character, 'unsupposing' them only in the sense that what is scientifically demonstrated is no longer merely supposed, is an outrage on the Greek, and as such was rightly denounced by the Cambridge commentator Adam, who in his edition of the *Republic*

(1902), vol. ii, p. 192, mildly protested that 'ἀναιρεῖν cannot be thus pared down'.

I do not mention the mistranslation in order to raise a smile at the Oxford commentators' expense for wanting to make Plato talk what they personally regarded as good sense. A commentator who does not want to make his author talk good sense has no business to be a commentator. I mention it partly as an example of the length to which commentators, and very good commentators, will go in order to satisfy this desire; which after all is nothing compared with the length to which a hostile reader will go in order to satisfy the desire to make out that his author is talking nonsense, especially if his hostility is not quite openly acknowledged, even to himself; but chiefly because it further illustrates what I have said above as to the relation between Bradley and John Stuart Mill.

The Oxford commentators belonged to the same school of thought as Bradley, and it is nowadays more or less *de rigueur* among English students of philosophy to misrepresent the entire work of that school, perhaps in order to justify them in ignoring it, as an attempt to grow a cutting from post-Kantian German idealism in the soil of Oxford. As I have already shown, Bradley's epigram about metaphysics, whether it represents a moment of despair or a settled conviction, expresses unambiguously a view as to the character of metaphysics which is identical with that of John Stuart Mill. It is an epigram which no post-Kantian idealist could have invented or even understood. Hegel, of whom Bradley is vulgarly and in spite of his own protests called a follower, would have thought it idiotic. The Oxford mistranslation of Plato's phrase about 'removing hypotheses', although to a person who insists upon catching at words it may seem a reminiscence of Hegel's term *aufheben*, is not an expression of Hegelianism, it is an expression of positivism. So intensely did the Oxford Platonists believe that it was the. business of metaphysics to find reasons for what we believe upon instinct, to raise the presuppositions of ordinary scientific thinking to the level of ascertained and demonstrated truths, that they allowed this belief to conquer their scholarship and induce them to put forward an interpretation of Plato which, by making him say the exact opposite of what he does say, makes him agree with John Stuart Mill.

XVI

SUICIDE OF POSITIVISTIC METAPHYSICS

IN Chapter XIV I have in effect defined the positivistic mistake about metaphysics as the mistake of thinking that metaphysics is the attempt to justify by appeal to observed facts the absolute presuppositions of our thought. This attempt is bound to fail because these things, being absolute presuppositions, cannot stand as the answers to questions, and therefore the question whether they are justifiable, which in effect is identical with the question whether they are true, is a question that cannot logically arise. To ask it is the hall-mark of pseudo-metaphysics.

Bradley's epigram shows that the greatest English philosopher of the nineteenth century had not yet overcome the tendency to indulge this positivistic error. It is the less surprising that the same error should reappear in a school of thought claiming the name of 'logical positivism'; a school in England at least deriving from Earl Russell, who began his brilliant philosophical career in close relation to Bradley. The error here takes an exacerbated form, committing public suicide like the legendary scorpion in a ring of fire. It has developed into the following syllogism. 'Any proposition which cannot be verified by appeal to observed facts is a pseudo-proposition. Metaphysical propositions cannot be verified by appeal to observed facts. Therefore metaphysical propositions are pseudo-propositions, and therefore nonsense.' The argument has been set forth with admirable conciseness and lucidity by Mr. A. J. Ayer in his book *Language Truth and Logic* (1936).

What is given us as an attack on metaphysics is an attack on pseudo-metaphysics. The minor premiss of the above syllogism expresses characteristically the characteristic positivistic error as to what metaphysics is: the error which converts metaphysical propositions (i.e. propositions about the history of absolute presuppositions) into pseudo-metaphysical propositions by omitting the metaphysical rubric. As I pointed out in Chapter XIV, this comes from a blunder in logic: the blunder of mistaking suppositions for propositions, and consequently thinking that logical efficacy, or the power of causing questions to arise, belongs exclusively to propositions, or things which are either true or false. Mr. Ayer, true to the positivistic tradition, does not possess the idea of supposing, and *a fortiori* not the idea of an absolute presupposition. Any statement of an absolute presupposition which he encounters in the course of his reading, therefore, he regards as a statement of a proposition; and for the metaphysical question 'Was this presupposition made on a certain occasion or not?' he substitutes the pseudo-metaphysical question 'Is this proposition true?'

How deeply Mr. Ayer stands committed to the position that 'metaphysics' means pseudo-metaphysics will appear even from a cursory examination of his text. On the second page of his preface he quotes as examples of metaphysical propositions 'that there is a non-empirical world of values', 'that men have immortal souls', and 'that there is a transcendent God' (op. cit., p. 12). I do not profess to understand all the words he uses, but I think I understand enough to be sure that he is repeating the familiar Kantian definition of the subject-matter of metaphysics, 'God, freedom, and immortality', with the implication that metaphysicians, when they speak of these things, profess to be asserting the existence of what he calls 'empirical matters of fact'. In his chapter on 'The Elimination of Metaphysics' (ch. i) he gives further examples: Bradley's sentence 'the Absolute enters into, but is itself incapable of, evolution and progress' (op. cit., p. 21), which he evidently takes to be the statement not of an absolute presupposition made on occasions of a certain kind but of a would-be proposition about an empirical matter of fact which 'is not even in principle verifiable' and therefore 'has no literal significance' (p. 22); the assertion, he does not say made by whom or in what context, 'that the world of sense-appearance was altogether unreal' (pp. 26–7); the positions maintained respectively by monists and pluralists, and by realists and idealists, in their 'metaphysical aspect', a qualification which by reducing his statement to a tautology leaves the reader in some doubt as to what positions he has in mind (p. 28); and all propositions about 'substance' (p. 32). Except in the case quoted from Bradley, he never in this chapter gives a single example of the propositions he is attacking; all we can be sure of is that he is attacking people who think that they are true (or, for that matter, false) whereas in fact, not being verifiable, they are neither true nor false and are therefore not propositions but pseudo-propositions, or as he calls them on p. 12 'putative propositions'.

Whether his own conception of 'verifiability' is sound I shall not consider. I shall assume for the sake of argument that it is; or at any rate that, if not quite immune from criticism as it stands, it is capable of being restated in some such way as to render it so immune. The points I wish to make are two: (1) that whether or not he derives his conclusion from true premisses it is a conclusion that I entirely accept and have already stated more than once in my own words, (2) that from this conclusion two questions arise which he ought to answer, but does not.

To call something a pseudo-x implies that it is not an x, but that somebody has mistaken it for one. If these 'metaphysical propositions' are, as Mr. Ayer says they are, and as I agree they are, pseudo-propositions, it follows that they are not propositions. Then what are they? What is it that in these cases somebody has mistaken for propositions? Mr. Ayer gives no answer. I answer, 'suppositions'.

If somebody has mistaken suppositions for propositions, who is it that has made the mistake? I answer, 'Mr. Ayer'. I do not mean that he initiated the mistake; I have already shown how Mill made it before him; I mean only that he has adopted it. The importance of Mr. Ayer's work on the subject (again not exclusively his own: the credit must be shared by a considerable group of so-called logical positivists) lies in the fact that he has not only made the mistake, he has also refuted it.

But he has not abandoned it. Had he done that, he would have said to himself, 'These things which I have proved not to be propositions are really something else. I will not rest until I have found out what they really are; and when I have discovered that, I shall understand what it really is that metaphysicians have all this time been doing. And then I shall know what the proper business of metaphysics is, and answer the question long ago asked by Kant: "How can metaphysics become a science?" All I have proved so far is that metaphysics is not what I with so many others have fancied it to be, a set of propositions claiming to give "knowledge of a reality which transcended the phenomenal world" (p. 16). Meanwhile, I abhor myself for having supposed it to be what I have now proved that it is not; and repent in dust and ashes.' Instead of which, he remains quite content with his half-finished analysis, and demands the 'elimination' of metaphysics.

Can it be that we are back once more in the atmosphere of the eighteenth century, listening to the cry *écrasez l'infâme*? Is this haste with tumbril and blade the outcome of a genuine desire to understand an enterprise which, to quote Kant once more, 'cannot be indifferent to humanity', or is it the outcome of a desire (not a rare desire, it must be admitted) to belittle what one cannot share, and destroy what one cannot understand?

The suspicion of some such motive is strengthened by finding (op. cit., ch. vi) that ethics and theology are later singled out as palmary instances of the metaphysics that is to be eliminated: ethics understood as consisting of 'exhortations to moral virtue' (p. 151) and theology understood as consisting of statements like 'Jehovah is angry' (p. 176), when this is understood not as merely meaning 'it is thundering', but as a statement about *un nommé Dieu*, a being like a human being in his mental powers and dispositions, but with the powers of a human being greatly magnified. These are notions of ethics and theology which have nothing to do with what the great moral philosophers and the great theologians have taught under those names. They are simply the foolish ideas many of us invented for ourselves, or picked up from foolish parents or foolish nurses, when we were small children. Many of us, again, look back on our childhood with bitter humiliation and resentment; in these cases, if our childhood has been passed in what is called a virtuous and religious home, the resentment attaches itself to what we (perhaps wrongly) believe to have been taught there, and *écrasez l'infâme* becomes a motive for rejecting in later life with contumely, and with argument, if we are trained to argue, the traces of that real or supposed teaching still discernible in ourselves.

The suspicion that resentment, not reason, may afford the true motive of the neo-positivists' anti-metaphysics is confirmed by the way in which we find them conceiving the relation between metaphysics and natural science. They seem to think of metaphysics as 'malicious' towards science (the word is Earl Russell's,[1] borrowed from Mr. Santayana) and to fear that unless metaphysics is destroyed it will destroy natural science. This implies a complete misreading of the present-day situation. Plenty of people have been protesting for a long time past against the dogma that natural science, and especially natural science as misunderstood by the positivists, is the only valid type of knowledge. But there has never been any ground for interpreting these protests as evidence of a conspiracy on the part of metaphysicians against the freedom and progress of natural science; and the suggestion that such a conspiracy exists can only cause or reinforce suspicions of persecution mania. No one is trying, or has tried within living memory, to tyrannize over natural science in the name of metaphysics. From metaphysics properly so called, the attempt to ascertain the absolute presuppositions of thought, a natural science that does its work conscientiously can have nothing to fear.

[1] *Mysticism and Logic*, p. 20. 'Mysticism', as Earl Russell here uses the word, is closely related to what Mr. Ayer calls 'metaphysics'; and I hardly think I should be far wrong if I were to conjecture that Mr. Ayer conceives metaphysics as not only pseudo-scientific but anti-scientific.

It is desirable, when A falsely accuses B of a certain frame of mind, intention, or emotion, to ask from what impression his idea of it is derived. Inquiry will often show that it is derived from his own 'bad conscience' or guilty self-knowledge. It is an interesting question whether these accusations of 'malice' towards science may not spring from a consciousness of precisely that malice in the accusers themselves *plus* a fantasy by which the guilt which one cannot face is transferred to another.

But this positivistic terror that metaphysics may injure natural science is, after all, not without a sort of lunatic foundation. If metaphysics were what the positivists mistake it for, if it were an attempt to provide empirical justification for the presuppositions of science, it might certainly, though without malice aforethought, prove detrimental to science itself, not by its success but by its inevitable failure; for when the discovery was made that no justification of this kind is to be had, the positivistic belief that it is nevertheless necessary might lead to the false conclusion that the whole fabric of scientific thought is rotten at the core. Thus understood, we may think of the positivist as, in a way, right to fear metaphysics as he does; but what he fears is not metaphysics as it really is, but metaphysics as he misconceives it; and further, what he fears is not this phantom itself, but the frightful consequences which, as he falsely imagines, would ensue upon its failure to do what he thinks to be its proper work: a work which in fact does not need doing and cannot be done. Such fears are a proper subject of study to the psycho-pathologist.

If by metaphysics is meant either (1) the absolute presuppositions of science, or (2) the attempt to find out what at any given time these presuppositions are, then clearly the positivistic attack on metaphysics, so far from aiding the cause of natural science, can only prove harmful to that cause in proportion to its own degree of success.

1. If by a metaphysical proposition is meant one

of the absolute presuppositions of science, such as that every event has a cause (I take that *exempli gratia*, without asserting that in fact the science of our own day does make any such presupposition), then the doctrine of the 'logical positivists' that metaphysical propositions are nonsensical will involve the bankruptcy of all thinking in which any use is made of absolute presuppositions; that is to say, the bankruptcy of all science. Any attack on metaphysics is an attack on the foundations of science; any attack on the foundations of science is an attack on science itself.

2. If by a metaphysical proposition is meant, as ought to be meant, the statement that a certain absolute presupposition is made by certain scientists in a certain piece of thinking, such a statement would be false if on the occasion referred to not that absolute presupposition was made but another; it would be nonsensical if on that occasion no absolute presuppositions at all were made. To call it nonsensical, therefore, would be merely an oblique and obscure way of repeating the old (and erroneous) positivistic dogma that thinking involves no absolute presuppositions. Let us see what follows.

There would be a certain plausibility in the statement that in its most completely unscientific form thinking involves no presuppositions at all, and therefore no absolute presuppositions, but proceeds by mere 'apprehension' or 'intuition' of something 'given'. But the disentanglement of presuppositions is precisely what distinguishes scientific thought from unscientific; so any attack on the doctrine that thought has presuppositions is a direct attack on science itself, and involves an attempt, whether conscious or unconscious, to reduce all thought to the standard of thinking at its most confused and unscientific level.

This is the real danger of the 'logical positivist' attack on metaphysics, and may conceivably be the real motive behind it. It is a mass of inconsistencies and confusions; but one thing which it may very well serve to express is an aspiration towards the destruction of science and its supersession by the most recklessly unscientific kind of thought. It may be that no such intention is cherished by its advocates. But where so much confusion has been found, it would be rash to assume that those in whom it has been found are perfectly clear about their own wishes. I have already suggested that a more or less concerted attack on reason as such is one feature of the contemporary world. Perhaps the 'logical positivists' do not mean to make themselves a party to it; but they have been at pains to put themselves in a position where, willingly or unwillingly, they are fighting on its side.

XVII

THE SON OF THE CHILD

IT was Wordsworth who wrote

> The Child is father of the Man;
> And I could wish my days to be
> Bound each to each by natural piety.

It was Samuel Alexander, one of two or three men in our time who have deserved to be called great philosophers, who took Wordsworth's lines as a kind of motto for his metaphysical work. When Alexander said that natural piety should be the clue to metaphysical thinking he meant to say, as many sound philosophers have said before him, that a metaphysician's business is not to argue but to recognize facts; and he meant to say also that these facts are not recondite or remote, to be recognized only after a long course of special training and specialized research, but simple and familiar, visible to the eyes of a child, and perhaps hidden from clever men because they are too clever. Certainly, he thought, they must remain hidden from those wise and prudent men who would accept nothing but what was 'proved'; and were revealed to any babe who would accept them as the child Wordsworth accepted the rainbow.

There is, I suspect, far more of wisdom and truth in this than I could ever hope to expound. Let me restate in my own way just so much of it as I believe I understand.

Metaphysics is concerned with absolute presuppositions. We do not acquire absolute presuppositions by arguing; on the contrary, unless we have them already arguing is impossible to us. Nor can we change them by arguing; unless they remained constant all our arguments would fall to pieces. We cannot confirm ourselves in them by 'proving' them; it is proof that depends on them, not they on proof. The only attitude towards them that can enable us to enjoy what they have to give us (and that means science and civilization, the life of rational animals) is an attitude of unquestioning acceptance. We must accept them and hold firmly to them; we must insist on presupposing them in all our thinking without asking why they should be thus accepted.

But not without asking what they are. That is the metaphysician's question, and Alexander does not mean to warn us against metaphysics. If we could hold firmly to the absolute presuppositions of our thought without knowing what they are, so much the better for us; we should be spared a troublesome inquiry. Alexander does not think we shall be spared it. What he wishes to tell us about it is that when we do undertake it we must do so in a spirit of natural piety. In our character as grown men, or metaphysicians, we must treat ourselves in our character as children, or non-metaphysicians, with filial respect. We must not now question, in the hope either of justifying them or of condemning them, the presuppositions which in that earlier stage of our life we were content to accept. The fact that we have learned what our absolute presuppositions are does not imply that our attitude towards them either should or can cease to be one of sheer presupposal. The rainbow is a rainbow still, and the man who knows it for an effect of refraction looks at it with the same eyes with which he saw it as a child, before he had ever heard of the spectrum and the prism.

All this I fancy Alexander meant, and meant consciously, when he recommended to metaphysicians an attitude of natural piety. And if he did mean it I am convinced that he was right, and that he spoke like the wise and good man he was. But there is another part of what he meant, in which I am not so sure that he was right.

Alexander the child accepts it as an absolute presupposition of all his thought that every event has a cause. I continue in this context to use my old example, the more confidently because it is one that he himself would have accepted. Alexander the man, the metaphysician, has come to know that he does this, but as the child's dutiful son he continues to do it in an unchanged spirit, that is, without asking for argument or justification. All the same, knowing that he does it means something more than being able simply to state the fact that he does it; it means also being able to explain what exactly it is that he is doing. To take a parallel: it is one thing to believe in God; that is what is called having faith. It is another thing to know that we believe in God; that is what is called knowing the creed of our faith. But a creed is the abstract or summary of a theology, and

to possess a theology means being able to explain
what exactly it is that we believe when we believe in
God, and what exactly it is that we say we believe
when we say that we believe in God.

If we ask Alexander what exactly he means by
saying he is sure that every event has a cause, we
shall get an answer in some such words as the
following:

'When I consider this sea I find it blue and rough.
When I consider this wind I find it warm and strong.
When I consider this table I find it hard and smooth
and heavy. These are characters which I find in some
things but not in others. Now there are some characters which I find not in some things only but in all
things. Thus whenever I consider anything at all I
find it somewhere and somewhen. Whenever I consider anything at all I find it lodged in a certain
tract of space and lasting for a certain tract of time.
Whenever I consider anything at all I find it due to
some other thing and productive of some third thing.
These pervasive characters, if I may use that name
for the characters I thus find in all things without
exception, are characters whose existence and per-
vasiveness I discover just as I discover the existence
and non-pervasiveness of blueness and warmth and
hardness, by experience: by considering the things
among which I find myself. When I say that everything has a cause I am making a statement which in
principle hardly differs at all from the statement that
every wave now in sight is blue; the only difference
of principle is that one statement applies to all the

things of a certain kind which I have before me at this present time, the other to all the things of every kind that I have ever had before me in my whole life.'

According to this, the statement that everything has a cause is not, logically considered, a statement of a different kind from the statement that all these sailors are washing the deck. It is not intrinsically a presupposition. Intrinsically, it is a summary statement of observed facts. Alexander need not deny that it may on occasion serve as a presupposition. But he does deny, and he must deny, that it necessarily serves as a presupposition and can be nothing else. The idea of absolute presuppositions has disappeared, and we are back in the atmosphere of positivism.

Thus considered, Alexander's metaphysics would seem to be a variety of positivistic metaphysics, whose difference from the commoner varieties consists chiefly in being the work of a very rich, very wise, and very profound thinker; but also in a kind of very subtle simplicity, or highly sophisticated *naïveté*, to which the results of intricate research and far-reaching inference appear as perfectly obvious facts which leap to the eyes as soon as they are opened.

Alexander's was, in fact, a mind of extraordinary power and energy, and his character one of extraordinary simplicity and candour. Intellectual difficulties meant nothing to him; problems were solved almost as soon as their presence was suspected; the labour of trying to get a problem disentangled, so that one could grasp it by the right end and untie in their logical order the knots of which it was composed, was a thing with which he seemed unacquainted. When he described knowledge as the mere 'compresence' of a mind with an object I can suppose that he was giving a truthful account of his own experience. It was as if he had found words in which to say without offending his own modesty 'put me in front of anything I don't understand, and I will promise to understand it in next to no time.'

I can suppose that Alexander's philosophy gives a truthful account of his own experience, because I knew him well. But I cannot pretend that it gives a truthful account of mine. In the light of what I have been saying I must even retract my earlier claim to understand and accept his notion of natural piety; for that claim depended on my assuming it to be his meaning that the proper place for natural piety was in our attitude towards our absolute presuppositions; and it now seems that for him there are no absolute presuppositions, there are only facts, and minds recognizing the facts when they are brought up against them.

Is that, according to my own experience, a true account of knowledge? It is not. It could at most serve for an account of what I do when I am thinking so vaguely and casually that what I am doing hardly deserves to be called thinking at all. How it may be with more powerful thinkers I will not try to say; but with a slow and feeble thinker like myself there is nothing, when I am thinking hard and efficiently,

that is like 'compresence' with any 'object' whatever. There is at first a whole nest of problems all
tangled up together. Then by degrees the tangle is
reduced to order. Here and there in it one problem
is seen to depend for its solution upon the solution
of another. Given luck and great patience and strict
attention to the rule of never asking two questions
together but always separating them out and asking
the first one first, I can sometimes solve the whole
lot. If I tried to deal with them according to Alexander's prescription I know by experience that I
should never solve any.

Here I had stopped; but I remember how Alexander used to say 'pitch into me', and I imagine the
face of quizzical regret with which he would meet a
friend who denied him that friendly office merely
because he was dead. So I will go on.

It is not on personal grounds alone, not only because my own experience differs from Alexander's,
that I find myself unable to endorse his views of
metaphysics. I think he was definitely wrong on a
point of crucial importance. If it had been true, as
he thought it was, that what I call absolute presuppositions of thought are simply statements of
fact, and that whatever is on my view presupposed
in them has an observable reality as a pervasive
character of everything that exists, then either the
same set of pervasive characters would have been
recognized *semper*, *ubique*, *ab omnibus*, or we should
have to believe in certain strange epidemic hallucinations to which all men are liable except ourselves.

Alexander, I believe because he was too much under the influence of eighteenth-century thinkers, constructed his metaphysics on the assumption that all human beings everywhere and always accepted what Mill calls the law of universal causation, and for that matter everything enunciated in Kant's 'System of Principles'. If every one had always uniformly accepted these principles it might be difficult to show reason why we should not believe them to be just empirical descriptions of pervasive characters in the real world. Kant, it is true, constructed an argument to meet exactly this demand; but I will assume that Kant's argument admits of valid refutation. This would not matter. For in point of fact the Kantian 'principles' are nothing more permanent than the presuppositions of eighteenth-century physics, as Kant discovered them by analysis. If you analyse the physics of to-day, or that of the Renaissance, or that of Aristotle, you get a different set.

Alexander does not seem to have known this. He allowed himself to be influenced by the quaint, characteristic eighteenth-century dogma that if anybody in any country or at any time arrived or had arrived in his thinking at conclusions unlike those arrived at by an eighteenth-century European brought up on Newton's *Principia*, it could only be because he was incapable of thinking straight. Characteristic of the eighteenth century, because derived from the eighteenth century's good conceit of itself combined with its extremely short historical perspective.

When once it is realized that the absolute presuppositions of eighteenth-century science, far from being accepted *semper, ubique, ab omnibus*, had only a quite short historical life, as we nowadays think of history, in only a quite limited part of the world, and that even inside Europe other systems of science worked before then and since then on different presuppositions, it becomes impossible for any one except for the most irresponsible kind of thinker to maintain that out of all these and all the other possible sets of presuppositions there is one set and only one which consists of propositions accurately describing observable characteristics everywhere present in the world, while all the other sets represent more or less systematic hallucinations as to what these characteristics are.

PART III
EXAMPLES

N

A

THE EXISTENCE OF GOD

XVIII

THE PROPOSITION 'GOD EXISTS'

In the last chapter but one I had occasion to comment on the way in which a 'logical positivist', wishing to recommend the doctrine that 'metaphysical propositions' not being verifiable by appeal to observed fact are pseudo-propositions and meaningless, quoted as examples propositions about God, such as the proposition 'God exists'. To him the proposition 'God exists' would seem to mean that there is a being more or less like human beings in respect of his mental powers and dispositions, but having the mental powers of a human being greatly, perhaps infinitely, magnified (cf. supra, p. 167).

In a sense any one is free to mean anything he likes by any words whatever; and if the writer whom I quoted had made it clear that this was only a private meaning of his own, the meaning he personally intends to convey when he says things about God, I should not have interfered. But he professed to be explaining what other people mean when they say the same things; and these other people, from what he says, I suppose to be Christians. In that case the question what the words mean is not one to be capriciously answered. It is a question of fact.

What Christians mean when they say that God exists is a complicated question. It is not to be answered except after a somewhat painstaking study of Christian theological literature. I do not profess to be an expert in theology; but I have a certain acquaintance with various writers who are thought to have been experts in their time; and I have no fear of being contradicted when I say that the meaning I suppose to be attached by this author to the proposition 'God exists' is a meaning Christian theologians have never attached to it, and does not even remotely resemble the meaning which with some approach to unanimity they have expounded at considerable length. Having said that, I am obliged to explain what, according to my recollection of their works, that meaning is.

But I shall not try to explain the whole of it. For my present purpose a sample is quite enough. According to these writers (I am speaking of the so-called Patristic literature) the existence of God is a presupposition, and an absolute one, of all the thinking done by Christians; among other kinds of thinking, that belonging to natural science. The connexion between belief in God and the pursuit of natural science happens to be a subject with which they have dealt at some length. I shall confine myself to it.

For the Patristic writers the proposition 'God exists' is a metaphysical proposition in the sense in which I have defined that phrase. In following them here, I am joining issue with my 'logical positivist', who evidently does not think it is anything of the kind. In his opinion it has to do not with the presuppositions of science but with the existence of a quasi-human but superhuman person. And the department of knowledge (or if you like pseudo-knowledge) to which a proposition concerning a matter of that kind would belong is, I suppose, psychical research; or what booksellers, brutally cynical as to whether these things are knowable or not, classify as 'occult'. There can be no conceivable excuse for classifying it under metaphysics.

If the proposition that God exists is a metaphysical proposition it must be understood as carrying with it the metaphysical rubric; and as so understood what it asserts is that as a matter of historical fact a certain absolute presupposition, to be hereafter defined, is or has been made by natural science (the reader will bear in mind my limitation of the field) at a certain phase of its history. It further implies that owing to the presence of this presupposition that phase in the history of natural science has or had a unique character of its own, serving to the historical student as evidence that the presupposition is or was made. The question therefore arises: What difference does it make to the conduct of research in natural science whether scientists do or do not presuppose the existence of God?

The importance of the metaphysical rubric has been well understood by those responsible for establishing and maintaining the traditions of Christendom. The creeds in which Christians have been taught to confess their faith have never been couched in the formula: 'God exists and has the following attributes'; but always in the formula: 'I believe' or originally 'We believe in God'; and have gone on to say what it is that I, or we, believe about him. A statement as to the beliefs of a certain person or body of persons is an historical statement; and since Christians are aware that in repeating their creeds they are summarizing their theology, one need only accept Aristotle's identification of theology with metaphysics to conclude that the Christian Church has always taught that metaphysics is an historical science.

I do not say that it has taught all the implications of this principle. For example, it has not consistently taught that there can be no proof of God's existence. Inconsistency on this point is easy to understand. The words are ambiguous. That God exists is not a proposition, it is a presupposition (Chap. IV, prop. 5). Because it is not a proposition it is neither true nor false. It can be neither proved nor disproved. But a person accustomed to metaphysical thinking, when confronted with the words 'God exists', will automatically put in the metaphysical rubric and read 'we believe (i.e. presuppose in all our thinking) that God exists'. Here is something which is a proposition. It is either true or false. If true, it can be proved: if false, it can be disproved. Unless it is proved it cannot be known at all; for like all absolute presuppositions a man's belief in God can never be discovered by introspection. If 'God exists' means 'somebody believes that God exists' (which it must mean if it is a metaphysical proposition) it is capable of proof. The proof must of course be an historical proof, and the evidence on which it is based will be certain ways in which this 'somebody' thinks.

A famous example lies ready to hand. If Gaunilo was right when he argued that Anselm's 'ontological[1] proof of the existence of God' proved the existence of God only to a person who already believed it, and if Anselm told the truth when he replied that he did not care, it follows that Anselm's proof, whatever else may be said either for it or against it, was sound on this point, and that Anselm was personally sound on it too. For it follows not only that Anselm's proof assumed the metaphysical rubric but that Anselm personally endorsed the assumption when it was pointed out to him, whether he had meant to make it from the first or no. Whatever may have been in Anselm's mind when he wrote the *Proslogion*, his exchange of correspondence with Gaunilo shows beyond a doubt that on reflection he regarded the fool who 'hath said in his heart, There is no God' as a fool not because he was blind to the actual existence of *un nommé Dieu*, but because he did not know that the presupposition 'God exists' was a presupposition he himself made.

Anselm's proof is strongest at the point where it is commonly thought weakest. People who cannot see that metaphysics is an historical science, and therefore habitually dock metaphysical propositions of their rubric, fancying that Anselm's proof stands or

---

[1] The name is Kant's. Invented seven centuries later than the thing named, and by a man who did not understand that thing, it has no authority. As a description it is not felicitous. Let us, or those of us who are not polysyllable-addicts, speak in future of 'Anselm's proof'.

falls by its success as a piece of pseudo-metaphysics, that is, by its success in proving the proposition that God exists, as distinct from the proposition that we believe in God, have allowed themselves to become facetious or indignant over the fact, as they think it, that this argument starts from 'our idea' of God and seems to proceed thence to 'God's existence'. People who hug this blunder are following Kant, I know. But it is a blunder all the same. When once it is realized that Anselm's proof is a metaphysical argument, and therefore an historical argument, it can no longer be regarded as a weakness that it should take its stand on historical evidence. What it proves is not that because our idea of God is an idea of *id quo maius cogitari nequit* therefore God exists, but that because our idea of God is an idea of *id quo maius cogitari nequit* we stand committed to belief in God's existence.

It is because Anselm's proof so explicitly takes its stand on history that it provides so valuable a test for a metaphysical turn of mind. A man who has a bent for metaphysics can hardly help seeing, even if he does not wholly understand it, that Anselm's proof is the work of a man who is on the right lines; for a man with a bent for metaphysics does not need to be told that metaphysics is an historical science, and at his first meeting with Anselm's proof he will realize that it is historical in character. I do not suggest that persons with a bent for metaphysics are the only ones who can do valuable work in metaphysics. Kant is an instance to the contrary.

XIX
RELIGION AND NATURAL SCIENCE IN PRIMITIVE SOCIETY

THE question I have undertaken to answer is primarily a question about the history of thought in the fourth century A.D., that being the time when the Christian world made up its mind by hook or by crook as to what it meant when it described itself as believing in God. Historical questions are questions in which one tries to understand what somebody was doing on a certain occasion. This can be done only if one understands what sort of an occasion it was; for every action arises out of the situation in which it is done, and there is no understanding the action unless one understands the situation. In metaphysics as in every other department of history the secret of success is to study the background.

It is through the historical background, therefore, that I shall approach the question what Christians mean by saying that they believe in God. Like an old-fashioned artist, I shall divide this background into two planes: an arbitrary simplification of what is in reality far more complex; but the best I can do. First I shall sketch in the 'distance', by saying something about the religion and science of primitive peoples; then the 'middle distance', by doing the same for the people of ancient Greece.

If there is to be anything at all which can in any sense be called natural science, the people in whose

minds it is to exist must take it absolutely for granted
that there is such a thing as 'nature', the opposite
(contradictory) of 'art': that there are things that
happen quite irrespectively of anything these people
themselves do, however intelligently or fortunately,
and irrespectively also of anything any one else may
do even with skill and luck greater than their own.
They must take it absolutely for granted that somewhere in the world there is a dividing line between
things that happen or can be made to happen or can
be prevented by art (and art never succeeds without
a certain support from luck), and things that happen
of themselves, or by nature. This line will doubtless
shift its position according to the degree of skill and
luck possessed by different people; for an extremely
powerful magician it will recede a long way; but
unless even in this extreme case it is supposed still to
exist somewhere, and to have beyond it a region in
which things happen that no magic can control, there
is not supposed to be any nature, and the ultimate
and fundamental presupposition on which depends
the very possibility of a natural science remains
unmade.

There is no reason to think that this presupposition is native to man. Except that it lies farther down
in the edifice of his intellectual habits, it is in principle
very much like other presuppositions which we know
that some groups of human beings have made while
others have not. To animals which physiologically
speaking are in either case human we can hardly
doubt that it is an open question whether they shall

suppose that this line exists and that beyond it lies a
world of nature, or whether they shall suppose that
there is no such line and that whatever happens in
the world happens by art; though certainly it is not
a question that could be decided by an act of choice
whereby a human animal actually in one of these two
alternative states abandons that state and embraces
the other. Anthropologists tell us of peoples who
believe that there is no such thing as natural death.
They think, we are assured, that every instance of
death is due to magic. If that is so there might be
peoples who hold the same belief about everything
whatever. No such people has been reported by
anthropologists, and very likely none exists; but if it
did it would afford an example of a society in which
no possible science of nature could arise until that
belief had disappeared; and it is at least conceivable
that this was once the belief of some or even of all
human beings.

It might be fancied that the mere course of experience would suffice to destroy it. Psychologists, or
some of them, if they read these words, will remind
me that according to themselves every child begins
life with a conviction of its own omnipotence, and
that this conviction is lost only by degrees, as its
baselessness becomes evident in the light of experience. But if that happens, this infantile conviction
of omnipotence is not at all like the absolute presuppositions which this book is about. An absolute
presupposition cannot be undermined by the verdict
of 'experience', because it is the yard-stick by which

'experience' is judged. To suggest that 'experience' might teach my hypothetical savages that some events are not due to magic is like suggesting that experience might teach a civilized people that there are not twelve inches in a foot and thus cause them to adopt the metric system. As long as you measure in feet and inches, everything you measure has dimensions composed of those units. As long as you believe in a world of magic, that is the kind of world in which you live. If any group or community of human beings ever held a pan-magical belief about the world, it is certainly not 'experience' that could shake it. Yet certainly it might be shaken. It might be shaken through the influence of a very powerful tribesman who found himself taking a different view; or by the prestige of some other community, accepted and revered in the first instance as extremely powerful magicians, and later found to reject and despise it.

The second step towards a science of nature is to organize your thoughts about this world of nature, where nature means the things that happen of themselves and not owing to anybody's art, by discriminating within it various realms or departments. Each of these realms will be a class of things or events resembling one another in certain recognizable ways and all agreeing to differ in these same ways from the things or events that make up the other realms. This step, once more, is a step in the development of absolute presuppositions; it is not a step which can be dictated, or even prompted, by any acquisition of 'experience'. For people like ourselves the habit of classifying things according to their resemblances and differences is so ingrained that we can hardly believe we are doing it. We can hardly believe that things do not present themselves to us whether we will or no ready labelled with reference-numbers to the classes in which we habitually put them.

It may help us to realize the arbitrary character of our own classifications if we study the very different classifications of the same material which other peoples have practised in the past or indeed still practise in the present; for example, the way in which the ancient Greeks and Romans classified colours not as we classify them, by the qualitative differences they show according to the places they occupy in the spectrum, but by reference to something quite different from this, something connected with dazzlingness or glintingness or gleamingness or their opposites, so that a Greek will find it as natural to call the sea 'wine-looking' as we to call it blue, and a Roman will find it as natural to call a swan 'scarlet' —or the word we conventionally translate scarlet— as we to call it white. It has been suggested that this is because the Greeks and Romans were colour-blind. But no sort of colour-blindness known to physiology would account for the facts. In both languages there are the rudiments of what we should call a true colour-nomenclature; and in both languages it happens that there are words for red and green, the colours that colour-blind persons cannot distinguish.

The problem I am suggesting for consideration is similar in principle to this, but it goes far deeper.

Instead of merely asking whether our conventional modern European way of classifying colours is the only possible way, a question which need only be asked to be answered in the negative, since records of other ways are actually in our possession, I am asking whether the age-old habit of considering the natural world (or world of things which happen of themselves) as a world consisting of various natural realms is the only possible way of considering that world. The answer is that any system of classification or division, whether the things classified or divided are colours or things that happen of themselves, is a system not 'discovered' but 'devised' by thought. The act of thought by which it is laid down is not proposition but supposition. The act of supposing the natural world to be divided into various natural realms is an act which for all human societies known to us has been habitual time out of mind; but it must have had a beginning. I do not see how we can ever hope to find out when or where so distant an event in human history took place; but I think we can be sure that it did take place; and I think we can describe with reasonable probability the kind of way in which human institutions are likely to have been affected by it.

The result of thinking systematically according to any given set of presuppositions is the creation of science; and this, like everything else that the human mind creates, grows for itself a body of institutions to keep it alive. In the case of science these are institutions for the pursuit of scientific research and for the education of young people in its methods and its

fruits. The result of thinking systematically about
what presuppositions are actually in use is the creation
of metaphysics or theology, and this too has its own
institutions, which in modern Europe (where 'theological colleges' are more concerned with vocational
training for the clerical profession than with theological or metaphysical instruction and research) have
been almost squeezed out of existence between scientific institutions on the one hand and religious institutions on the other, but flourished once in Europe as
they still flourish in the East, though even there the
influence of European example threatens them. It is
because they hardly exist in Europe that pseudo-
metaphysics of various kinds is so rife there. The
result of simply presupposing our presuppositions,
clinging to them by a sheer act of faith, whether or
not we know what they are, whether or not we work
out their consequences, is the creation of a religion;
and the institutions of a religion have this as their
object, to consolidate in believers and perpetuate in
their posterity the absolute presuppositions which lie
at the root of their thought.

It is because absolute presuppositions are not
'derived from experience', but are catalytic agents
which the mind must bring out of its own resources
to the manipulation of what is called 'experience'
and the conversion of it into science and civilization,
that there must be institutions for perpetuating them.
If they were once lost, they could never be recovered
except by repeating the same kind of process by which
they were originally created. As to the nature of this

process very little is known. That is one of the questions on which light will be thrown by the reformed metaphysics described in Chapter VII. At present there is little we can say about it except that it must have been extremely slow. Granted the preservation of what may be called the 'scientific frame of mind' characteristic of European civilization, the whole of modern European science could be reinvented in a very few thousand years, or even in a matter of hundreds, if all record of its achievements should be lost. But if the 'scientific frame of mind' were lost it would be a question of perhaps tens or hundreds of thousands before any tolerable substitute for it could be invented.

The guardianship of the European 'scientific frame of mind' is vested in the religious institutions of European civilization. In any civilization it is man's religious institutions that refresh in him from time to time the will (for it is a matter of will, though not a matter of choice) to retain the presuppositions by whose aid he reduces such experience as he enjoys to such science as he can compass; and it is by dint of these same religious institutions that he transmits these same presuppositions to his children. For if science is 'experience' interpreted in the light of our general convictions as to the nature of the world, religion is what expresses these convictions in themselves and for their own sake and hands them on from generation to generation. And it does this irrespectively of whether we know by means of metaphysical analysis what these convictions are.

Whenever and wherever men first acquired the habit of dividing the natural world into realms according to resemblances and differences among the things and events which they regarded as composing that world, we may be sure that this new habit of mind had its expression in their religious practices. We may assume with a certain degree of confidence that its effect was to split these up into a plurality of different cults practised, perhaps, by different sections of society, where each section regarded the others not as practising a rival religion to their own but rather as combining with themselves to maintain a single complex of religious institutions each one of which was necessary to the total welfare of society.

It is a mark of ignorance in anthropology to speak as if there were one single institution or set of institutions called 'totemism', or one single stage of human history or civilization to which the name 'totemistic' can be applied; but it is certainly true that in many different parts of the world, where peoples have been studied in what seems a very low and primitive grade of civilization, a single society has been found to regard itself as divided into a number of lesser units each having its own special religious institutions and each thus co-operating with all the rest in the collective maintenance of a religion which is not perhaps exactly polytheistic, for the idea of a god has hardly at this stage taken a definite shape, but is certainly polymorphic in respect of its ritual activities.

In a society of this kind there would be a sort of natural science; but in certain ways it would be very much unlike what we call natural science. In each 'totemic clan', or whatever name we like to use for a single one of the various religious groups within a society thus organized, there would be persons who achieved at least a quasi-scientific point of view towards their 'totem'. One such group, taking a special interest in one class of natural things or events, would become the repository of information about it; and in this way there would grow up a kind of departmentalized science of nature whose polymorphism would repeat the polymorphism of ritual activities.

What would make this extremely unlike the specialization of modern science is that modern specialization arises and runs its course within a unity logically prior to it which it never attempts to break up. The mutual independence of departmental specialists in modern science depends for its very existence on the presupposition that one and the same set of laws hold good throughout the entire world of nature. Unless it were thought an absolute certainty that in this sense nature is one, and therefore that natural science is one also, relations between the various departmental sciences would be as chaotic as the relations between various communities whose frontiers had never been agreed upon, which had never made any treaties, and whose respective positions had never been marked on any map. In the polymorphic science which I am trying to envisage there would be chaotic interrelations of this kind between any one set of inquirers and any other.

XX
POLYTHEISTIC AND MONOTHEISTIC
SCIENCE

WHEN first our evidence enables us to discern the thing we call Greek science it already shows marks of maturity. We have no direct evidence as to what it was doing before the lifetime of the Ionian 'philosophers' in the late seventh and early sixth centuries B.C.; but what we know about their work gives us plenty of indirect evidence both as to the existence and as to the character of the science which they set out to reform. There is also, as I shall point out towards the end of this chapter, evidence of another kind.

Greek religion was polytheistic; the Greek 'philosophers' from Thales onwards almost uniformly preached a monotheistic religion, and in many cases did so in conscious opposition to the current beliefs and institutions of their time. It would hardly be an exaggeration if one should describe the Greek 'philosophers' as a dissenting and sometimes persecuted sect of monotheists in a polytheistic society. Nor would it be much of an exaggeration if one should describe them in their scientific capacity as a succession of thinkers all bent upon showing that the world is one. Their monotheistic religion went hand in hand with a monomorphic science. And when we look at this science in some detail we find it so framed as to show that it must have arisen out of a pre-existing polymorphic science in the same kind of way in which their monotheistic religion arose out of a pre-existing polytheistic religion.

Thales is famous as the 'philosopher' who maintained that the world and everything in it was made of water. His contemporaries thought him a great man, and that opinion represents the popular judgement of which an ounce is worth more than a ton of academic or professional reputation. To have said in the time of Thales that the world is made of water must, therefore, have been regarded as an intellectual achievement of the first magnitude. To us it sounds rather childish. But that is because we, as heirs to the scientific tradition of Christendom, inherit a full and satisfactory solution, being in fact the fourth-century Greek solution, of what the Greeks called the problem of the one and the many. Thales was just beginning to tackle that problem.

If you got hold of any intelligent but 'uneducated' man to-day, and asked him why he thought it childish to say that everything was made of water, he would give you some such answer as this: 'I suppose it is true that in the long run everything is made out of the same sort of stuff. And I dare say water is as good a name for it as any other. But why make such a song about it? It is the differences between things that are interesting. If you told me why the piece of water that I call a stone sinks to the bottom of the sea when the piece of water that I call a flame jumps up into the air, or why the piece of water that I call a caterpillar turns into a butterfly when the piece of water that I call an egg turns into a hen, you would be telling me the kind of things I want to know.'

This is as much as to say that nowadays we take the oneness of things for granted and are chiefly interested in their manyness. If we repeat the mistake which in an earlier chapter I ascribed to the eighteenth century, and fancy that the way in which we think nowadays is the way in which all human beings think and always have thought, we shall infer that in the time of Thales, too, 'human nature' being what it is, people took the oneness of things for granted and were chiefly interested in their manyness. If they had, it would certainly have been childish of Thales to go on in this way about the oneness of things. As they did not think him childish for doing that, we may infer that they did not draw the line between the things one takes for granted and the things one wants to know in quite the same place as ourselves.

The work of the Ionian 'philosophers' becomes intelligible when we think of it as an attempt to introduce unity into a pre-existing mass of scientific work which was polymorphic in character. Being polytheistic in their religion but already quite capable of scientific work (for the existing fragments of Thales are no more the work of a 'primitive' than are the existing poems of Homer; and if Homer implies a pre-existing tradition of literary art, Thales no less implies a pre-existing tradition of scientific thought) the Greeks must already have worked out a number of departmental sciences of the kind roughly described in the preceding chapter; but with this difference, that in the preceding chapter I was describing a very primitive state of society in which the 'information', as I called it, that went to make up one such 'science' would be from our point of view less like a collection of scientific observations than like a collection of folk-lore, and pretty savage folk-lore at that; whereas the Greeks of a time not long before Thales were very far from being savages; they were already Greeks, already heirs to the Minoan world with its accurate observation of natural detail, already pupils to the scribes and star-gazers of Mesopotamia, the sculptors and engineers of Egypt.

It is something more than a guess, then, to say that before the time of Thales there already existed in Greece, and especially in the Greek cities of the Asian coast, a well-founded and well-developed science of nature, or rather a number of departmental sciences of this, that, and the other natural realm; and that the professional and educational organization of these sciences must have been focused in the specialized cult-centres of polytheistic religion; a state of things which survived here and there to a much later date in such examples as the college of medical men attached to the temple of Asklepios at Epidauros. And Thales would not have produced on the history of Greek thought the effect which he did produce unless this departmental and polymorphic natural science had reached a point of development, necessarily a rather high point of development, at which the lack of any co-ordinating authority to draw up a map of the sciences and arbitrate in frontier disputes between them was beginning to be acutely felt. People had become a little tired of the manyness of things. It was when Thales began talking about the oneness of things that they began to hear the kind of things they wanted to hear.

To drop the political and cartographic metaphor, the collection and study of isolated blocks of material, each drawn from a single realm of nature, was finding itself handicapped by the obscurity of the relations between one such block and another. It is not easy for us to grasp such a state of things, because for us it is an axiom that rules of method which are valid in one science will hold good, either without modification or *mutatis mutandis*, in those most nearly akin to it. But this is because science is for us no longer polymorphic. In a polymorphic science there is no sense in calling one science nearly or distantly akin to another. They are all just different. If anybody after a training in one science began to study another, his previous training would be valueless; he would have to start again at the beginning. It is an axiom for us that in any realm of nature there are certain laws which hold good not only there but in all other natural realms without exception, and others which hold good either without modification or *mutatis mutandis* in the realms nearest akin to it. In a polymorphic science there is no such axiom. There is no more ground for expecting discoveries in one science to point a way towards discoveries in another than for expecting methods in one science to indicate methods in another. And where it is impossible for one science to come to another's help with hints and suggestions depending on assumed analogies between their respective subject-matters or their respective methods it will be impossible for any one science in this isolated condition to attain more than a very low degree of orderliness and method in its inquiries, or of certainty in its results.

All modern scientific work rests on the absolute presupposition that nature is one and that science is one: that the different realms of nature are in part governed by one and the same code of absolutely identical laws, the laws of mathematics, and in part by special codes which do not differ radically among themselves but are so linked together by analogies and similarities that they may be regarded as so many local variants of laws which in spite of these variations can still be called 'laws of nature'; while the various sciences that investigate the various realms of nature are not independent sciences but only modifications of one and the same thing, a single thing which we call by the single name of natural science. What Thales was fighting for, when he 'childishly' said that the world was made of water, was this principle we so lightly take for granted: the principle that in spite of all the differences between different natural realms and the different sciences that study them there is one thing that is nature, and one science that is natural science.

The attempt to replace a polymorphic by a monomorphic natural science was logically bound up with the attempt to replace a polytheistic by a monotheistic religion. Or rather, since even in Homer a kind of monotheistic tendency exists side by side with a polytheistic, an attempt to develop the monotheistic tendency already present in popular religion, and to prevent it from being choked by the polytheism which prevailed over it in popular ritual practice. Perhaps to avoid this danger, the 'philosophers' did not, as certain poets like Aeschylus did, graft their monotheism upon the monotheistic element in Homer by giving to their one God the name of Zeus. They did not constitute themselves a sect of Zeus-worshippers. They declined to use any personal name at all, and spoke simply of ὁ θεός, God.

This was in effect a refusal to allow certain poetical motives to interfere with the motives of religion on the one hand and those of theology or metaphysics on the other. The Greeks were a people whose artistic genius was not less remarkable than their scientific. In the work of the Greek mind it is not always easy to distinguish the respective operations of their artistic and their scientific genius. Their habit of representing their gods in vividly realized human form was not a piece of theology, it was a piece of poetry. When they described or portrayed Aphrodite, for example, they did not think they were describing or portraying a magnified and non-natural woman who, by the exercise of something like will, but a superhuman will, brought about the various events which together made up her realm, namely the events connected with sexual reproduction. They did not think they were describing or portraying a person who controlled or produced these events, they thought they were describing or portraying these events themselves, regarded generically as natural events, or events not under human control, and specifically as sexual events. The human or quasi-human figure of Aphrodite is merely the poetical way in which they represented these events to themselves. The power or might or royal status annexed to that figure is merely the poetical way in which they represented to themselves their conviction that events of this kind are not only beyond our control but are also of the utmost importance in our lives; so that we must adjust ourselves to them as best we can, since a successful adjustment will mean a happy and successful life for ourselves so far as that realm of nature is concerned, whereas an unsuccessful adjustment will entail our misery or destruction.

There can be no more fatal misunderstanding of Greek literature than the failure to grasp this principle. In the *Hippolytus* of Euripides, for example, a young man is cruelly done to death because he refuses to gratify the incestuous passion of his stepmother. In terms of poetry, his destruction is compassed by a quasi-human person called Aphrodite, in the execution of her vengeance upon him for refusing, not then only but always, to take part in sexual intercourse; a refusal which she regards as insulting to herself as the patron of sex. In order to achieve her vengeance this goddess deprives his stepmother first of her happiness and self-respect and then of her life, and robs his father both of wife and of son, making him his son's murderer.

Simple-minded modern readers can hardly restrain their indignation; allow themselves strong language about the low moral quality of Greek religious ideas; and hint a suspicion that Euripides may have been deliberately attacking the beliefs of his countrymen. Yet if these same readers heard somebody say that a steeple-jack, notoriously careless about the condition of his ropes, fell one day by the operation of the law of gravity from the top of a church tower, so that himself and a harmless passer-by were killed, and his aged father ended his days in the workhouse, they would hardly suspect their informant of meaning to suggest that so inhuman a law ought to be repealed. They have simply been deceived by the Greek habit of personification. The story of the *Hippolytus* would be exactly the same if you left the goddess out. Here it is.

'Once upon a time there was a young man who had a horror of women. To persuade himself that there was nothing wrong with him, he devoted himself to blood-sports. His mother was dead, and his father married again, a nice young woman, good-looking and of good family, though there were odd stories about them. . . . Well, as luck would have it, or perhaps it was that queer streak in her family, she fell violently in love with her stepson. She was almost dying of love, when her old nurse found out about it and persuaded her to speak to the young man. He refused her with such disgust that she didn't know what to do. So she committed suicide, leaving a letter for her husband saying that it was because her stepson had made love to her. The old man believed it; so he had him murdered.' The moral is that sex is a thing about which you cannot afford to make mistakes.

These stories, already hundreds of years old when they were piously preserved in the Greek literature of the fifth century before Christ, a literature which was consciously and professedly the handmaid of Greek polytheistic religion, are often found to inculcate such morals as this, and may be regarded as documentary relics of the polymorphic science which the 'philosophers' set out to reform. Refracted as they are through the atmosphere of fifth-century Greek civilization, they can hardly be called direct evidence as to what that polymorphic science was like; but indirectly they are evidence of a very valuable kind, and enable the metaphysician who is conscious of the historical character of his own work to carry the history of the absolute presuppositions involved in Greek science back beyond the point to which it was brought by the reformation that Thales initiated.

The high-water mark of this reformation is recorded in Aristotle's *Metaphysics*, where the central problem is to expound the presuppositions of a science of nature (the science of nature which was pursued by Aristotle himself, the foremost natural scientist of his age, and those whom he regarded as his fellow workers in that field) in which the balance was evenly held between the oneness of things and their manyness. Aristotle's *Metaphysics*, openly and professedly a theology, reminds the reader by this fact of the intimate connexion that there must always be between the doctrines of religion and the foundations of natural science. In it Aristotle tries to express both the genuine unity of the natural world, as envisaged by this science, and also the genuine plurality of the realms within it, in other words, both the genuine unity of natural science and the genuine plurality of the natural sciences, as these things existed in his own time, by affirming the following propositions. The reader will understand that my purpose is only to summarize a few of Aristotle's points, and that in every case I leave it to him to insert the metaphysical rubric.

Of Nature

1. (DEF.) *The 'world of nature' is a world of movements which happen of themselves.*

Note on prop. 1. That there is such a world is a thing we discover by the use of our senses.

Of the Unity of Nature, or of God

2. *There is one God, and only one.*

3. *God is not a creator from whom natural movements receive their origin (for if so they would not happen of themselves); he is the perfect being whom all the things in nature are trying to imitate.*

4. *God is mind; but all these imitations are movements; therefore natural movements imitate God in the only way in which movements can imitate the activity of mind.*

5. *The activity of mind is rational activity; therefore*

natural movements in general, as imitations of God, are rational movements, i.e. movements taking place according to laws.

Of the Plurality of Natural Realms, or of the Intelligences

6. *There are various realms of nature, in which various different kinds of movement obtain.*

7. *There is only one realm of nature, the sphere of the fixed stars, which directly imitates God.*

8. *It does so by moving with a uniform rotation, this being the only kind of motion which can go on uniformly for ever, and thus serve to imitate the eternal and unchanging activity of God.*

9. *The non-circular and non-uniform movements characteristic of other natural realms are imitations, in terms of movement, of other kinds of mental activity.*

10. *They are imitations, in terms of movement, of the activities of certain Intelligences, which are minds themselves imitating in various partial and incomplete ways in terms of mental activity the one activity of God; these Intelligences being neither divine nor human, but belonging to an order intermediate between the two.*

Note on prop. 10. The statement that there are many different ways in which God's single activity can be imitated by other minds implies that all these different forms of mental activity already exist within God's single activity. This may be expressed by saying that the unity of God's activity is a 'self-differentiating unity', like the unity of the logical universal (see p. 6).

XXI
QUICUNQUE VULT

IF Aristotle's account of the presuppositions underlying natural science as he understood it are compared
with those of modern European science, certain points
of agreement and certain points of difference will be
found. I will begin with the most important points
of agreement.

I. That *there is one God*; in other words, that there
is one world of nature with one system of laws running all through it, and one natural science which
investigates it.

II. That *there are many modes of God's activity*; in
other words, that the oneness of nature does not
preclude, it logically implies, the distinction of many
realms within nature, and the oneness of natural
science does not preclude, it logically implies, distinctions between many departmental sciences.

This solves the 'problem of the one and the many'.
The solution in terms of religion is not to be found
in a polytheism which asserts a diversity, however
harmonious, of departmental gods; it can only be
found in a monotheism which regards the one activity
of the one God as a self-differentiating activity. This
solution has the minor drawback, if you think it a
drawback, that although you can quite well understand how a single activity differentiates itself into
various activities (Plato had already made this clear
when he showed that the four 'virtues' of temperance,

courage, wisdom, and justice were differentiations of one single 'virtue' which includes them all, so that a man is properly called 'good' not because he is either temperate or brave or wise or just but because he is alike temperate and brave and wise and just) you cannot personify this in sculpture or painting or poetry; so that people who fancy they cannot understand a thing unless they can see it mythologically represented in a picture will fancy they cannot understand this. When a sculptor, for example, wishes to express the idea that the divine activity is one, he will personify it in a single human figure invested with conventional attributes of divinity: when he wishes to express the idea that this one activity diversifies itself into many activities, he will personify it in a group of figures, rather comic to an irreverent eye, appearing to represent a committee of perhaps strangely assorted gods. An unintelligent spectator will think that there is inconsistency here, and will complain that he cannot tell whether monotheism or polytheism is being expounded.

There are at least two points, however, where Aristotle's account of his own presuppositions fails to agree with the presuppositions of modern natural science. When these points are examined it will be seen that Aristotle was not so much failing to anticipate the absolute presuppositions of a future age as failing correctly to define his own.

III. When Aristotle says that *God did not create the world*, this means that the existence of nature is not a presupposition of natural science but simply an observed fact. For if it had been said that God created nature, this would have meant that the existence of nature is a presupposition of natural science; since God is such a presupposition, and any activity which we ascribe to God is an integral part of what we believe about Him, and therefore when we presuppose Him we simultaneously presuppose anything which we regard as the product of His activity.

Aristotle thought, and he was not the only Greek philosopher to think it, that by merely using our senses we learn that a natural world exists. He did not realize that the use of our senses can never inform us that what we perceive by using them is a world of things that happen of themselves and are not subject to control by our own art or any one else's. I have already pointed out that the existence of such a world is a presupposition, the first and fundamental presupposition, on which alone any science of nature can arise. When Aristotle described it as a fact discovered by the use of the senses, therefore, he was falling into a metaphysical error. For his own science of nature, no less than for any other, the thing was in fact an absolute presupposition. This metaphysical error was corrected by Christianity.

If metaphysics is our name for the statement of absolute presuppositions, and if metaphysics and theology are the same, there are three ways in which the existence of a world of nature might be made to figure among the doctrines of theology.

1. It might be a proposition in metaphysics, as it is for Spinoza, that God and nature are the same.

But this would entail the consequence that natural science is the same thing as metaphysics: which cannot be right if the business of metaphysics is to state the absolute presuppositions of natural science.

2. It might be a proposition in metaphysics that the world of nature exists, but this proposition might be left wholly unrelated to the proposition that God exists. But then it would not be a proposition in theology; and therefore, if theology and metaphysics are the same, not a proposition in metaphysics. And what about the presupposition of which it was the statement? The act by which we hold such presuppositions, I have said elsewhere, is religious faith; and God is that in which we believe by faith; therefore all our absolute presuppositions must be presuppositions in holding which we believe something about God.

3. It might be a proposition in which the existence of the world of nature was stated in the form of an attribute or activity of God; and this seems the only possible alternative.

IV. The second point of discrepancy between Aristotle's metaphysics and the presuppositions of modern science is concerned with *motion* as a feature of the natural world.

Let it be granted that there is a natural world, no matter what our reasons for believing it. Greek and modern physics are agreed that the most universal characteristic of this world is motion. Now, if we ask how we know that in the natural world there is such a thing as motion, the Greek answer is that we

know it by using our senses. That is how we know
that there are natural things; that is likewise how we
know that they move. But if the existence of natural
things is not a fact discovered by experience but a
presupposition without which we could never convert the data of experience into a science of nature,
the idea that these things move must be a part of that
same presupposition. For when we speak of the
existence of natural things we mean (as Aristotle
very truly says) the existence of things that move of
themselves or events that happen of themselves. The
idea of movement or happening, and self-movement
or automatic happening at that, is contained in the
idea of a natural world. The idea of motion, therefore (for if the world of nature is a world of bodies
all the events in nature are motions), cannot be an
idea which we obtain, as the Greeks thought we
obtained it, through the use of our senses. It is an
idea which we bring with us in the shape of an
absolute presupposition to the work of interpreting
what we get by using our senses. The proposition
that there is motion in nature is a metaphysical
proposition.

How could this proposition be incorporated in a
theology? Obviously by saying that God, when he
created the world of nature, set it in motion. The
other alternatives, (1) that God is nature and that the
movement of nature is God's activity of self-movement, and (2) that science involves this presupposition among others, that natural things move, have
been in principle already considered and rejected.

But if we say that God set the world in motion when he created it, we are saying that his thus setting in motion the world he created is an integral part of his creating it, and therefore arises out of something in his essential nature. Aristotle did not think that movement, as such, in the natural world arose out of anything in God's nature; he thought it happened of itself. He only thought that the orderliness or regularity or 'rationality' of such movement arose from something in God's nature, namely from the rationality of God's thought, which things in nature imitated. But if we drop the idea of natural movements as first (logically first, of course) occurring of themselves, and only secondly acquiring their orderliness through imitating God, and substitute the idea of these movements as created by God, we are saying in effect that to be the creator of movement in the natural world is just as much a part of God's nature as to be the source of diversified orderliness in the natural world.

Here again, it will be seen, Aristotle failed in his metaphysical analysis; and his failure was not limited to himself alone; the metaphysical mistake which he made was a commonplace of Greek thought. And since metaphysics is inseparable, as regards success or failure, from ordinary thinking, this breakdown of Greek metaphysics implied a breakdown of Greek science.

This was very clearly seen by the Patristic writers, who made all the four points I have enumerated, consciously and deliberately emphasizing their im-

portance for natural science. I will go over the points
in a slightly different order.

I. *There is one God.* Here they agreed with the
philosophical tradition of the Greeks, and also with
the prophetic tradition of the Hebrews, which resembled it in asserting a monotheistic religion against
a background of popular polytheism.

II. *God created the world.* Here they accepted the
Hebrew tradition and departed from the Greek. For
Plato, God is not the creator of the world, he is only
its 'demiurge'; that is to say, he made it, but made
it on a pre-existing model, namely the eternal hierarchy of Forms. For Aristotle, he did not even make
it; he is only the model on which it tries to make itself.

In order to understand what the Christian metaphysicians were doing, and why the thing they did
was ultimately accepted by the Greco-Roman world,
in other words why that world was converted to
Christianity, it is necessary to bear in mind that at
this point they were correcting a metaphysical error
on the part of the Greek philosophers. I have already
explained that the article of faith 'God created the
world' meant 'the idea of a world of nature is an
absolute presupposition of natural science'. In maintaining that article of faith, the Christians were substituting a correct piece of metaphysical analysis for
the incorrect piece of metaphysical analysis whereby
the Greek philosophers had been led to the doctrine
that we learn of the natural world's existence by the
use of our senses.

III. *The activity of God is a self-differentiating*

activity, which is why there are diverse realms in nature.
This doctrine was a blend of the foregoing with a
notion which Christianity owed to the Greek philosophers. The notion of a self-differentiating unity
was characteristically Platonic; and from Platonism it
had already found its way into the Jewish Platonism
of Egypt. The technical term in Greek for a self-
differentiating unity is λόγος, and this word was taken
over by the Egyptian schools, and later by Christianity itself in the Fourth Gospel. Everybody knows
Gibbon's gibe to the effect that this notion was
taught 300 B.C. in the school of Alexandria, revealed
A.D. 97 by the Apostle St. John. Most people know,
too, that Gibbon lifted this statement out of St.
Augustine's *Confessions*, characteristically omitting
to acknowledge it and at the same time falsifying
the facts by suppressing Augustine's point, which
is that the notion of the λόγος was a commonplace
familiar to every Platonist, but that the Johannine
doctrine according to which 'the λόγος was made
flesh' was a new idea peculiar to Christianity.[1]

---

[1] Gibbon's remark occurs in his table of contents to chapter xxi.
'My personal acquaintance with the Bishop of Hippo', he says in
note 30 to chapter xxxiii (Bury's ed., vol. iii, p. 607), 'does not
extend beyond the *Confessions* and the *City of God.*' Here is the
passage from the *Confessions*, vii. 9: 'et ibi [sc. in libris Platoni-
corum] legi non quidem his verbis, sed hoc idem omnino, multis
et multiplicibus suaderi rationibus quod *in principio erat verbum,
et verbum erat apud Deum, et Deus erat verbum; hoc erat in principio apud Deum* (and so on, quoting John i. 1–5, then omitting
the reference to the Baptist and beginning again at verse 11).
Quia vero *in sua propria venit* . . . (quoting verses 11–12) non ibi
legi. Item ibi legi . . . (quoting verse 13) sed quia *verbum caro*

IV. *The creative activity of God is the source of motion in the world of nature*. This, like number II, was a departure from Greek precedents and a point borrowed from the Hebrew creation-myth, where 'the spirit (breath) of God moved upon the face of the waters', and where God after modelling Adam out of clay 'breathed into his nostrils the breath (spirit) of life'. God is pictured as blowing over the world he makes, thus setting it in motion; blowing into the living creature he makes, thus giving it power to move itself.

This point is logically connected with number II. If the world of nature is by definition a world of movements, and if the existence of that world is an absolute presupposition of natural science, the movement which is its essence must be an absolute presupposition too. Once it was seen that Greek natural science did in fact absolutely presuppose the existence of a natural world, although by an error in metaphysical analysis the Greek philosophers had overlooked the fact; and once the fact had been stated, strictly in accordance with the Aristotelian principle that metaphysics and theology are the same, by saying that the world of nature exists in virtue of a

factum est . . . (quoting verse 14) non ibi legi.' The extreme care with which Augustine details every point in which the Evangelist is merely repeating the commonplaces of current Platonism throws into sharp relief the points in which he claims that the Christian doctrine departs from the Platonic; and makes one regret the slipshod way in which Gibbon speaks of Plato as having 'marvellously anticipated one of the most surprising discoveries of the Christian revelation'.

creative act on the part of God; it followed inevitably that this creative act should be defined as not merely (*a*) creative of nature in general, nor merely (*b*) creative of distinct realms in nature, but also as (*c*) creative of motion in nature.

When a Christian theologian to-day says that God exists, or (to be precise by making explicit the metaphysical rubric) that we believe in God, he is consciously using words in the sense in which they were defined by the Patristic writers who worked out the notions I have been describing. When an uneducated Christian makes the same statement, he too is using words in the same sense, unless indeed he is attaching to them some private and heretical (that is, historically unjustified) sense of his own. What the words do actually and historically mean is by now, I hope, clear. I will try to summarize it briefly, bearing in mind that I have undertaken to deal only with their application to the absolute presuppositions of natural science.

They mean that natural scientists standing in the Greek tradition absolutely presuppose in all their inquiries

1. *That there is a world of nature*, i.e. that there are things which happen of themselves and cannot be produced or prevented by anybody's art, however great that art may be, and however seconded by good luck.

2. *That this world of nature is a world of events*, i.e. that the things of which it is composed are things to which events happen or things which move.

3. *That throughout this world there is one set of laws according to which all movements or events, in spite of all differences, agree in happening*; and that consequently there is one science of this world.

4. *That nevertheless there are in this world many different realms*, each composed of a class of things peculiar to itself, to which events of a peculiar kind happen; that the peculiar laws of these several realms are modifications of the universal laws mentioned in 3; and that the special sciences of these several realms are modifications of the universal science there mentioned.

Christian writers in the time of the Roman Empire asserted, and no historian to-day will deny, that in their time the science and civilization of the Greco-Roman world were moribund. Some modern writers, purveyors of sensational fiction rather than historians, say that this was because the Greco-Roman world was being destroyed by barbarian attacks. The causes of historical events are sometimes clearer to posterity than to contemporaries; but not in a case like this. If a man's friends have left it on record that he died of a lingering disease, and a group of subsequent writers, in an age for which it is a dogma that no such disease exists, agreed to say that he was shot by a burglar, a reader might admit that the story told by posterity was more entertaining than that told by the contemporaries, without admitting that it was truer. The Patristic diagnosis of the decay of Greco-Roman civilization ascribes that event to a metaphysical disease. The Greco-Roman world, we are told, was

moribund from internal causes, specifically because
it had accepted as an article of faith, as part of its
'pagan' creed, a metaphysical analysis of its own
absolute presuppositions which was at certain points
erroneous. If metaphysics had been a mere luxury
of the intellect, this would not have mattered. But
because metaphysical analysis is an integral part
of scientific thought, an obstinate error in metaphysical analysis is fatal to the science with which
it is concerned. And because science and civilization,
organized thought in its theoretical and practical
forms, stand or fall together, the metaphysical error
which killed pagan science killed pagan civilization
with it.

This diagnosis is naturally repugnant to an age like
the present, when the very possibility of metaphysics
is hardly admitted without a struggle, and when,
even if its possibility is admitted, its importance
as a *conditio sine qua non* of science and civilization
is almost universally denied. Naturally, therefore,
this anti-metaphysical temper has produced an
alternative explanation for the collapse of the 'pagan'
world: that it was destroyed by the barbarians. But
this explanation cannot be taken seriously by any
one with the smallest pretensions to historical learning. A good deal of information about barbarians
and Romans in the later Empire is now accessible
even to persons who profess no special interest in the
subject; and any reader who will spend a little time
upon it can satisfy himself that it was not barbarian
attacks that destroyed the Greco-Roman world.

Further research will convince him that to this extent
the Patristic diagnosis was correct: the 'pagan' world
died because of its own failure to keep alive its own
fundamental convictions.

The Patristic writers not only saw this, but they
assigned to it a cause, and proposed a remedy. The
cause was a metaphysical cause. The 'pagan' world
was failing to keep alive its own fundamental convictions, they said, because owing to faults in metaphysical analysis it had become confused as to what
these convictions were. The remedy was a metaphysical remedy. It consisted, as they formulated it,
in abandoning the faulty analysis and accepting a
new and more accurate analysis, on the lines which
I have indicated in this chapter.

This new analysis they called the 'Catholic Faith'.
The Catholic Faith, they said, is this: that we worship
(note the metaphysical rubric) one God in trinity,
and trinity in unity, neither confounding the ὑποστάσεις
and thus reducing trinitarianism to unitarianism, nor
dividing the οὐσία and thus converting the one God
into a committee of three. The three ὑποστάσεις, that
is to say the three terms in virtue of whose distinctness
they spoke of a trinity, they called respectively the
Father, the Son, and the Holy Ghost. By believing
in the Father they meant (always with reference
solely to the procedure of natural science) absolutely
presupposing that there is a world of nature which
is always and indivisibly one world. By believing in
the Son they meant absolutely presupposing that
this one natural world is nevertheless a multiplicity

of natural realms.[1] By believing in the Holy Ghost
they meant absolutely presupposing that the world
of nature, throughout its entire fabric, is a world not
merely of things but of events or movements.

These presuppositions must be made, they said,
by any one who wished to be 'saved'; saved, that is
to say, from the moral and intellectual bankruptcy,
the collapse of science and civilization, which was
overtaking the 'pagan' world. The disease from which
that world was suffering they regarded as a fatal
disease. A civilization is a way in which people live,
and if the way in which people live is an impracticable
way there can be no question of saving it. What has
to be saved is not the way of living but the people
who live in that way; and saving them means inducing them to live in a different way, a way that is
not impracticable. The different way of living which
these writers proposed for adoption was the way of
living based upon the absolute presuppositions I

[1] This is why, as everybody knows who has ever looked at the
sculptures of a French cathedral, the specialized creative work
done on the Days of Creation is represented in medieval Christian
art as being done not by the Father but by the Son. The second
'Hypostasis' of the Trinity is the λόγος, the self-differentiation of
the divine creative activity. 'Dieu a créé, mais il a créé par son
Verbe ou par son Fils. C'est le Fils qui a réalisé la pensée du
Père, qui l'a fait passer de la puissance à l'acte. Le Fils est le vrai
créateur. Pénétrés de cette doctrine, les artistes du moyen âge
ont toujours représenté le créateur sous les traits de Jésus-Christ':
Émile Mâle, *L'art religieux du xiiie siècle en France*, 1925, p. 29.
Cf. Augustine, *Conf.* xi. 5, for the origin of the doctrine: 'quoniam
tu Pater in principio quod est tua sapientia de te nata, aequalis
tibi et coaeterna, id est in Filio tuo, fecisti caelum et terram'.

have tried, in a partial and one-sided manner, to describe. The new way of living would involve a new science and a new civilization.

The presuppositions that go to make up this 'Catholic Faith', preserved for many centuries by the religious institutions of Christendom, have as a matter of historical fact been the main or fundamental presuppositions of natural science ever since. They have never been its only absolute presuppositions; there have always been others, and these others have to some extent differed at different times. But from the fifth century down to the present day all these differences have played their changing parts against a background that has remained unchanged: the constellation of absolute presuppositions originally sketched by Aristotle, and described more accurately, seven or eight centuries later, by the Patristic writers under the name of the 'Catholic Faith'.

Note to pp. 223–5.—There may be readers who find strange or even shocking my denial of the vulgar error that Roman civilization was destroyed by barbarian attacks. In the text I remarked that this impression would be dispelled by looking up what modern writers have to say on the subject. Such readers can now be referred to an authoritative discussion of this very point in a book which has placed its author among the foremost living historians: A. J. Toynbee, *A Study of History*, vol. iv, pp. 56–63, published while this Essay was in the press.

B

THE METAPHYSICS OF KANT

XXII

KANT'S PROBLEM AND THE PROBLEM OF TO-DAY

WHEN Kant wrote the *Critique of Pure Reason* he meant to place it before the public not as a piece of constructive metaphysical thinking but as a clearing away of errors which had impeded and still did impede metaphysical thinking.

His view of metaphysics, as stated in his preface, was (1) that it was concerned with God, freedom, and immortality; (2) that as dealing with these supremely important subjects it represented an inquiry to which men could never be indifferent and which they would never renounce, so that the question was not whether people should have metaphysics or no metaphysics, but whether they should have good metaphysics or bad metaphysics; (3) that the 'illuminists' of his own century, in attacking metaphysics, were really attacking the foundations of all knowledge and in effect if not in intention acting as enemies of the science whose friends they professed to be; (4) that metaphysicians were to blame for this state of things, because they had misunderstood their own problems and their proper methods, and had consequently given the public not genuine metaphysics but pseudo-metaphysics; (5) and lastly, that a sounder metaphysics was not to be looked for until those errors had been cleared away which had vitiated the work of past metaphysicians.

The resemblance between Kant's problem and our own will appear from the following comments on these five propositions.

1. To say that metaphysics deals with 'God, freedom, and immortality' is to invite the ridicule of every one who prides himself on being what William James called 'tough-minded', or in the slang of to-day 'hard-boiled'. It suggests to people of this kind that metaphysics is a game in which senile sentimentalists play at taking seriously the old wives' tales they heard when they were children. In the last chapter I have shown that, interpreted historically, the proposition 'God exists' takes its place not among old wives' tales but among the absolute presuppositions of science and civilization. Similar interpretations could be given, granted adequate historical equipment, for the beliefs in human freedom and human immortality; which, thus metaphysically expounded, are by no means the mere wish-fulfilment fantasies for which they are too often taken.

But (a) I do not suggest that, for any of the three, Kant himself had any such interpretation in mind; (b) even if such interpretation is given and accepted, Kant's formula remains objectionable as conveying the suggestion that metaphysics has a closed repertory of problems, which is wholly false (see p. 64). The most I can say for Kant on this point is that if the terms 'God, freedom, and immortality' are interpreted as the term 'God' has been interpreted in the foregoing chapters, his formula gives a sample of the problems with which any modern metaphysics must deal.

2. It is still as true as it was in Kant's time that there must be metaphysics. Kant seems to suggest that the necessity for it is a psychological one, arising out of men's desires; but this is not the case. It is a logical necessity. It arises out of the mere pursuit of knowledge. That pursuit, which we call science, is an attempt to think in a systematic and orderly manner. This involves disentangling the presuppositions of our thought. This again involves discovering that some of them are relative presuppositions which have to be justified, and that others are absolute presuppositions which neither stand in need of justification nor can in fact be justified; and a person who has made this discovery is already a metaphysician. No metaphysician, no scientist.

3. It is still true that the professed enemies of metaphysics are attacking the foundations of science. Perhaps the danger from such attacks is graver to-day than it was in the time of Kant. I say perhaps, because I am aware of the tendency to think the danger in which one stands to-day graver than the danger which yesterday was successfully weathered. But it is in fact my opinion that the danger to science from anti-metaphysics is more serious now than it has ever been before. I have already tried to explain the kind of issue which seems to be involved by what I have called the irrationalist movement of the present day. It is not comparable with the scepticism of the eighteenth century. That did not express a revolt against the life of scientific thought; it expressed only a sense of its difficulty. It was not an attempt to

overthrow science. Even Hume, for all his scepticism, was as thoroughly convinced as any of his contemporaries that the Newtonian physics was valid. Where he showed himself a sceptic was in rejecting the ordinary view as to the grounds of that conviction, not in rejecting that conviction itself. The situation to-day is quite different. Metaphysics came under fire in the eighteenth century because people fancied that in a world without metaphysics conditions would be more favourable to the development of science. To-day metaphysics is under fire because in a world without metaphysics conditions will be more favourable to the development of irrationalism.

I spoke in Chapter XIII of obstacles which hinder this development. Prominent among these is a conviction on the part of educated persons, including both the class of professional thinkers and the class of persons who, though not thinkers by vocation, are qualified by training and inclination to understand what the thinkers by vocation are doing, that truth is supremely worth pursuing and that scientific thinking must at all costs go on. If this conviction holds, the epidemic of irrationalism will be stayed. But if educated persons commit themselves to the view that truth is not worth pursuing, and this is what they do commit themselves to, knowingly or unknowingly, if they decide that metaphysics is impossible, they will surrender their faith in science, and thus remove what may prove the only serious obstacle to the overthrow of European civilization.

4. It is still true to-day that metaphysicians, by

propagating erroneous views as to the nature of meta-physics, have played into the hands of their enemies. But it is less easy to-day than it was in the eighteenth century to acquit their enemies of blame on that account.

The most 'valuable discovery' that has been made since Kant's time in what Hume called 'the republic of letters' has been the discovery of a scientific technique in history. In the eighteenth century historical research was still conducted by the use of scissors and paste. The historian was still a person whose business was to know what his 'authorities' had said on the subject in which he was interested, and to repeat this in his own way and with his own comments. To-day the very notion of 'authorities' has disappeared. The twentieth-century historian is a person who takes no man's word about the subject into which he is inquiring. The statements he makes about that subject are made on no one's authority but his own. The process by which he arrives at them is not a process of deciding to believe what somebody has told him, it is a process of making up his mind what the evidence in his possession proves. For a man of the twentieth century it is inexcusable to take a metaphysician's word for what he is doing. You must settle that question for your-self by studying his works.

And when you read the works of an anti-meta-physician, you can and must demand of him what in the eighteenth century no reasonable man would have demanded, an accurate knowledge of what metaphysicians have in fact been doing, based not on hearsay but on a critical study of their works conducted according to the well-known methods of historical inquiry. 'If we take in our hand any such volume'—I adapt another saying of Hume's—'let us ask, does it contain, I will not say evidence that its author is well read in metaphysical literature, but evidence that he has thought historically about what he has read?—No.—Commit it then to the flames; for it can contain nothing but sophistry and illusion'.

5. Nevertheless, it is still true that errors as to the proper method and true definition of metaphysics have hampered metaphysicians in their work, encouraged and indeed generated anti-metaphysicians, and thus given assistance to the irrationalists by fostering treason among those who ought to have unitedly opposed them. Kant's problem may or may not be less urgent than the problem of to-day; but they are problems of the same kind. That is why in the chapters that follow I shall from time to time insert observations on the anti-metaphysicians of to-day, as a kind of running commentary on the metaphysical statements that I find in the *Critique of Pure Reason.*

XXIII
METAPHYSICS AND CRITICAL
PHILOSOPHY

KANT intended when he wrote his first *Critique* to clear the way for a future metaphysics by criticizing the errors that had vitiated metaphysics in the past. In writing it he actually promised that when it was done he would write and publish the new system of metaphysics for which it would have prepared the way. But he never did so; and when reminded of his promise he answered that the *Critique* was itself that system. This remark admits of more than one interpretation. But there is one possible interpretation of it which would harmonize with the view of metaphysics I find in Aristotle and am trying to expound in this essay; and therefore I shall set forth that interpretation without professing to know whether Kant would have accepted it.

Kant wrote the *Critique of Pure Reason* in order to review the contemporary position of metaphysical studies, very much as a man might approach any difficult problem in any kind of science by reviewing the more important attempts to solve it; asking how far they had succeeded and why they had not succeeded more completely; considering the state in which they had left the problem; and in general making quite sure he knew what the problem was that he wanted to solve, and upon what conditions he would be able to claim in the future that he had solved it.

It had been a commonplace ever since the time of Descartes that there were three kinds of science: mathematics, physics, and metaphysics. Kant observed that mathematics had been firmly established on the path of scientific progress ever since the days of the early Greeks, and physics ever since the time of Galileo. Metaphysics had not yet reached that state. Something had therefore to be done in metaphysics, he argued, corresponding to what the early Greeks had done in mathematics, and to what Galileo and his contemporaries had done in physics. What was it, then, that these people had done?

In mathematics, Kant replied, the early Greeks had discovered the path of scientific progress by treating geometry not as an affair of making measurements but as an affair of arguing out the consequences of assumptions. Instead of saying 'Here is a piece of land, let us measure it up', they said 'Let ABC be a triangle, and let AB = AC.' In physics Galileo had discovered the path of scientific progress by rolling a ball down an inclined plane. Instead of first making observations and then asking what they proved, he first framed hypotheses and then devised experiments to test them.

The feature common to these two discoveries was that people gave up the attempt to construct a science by arguing from their observations of things they discovered under their noses, and set to work instead by asking questions and demanding answers to them. This had been said before. It was Bacon who insisted that the science of nature begins when man begins 'putting nature to the question' (that is, the torture; Bacon was a lawyer and knew what 'the question' meant in his own profession), extorting from her an answer to the questions he chose to ask, instead of contenting himself with noting down whatever she elected to reveal. And Kant took care to acknowledge his debt by using a quotation from Bacon as the motto of the *Critique*.

The moral Kant meant to convey was that in metaphysics too the path of scientific progress would be found when metaphysicians began putting their questions in an orderly and systematic way, instead of arguing blindly, as they now did, in the hope of seeing what came of it. This advice was extremely sound; but it would not have done metaphysicians much good unless it had been accompanied by further advice as to what kind of questions they should ask. And on this matter Kant's mind was not, I think, perfectly clear. Consequently, although he was able to state in this general way what the conditions were under which alone metaphysics could become a science, I doubt whether at this stage he had any definite idea what, when it had become a science, it would be like.

Fortunately he was a man with a passion for detail. Having made up his mind that there could be no science unless definite questions were asked, and that scientific technique meant simply the skilful asking of questions; having seen that all questioning involved presuppositions; and having seen that mathematics and physics in so far as they had become sciences of the modern type had done so by developing a technique of questioning which depended on the acceptance of a definite set of absolute presuppositions, he was not content to leave the matter there. He had to enter at enormous length, and with an apparent irrelevance which exasperates some readers and delights others, because it makes them think he is losing sight of metaphysics altogether, into the question what these presuppositions were. Both classes of readers are mistaken. He never lost sight of metaphysics for a moment.

With the presuppositions of mathematics he dealt rather briefly. In this he was wise, for he was not very much of a mathematician; and no philosopher can acquit himself with credit in philosophizing at length about a region of experience in which he is not very thoroughly at home. With physics it was different. He was a first-hand physicist of considerable distinction, and teaching the subject had long been an important part of his professional work. He therefore threw himself with zest into the work of stating as fully and accurately as he could what exactly the presuppositions were which in his work as a physicist he found himself making.

The statement of these presuppositions occupies that part of the *Critique* which is called 'Transcendental Analytics'. The reader will observe that here Kant was doing what, according to Aristotle himself, it is the business of a metaphysician to do. Kant did not leave his metaphysical system unwritten; he wrote it under the title of 'Transcendental Analytics'.

And what I am suggesting in this chapter is that owing to a certain change in his view of the relation between metaphysics and critical philosophy Kant came to see this for himself.

When he wrote the Transcendental Analytics, it is clear that he did not mean it for metaphysics. He meant it for a kind of clue to metaphysics. The relation between physics and metaphysics, he meant his readers to think, was one of analogy. Physics had become a science by obtaining a firm grasp on its own presuppositions, asking questions that arose from them, and devising experiments by which these should be answered. Metaphysics must follow suit. Metaphysics must obtain a firm grasp on its own presuppositions, ask questions that arise from them, and devise experiments by which these shall be answered. Unless I am mistaken, it was in order to give metaphysicians the full benefit of this analogy and enable them to pick up any hint the procedure of physics might afford, that he indulged himself in the luxury, as it must surely have been, of describing the presuppositions of physics at such length.

Later, when he said that the *Critique* was his metaphysical system, what he meant by this remark was, I suggest, that the relation between the Transcendental Analytics and his own metaphysical system was, after all, not one of analogy but one of identity. It had been said often enough that the business of metaphysics was to state the presuppositions of physics. Kant had only to recollect that the science whose subject-matter he had been in the habit of defining as God, freedom, and immortality was alternatively known as the science which studies the presuppositions of physics; and it would flash upon his mind that he had been writing metaphysics *sans s'en apercevoir*. He had given his metaphysical system to the world under the newfangled name of Transcendental Analytics.

XXIV

METAPHYSICS AS TRANSCENDENTAL ANALYTICS

THERE is one possible objection which ought to be answered before it would appear justifiable to subsume Kant's Transcendental Analytics under the conception of metaphysics as defined in Part I, the conception of metaphysics as an historical science. That definition had to some extent, as appeared from Chapter VII, the character of a programme: it was partly intended to serve as the basis for a reform of metaphysics by extruding from it non-historical elements. But it had this character in a secondary and incidental way. Primarily it was meant for a statement of fact, a statement that metaphysics actually was and always had been an historical science. 'Now', it may be objected, 'this is a statement which, if made about the Transcendental Analytic, is simply not true. We know an historical essay when we see one; and we have only to look at the Transcendental Analytics to see that it is not an historical essay.'

A second look will, I think, convince the reader that it is one; though I do not suggest that its author was aware of this.

What Kant was doing in the Transcendental Analytics was to set forth in detail the absolute presuppositions he was able to detect in his own thinking as a physicist. If we assume, as the evidence entitles us to do, that his own thinking as a physicist proved on the whole acceptable to the other physicists of his time, it will follow that an account of his own absolute presuppositions as a physicist was on the whole an account of the absolute presuppositions made by his scientific colleagues. The statements made in the Transcendental Analytics are not personal statements about Kant himself, they are statements about how a certain business (the business of making absolute presuppositions in natural science) was done by everybody in his time. Everybody, that is to say, within the circle of Europeans, and civilized and educated Europeans at that.

'But surely they are not on that account historical statements, except in an accidental way. Essentially they are statements about certain necessary conditions under which alone thinking can be scientifically done. If thinking was scientifically done in Europe between 1600 and 1800, those conditions were no doubt fulfilled in Europe at that time, and therefore a description of them is in an accidental way a description of something which happened in Europe at that time. If thinking had never been scientifically done except in Europe between 1600 and 1800, a description of these conditions would be in an accidental way a description of something that never happened except in Europe, and even there never except between 1600 and 1800; but essentially it would be not a description of something that happened at a certain time in modern European history; essentially it would be a description of the necessary conditions of scientific thought.'

This objection assumes what it professes to prove. It proceeds on the assumption that no thought is genuinely scientific unless it proceeds according to the principles and methods accepted at a certain place and time; and then argues that a description of the principles and methods accepted at that place and time is not an historical description because it is a description of all thought, no matter where or when, which is genuinely scientific. It ends by asserting that if in actual fact genuinely scientific thought has never been done at any other place or time, that is a mere accident. It is not a mere accident. We are no more entitled to call it a mere accident than some one who began by assuming that all endeavours after civility, decency, justice, or comfort were attempts to realize the standards recognized in his own country would be entitled to call it a mere accident that his own country was the only one in which manners were polite, clothes decent, legal decisions just, or houses comfortable. It would not be an accident; it would be a prejudice coming home to roost.

The truth is that the Transcendental Analytics is an historical study of the absolute presuppositions generally recognized by natural scientists in Kant's own time and as a matter of fact for some time afterwards. I cannot add, 'and for some time before', because there is one of them which I do not know that anybody ever accepted, in the precise form in which he states it, before himself. Some of them go back to Galileo. Some of them are to-day fallen into desuetude. If the unity of the whole constellation is insisted upon, there is nothing for it but to say that it forms a set of absolute presuppositions not actually made as a whole until Kant's own lifetime, which lasted for about a century after he formulated it, but whose proper place to-day is among the interesting occupants of that 'Anchorage for Obsolete Vessels' which may be found marked in the Admiralty Charts of the Isle of Wight.

In the following four chapters I shall try to show how the Transcendental Analytics can be read as a history of the absolute presuppositions of natural science from Galileo to Kant himself. From the point of view of a twentieth-century historian this is not a long period in the history of natural science; but for Kant it would be hardly an exaggeration to say that the history of natural science from Galileo to his own time was equivalent to the history of natural science as a whole; and in that case the inter-pretation of the Transcendental Analytics which I am about to offer would make it in Kant's eyes no mere monograph on one short period in the history of natural science but a comprehensive history of the entire subject. We must not forget the character of the historiographical tradition on which Kant was working. He was brought up in the Prussia of Frederick the Great; and Frederick the Great was the friend, and his more intelligent subjects all more or less the disciples, of Voltaire. The 'illuminism' of which Voltaire was the apostle was not the only determining influence in the formation of Kant's mind, but it was one of them, and as regards history the most important.

The 'illuminists' were keenly interested in historical studies. Their leader Voltaire not only distinguished himself as an historian, he originated a new and important school of historical thought. It was characteristic of this school that it took little interest in the remoter past. One of Voltaire's own declared principles in historiography was that only the recent past was knowable. Hume, the second great 'illuminist' historian, thought it worth while to begin his *History of England* with an account of distant times; but this was so perfunctory and superficial that in effect it proclaimed his agreement with Voltaire. If Voltaire's considered and declared opinion was that French history began to be worth studying, both as regards the extent of its subject-matter and as regards the volume and trustworthiness of its authorities, with Francis I, and if Hume taught his readers more by example than precept that in England serious history began with the Tudors, it is hardly surprising that for Kant the history of natural science should be, as it were, officially deemed to begin with Galileo.

XXV

AXIOMS OF INTUITION

KANT divides Transcendental Analytics into two parts: the Analytics of Concepts and the Analytics of Principles. I am concerned only with the second. Here he offers his reader an account of all the 'principles' which, according to his own experience, are absolutely presupposed in physical science. Before looking at these in detail, I will make two preliminary observations.

First: Kant here professes only to enumerate the absolute presuppositions of natural science, or theoretical thinking in its special application to the world of nature. Practical thinking also has its presuppositions, and the investigation of these he calls the 'metaphysics of morals'. As in Part III A, I shall here confine my attention to what he distinguishes as the 'metaphysics of nature'.

Secondly: Kant makes a point of insisting that the various presuppositions enumerated in such an inquiry as this must not be discovered by haphazard search, but must be systematically 'deduced' from a principle, so that we can be sure, when we have enumerated them all, that our task is done. I shall not here consider the justice of this view, because I have already said in Chapter VII that I think it an illusion, and stated the grounds on which I think so. Here I will only say that there were two things which, acting together, made it possible for Kant to be deceived in this particular way.

1. He was predisposed to this particular illusion by the influence of that very habit which, on occasion, he so strongly and justly condemned: the habit of using in metaphysics methods modelled on those of mathematics. This was the habit of the metaphysical school in which as a young man Kant had enjoyed what he was to call his 'dogmatic slumber'. His revolt against it, as is often the case with such revolts, was not complete.

2. He would have been saved from this illusion, despite a predisposition towards it, if he had known more history. So acute and conscientious a thinker could not possibly have thought that the absolute presuppositions of eighteenth-century physics were the only ones which human understanding could make had he given to medieval physics and ancient Greek physics the same attention he gave to Galileo or Newton. I have said something on this matter at the end of Chapter XVII. The short historical perspective which Kant inherited from Voltaire was at this point his undoing, and made it possible for him to write what was in reality neither more nor less than a history of the absolute presuppositions of physics from Galileo's time to his own, without being aware that this was what he was doing, and in the mistaken belief that he was writing an account of the absolute presuppositions of any possible physics.

He groups his subject-matter under four heads, of which this chapter deals with the first.

'Axioms of Intuition' are absolute presuppositions of science (or, with the metaphysical rubric, propositions of metaphysics) depending on the principle that mathematics can be applied to the world of nature; in other words, that natural science is essentially an applied mathematics. It is, strictly speaking, this principle alone that is an absolute presupposition, and therefore it is the proposition that this principle is absolutely presupposed which alone is a metaphysical proposition. The 'Axioms', in so far as they are not mere ways of restating this principle but presuppositions dependent upon it, are only relative presuppositions. But so long as the reader is clear about this point, there is no need to insist upon it, and I shall not insist upon it henceforth.

Historically considered, this takes us back to Galileo's famous pronouncement that the book of nature is a book written by the hand of God in the language of mathematics. When Galileo said this, he was neither repeating a platitude nor giving vent to a pious or sham-pious sentiment. He was making a fighting speech. Medieval science of nature, following the lead of Aristotle, had seen in the natural world a world of quality, and had dealt with this world in the only possible way, by constituting itself a science of quality. But Aristotle's view of the natural world was very far from being the unanimous view of Greek scientists. It was not even a majority report. That name must be reserved for the Pythagorean view, of which Plato and the Atomists were adherents, to the effect that all science is mathematical. The God of Plato 'always geometrizes'. The natural science of the Renaissance represents a Pythagorean-Platonist reaction against the Aristotelianism of the Middle Ages; and Galileo's pronouncement was a deliberate echo of Plato's and a declaration of war on the Aristotelians.

This revival of Platonic science in a world that had gone Aristotelian is an event of extreme interest to the historian, and one which is very little understood. It is the inner or theoretical side of that event which on its outer or practical side we call the end of the Middle Ages, or the Renaissance. I cannot avoid making a few observations on it here; but they shall be very brief, in order to avoid hopelessly breaking the thread of what I have to say about Kant's metaphysics.

1. There is something paradoxical about the whole thing. It seems obvious that nature is a mass of qualities—hot and cold, wet and dry, colours, sounds, smells, tendencies and appetites—and that a natural scientist who turns his back on quality and devotes himself to the study of quantity is turning his back on nature itself and plunging into a shadow-world of abstractions. Aristotelian natural science seems to have on its side all the facts of the world and all the common sense of mankind. On the other side there seems to be nothing except a perverse fanaticism which delights in saying what is obviously untrue. No one can really believe that God is a mathematician.

2. And in fact the victory of Platonism was never complete. Throughout the seventeenth century, a large proportion of the ablest scientists, especially biologists and 'naturalists', were Aristotelians. And

the biological sciences, in spite of the materialism which invaded them in the eighteenth century, remained a more or less permanent stronghold of the Aristotelian spirit.

3. Like other incomplete victories, it had to reinforce itself with a campaign of calumny. Eighteenth-century 'illuminism' knew little about Aristotle and less about the Middle Ages, and was proud of its ignorance; but it repaired this deficiency by enrolling 'Aristotle's friends' among the worshippers of the goddess Dullness, and converting the name of one of the greatest medieval thinkers into the title of Dunce. And the campaign of calumny is still going on. It is still taught to-day that the true justification of Renaissance Platonism rests on the appeal to its success in replacing by genuinely scientific investigation of nature what had been no science at all, but merely a futile groping in the intellectual darkness of the Middle Ages.

4. For the historian of thought, it is an interesting question how the Platonic revival in natural science was possible. It was possible only because the revived Platonism was Platonism with a difference. Genuine Platonism holds out no hope of a scientific applied mathematics. It teaches that nothing in nature admits, strictly speaking, of mathematical description; for in nature there are no straight lines, no true curves, no equalities, but only approximations to these things, approximations which no refinement in mathematical methods could ever reduce to a mathematical formula. Genuine Platonism does not believe

in a science of nature at all. It believes that nature is the realm of imprecision, no possible object for scientific knowledge. The mathematician cannot portray nature as it is, he can only portray nature as it would be if it had that precision which, as nature, it essentially lacks. What he does portray, therefore, is not the world of nature, it is the world of pure mathematics.

5. Genuine Platonism, therefore, could offer no science of nature. Even the *Timaeus* does not profess to give a science of nature; it only professes to say something about nature which shall in some way approximate to the facts. Aristotle, therefore, in constructing a qualitative science of nature, was not controverting Platonism; by an admirable effort of creative genius he was filling up a space in the map of knowledge that Platonism had left blank.

6. Christianity, by maintaining that God is omnipotent and that the world of nature is a world of God's creating, completely altered this situation. It became a matter of faith that the world of nature should be regarded no longer as the realm of imprecision, but as the realm of precision. To say that a line in nature is not quite straight means for a Platonist that it is an approximation to a straight line, the result of a praiseworthy but not altogether successful attempt on the part of some natural thing to construct a straight line or to travel in one. For a Christian it cannot mean that. The line was drawn or constructed by God; and if God had wanted it to be straight it would have been straight. To say that

it is not exactly straight, therefore, means that it is exactly something else. The natural scientist must find out what it exactly is.

7. Thus the possibility of an applied mathematics is an expression, in terms of natural science, of the Christian belief that nature is the creation of an omnipotent God. This belief is what replaced the Greek conception of nature as the realm of imprecision by the Renaissance conception of nature as the realm of precision. The Platonism of Renaissance natural science is not fundamentally Platonic, it is fundamentally Christian. Christian thought is adapting Platonism to its own ends, or begetting upon Platonism an idea which Platonism proper could never have originated or even tolerated.

The principle that natural science is essentially an applied mathematics is thus by no means an indispensable presupposition for any science of nature. A presupposition it certainly is, and an absolute presupposition. It could not possibly be learnt from experience or justified by research. The only sense in which it can be justified by research is the pragmatic sense. You can say, and rightly, 'See what noble results have come from its being accepted for the last three hundred years! One must surely admit that it works; and that is sufficient justification.' Perhaps. It depends on what you want. If all you want is to congratulate yourself on having the kind of science that you have, you may do so. If you want to congratulate yourself on having the best of all possible kinds of science, that is not so easy; for nobody knows what all the possible kinds would be like.

Galileo's principle still holds to-day. Scientists still presuppose in all their work that the more closely a science of nature approximates to the condition of consisting in its entirety of applied mathematics, the more closely it approximates to the ideal of what a natural science ought to be. In pure physics, including astronomy, the principle seems to have triumphed to-day as never before. Yet there is at least one symptom of revolt against it in the heart of its main stronghold. Physicists have begun within recent years to say that the laws of nature are 'statistical' laws, laws (that is to say) not obeyed by each and every physical body, but obeyed only by that *ens rationis*, the average of a number of such bodies. If this idea has come to stay, Galileo's principle is doomed. In any case, it is subject to strain.

In the biological sciences, the present tendency is towards emphasizing applied mathematics, as in biochemistry, and also in genetics, where the Platonism of Mendel has succeeded the Aristotelianism of Darwin. The biological controversy between 'mechanists' and 'vitalists' is in effect a struggle between Platonists and Aristotelians, friends of applied mathematics and friends of quality, for the last citadel of Aristotelian natural science. To the mere spectator, there seems to be evidence that the 'mechanists' are winning.

But a biological 'mechanist', like any other scientist in the tradition of Galileo, is working on presuppositions that no experience can confirm and no experiment verify. When he says that the book of nature is written in the language of mathematics, he does not mean only that the pages of this book which have been read in the past have been found to be written in this language, nor even only that this is true of the pages that have been read in the past and also, probably, of those which he is just about to read. He means that the book of nature is quite certainly written in that language from end to end. And no one thinks that this will ever be 'verified'. It is an absolute presupposition, in other words a matter of 'faith'. Galileo is deliberately applying to 'nature' the principle which Augustine laid down with regard to the Holy Scriptures, the book *par excellence* 'written by the hand of God': that whatever doubts may arise about the meaning of this or that passage, it has a meaning, and the meaning is true (*Conf.* xii. 23–4).

Here, accordingly, a 'logical positivist' who was in earnest with his principles would lift up his voice. 'You are affirming a proposition', he would say, 'which applies to an indefinite number of instances, described as observable, which nevertheless have not all been observed and in fact never will be all observed. Tell me that mathematics has been applied by this or that person to this or that thing in the world of nature, for example to colours by Newton, or to heredity by Mendel, and I know what you mean and can admit that what you say is either true or false. But tell me that mathematics is applicable to everything in nature, and I cannot either agree or disagree: the proposition you are affirming is one which can never be verified, and therefore I maintain that it has no meaning.'

I do not know why the logical positivists have not thus pilloried as nonsensical the principle that mathematics is applicable to everything in nature; unless it is that they know this principle to be one upon which natural science ever since Galileo has depended, and still depends, for its very possibility. Being the declared friends of natural science, they would never dream of making a fuss about anything which natural scientists find it necessary to take for granted. So they let it pass, and to ease their consciences drop heavily upon the proposition 'God exists', because they think nobody believes in God except poor miserable parsons, whose luggage enjoys no such diplomatic immunity. If they knew a little more about the history of science, they would know that the belief in the possibility of applied mathematics is only one part of the belief in God.

XXVI

ANTICIPATIONS OF PERCEPTION

THIS is Kant's name for those propositions about things in the world of nature which depend on the principle of continuity, the principle that between any two terms in a series, however close together they are, there is always a third term. If at a time t_1 a body is moving with a velocity v_1 and at a later time t_2 with a higher velocity v_2 there must according to the principle of continuity have been times between t_1 and t_2 at which it was moving respectively with every intermediate velocity between v_1 and v_2. This will happen irrespectively of whether its acceleration has been uniform or not. If its acceleration has been uniform from t_1 to t_2 then at the time midway between t_1 and t_2 its velocity will have been midway between v_1 and v_2; and so on. If the acceleration was not uniform there will of course be no such constant relation between lapse of time and increase of velocity; but there will still be some time somewhere between t_1 and t_2 at which any velocity you like to name between v_1 and v_2 will be reached. If the acceleration was interrupted by a period or periods of deceleration, some of these intermediate velocities will have been reached more than once; but whatever happens every one of them must have been reached once at least.

With this principle Kant has moved a step forward in the history of science. He has moved from Galileo and the general principle that a science of nature must be an applied mathematics, to Leibniz and Newton and the special principle that a science of nature must consist of differential equations.

Once more, 'logical positivists' ought to object. If they stuck to their guns they would say at this point: 'I refuse to admit that in the case considered above there must, whether it is observed or not, be a time at which the body was moving with a velocity midway between v_1 and v_2. I see no reason which could entitle anybody to say that there was such a time, except the testimony of some one who said that he had observed it; in other words, that there had been a time at which he had measured the velocity and discovered it to be just midway between v_1 and v_2.'

The historical interest of this protest, if it were made at the present time, would arise from the fact that what the 'logical positivist' would here be saying is a commonplace of the quantum theory. For the quantum theory is in principle a mechanical theory based on denying the applicability of the differential calculus *à outrance* to the world of nature. But for a 'logical positivist' to argue like this might be dangerous. His professions of loyalty to natural science would be rendered liable to interruption by a voice from the audience: 'Under which king, Bezonian? Harry the fourth, or fifth?' It is difficult to keep up the pretence of thinking natural science the only valid form of knowledge if somebody points out that there is natural science and natural science, and that if quantum theory is true classical physics is false and all the sciences which share the method and presuppositions of classical physics false too.

Further reflection will show that 'logical positivism' is incompatible with loyalty to either king. The principle of continuity, asserting as it does that all change in the world of nature is continuous, is unverifiable and therefore to a 'logical positivist' unmeaning. It follows that he cannot tolerate the classical physics; but it does not follow that he can patronize the quantum theory. The principle of continuity is, or rather ought to be, objectionable to him not because it is false but because it is unmeaning. If it had been false, its contradictory would have been true and the quantum theory, as based on this contradictory, would have been acceptable. But as it is unmeaning, its contradictory is just as unmeaning as itself. Quantum theory is just as nonsensical as classical physics. For, in Kantian language, quantum theory commits us just as definitely as classical physics to anticipating perception; the only difference is that it anticipates perception on a different principle. In the language of 'logical positivism', both classical physics and quantum theory are 'metaphysical'. Each of them pins its faith to an unverifiable principle. Since 'logical positivism' does not distinguish between good metaphysics and bad metaphysics, but regards all metaphysics as equally nonsensical, quantum theory would be in the eyes of a consistent 'logical positivist' just as nonsensical as classical physics, and no more.[1]

---

[1] Mr. O. T. Gnosspelius has called my attention to a practical

problem which brings into relief the question whether the physics of to-day can be content with the conception of continuity from which calculations can be made by the methods of the differential calculus. He tells me that the design of aeroplanes is still entirely without a scientific basis. We have arrived by trial and error at designs which give a certain degree of efficiency, but a very low one; beyond this very low standard we seem unable to go; and of the most notorious facts with regard to the flight of birds we can give no theoretical account at all. He suggests that advance in these respects is conditional on the establishment of a satisfactory theory of the flow of air, and that our inability to frame such a theory at present may be due to the fact that we only formulate theories about such things assuming the continuity of the medium and then apply the reasoning of the differential calculus. According to our own orthodox view as to the structure of gases, air is not continuous in its structure. With what justice, then, do we assume that it is continuous in its motion?

XXVII

ANALOGIES OF EXPERIENCE

KANT'S third set of principles are based on the idea of necessary connexion: not necessary connexions between 'ideas', to quote Hume's distinction, such as are found in the realms of logic and mathematics, but necessary connexions between 'matters of fact', necessary connexions between perceptible things such as go to make up the world of nature. Of these necessary connexions between perceptible things Kant distinguishes three species.

(*a*) Where two perceptible things are considered by a person thinking about them to be two possible appearances of the same thing. Here the presupposition which makes him think about them in this way is stated by saying that he believes in the permanence or indestructibility of substance. If you hit a golf-ball into the rough, and cannot find it, and encourage yourself to go on searching for it by saying 'It must be somewhere hereabouts', you are asserting a necessary ('must', you said) connexion between your past perception when you saw it flying in this direction and a possible perception of seeing it somewhere hereabouts in the future. When after some more unrewarded searching you say 'It can't have vanished into thin air', what you are saying is (i) that this is just the sort of occasion on which you realize that you must hold firmly to the principle of the indestructibility of substance; for you are saying in effect that even if it had turned into 'thin air' that 'thin air' would still be your golf-ball transformed into a new shape, as happens when water evaporates or when oil is burnt; (ii) that so far as analogies from experience afford any guide you do not think that in this case any such transformation can have happened; so that since, as aforesaid, the ball must still exist in some shape or other analogies from experience lead you to think that its shape will still be the same as when you last saw it, and therefore you continue to look for a recognizable golf-ball.

Kant is making two points. First, that the 'indestructibility of substance' is a principle taken for granted by all scientists, and 'scientists' here includes not only professional scientists working at carefully formulated problems under carefully regulated conditions, but ordinary people as well, grappling with golf-balls and collar-studs under the haphazard conditions of daily life. Secondly, that this principle is thus taken for granted not because it has been established once for all by scientific research, for it never has been; nor because we think that it could be so established if it were worth our while, for it never could be; nor because it has already been established, before specialized scientific work begins, in the experience of daily life, for that again has not happened and could not happen; it is taken for granted as one of the absolute presuppositions without which we should not have our science of nature, and indeed not even that 'daily life' of searching for golf-balls and collar-studs of which our science of nature is a development and extension.

If metaphysics is understood as an historical science, Kant is absolutely right on both points. The 'indestructibility of substance' was in fact unanimously taken for granted in his own time both by ordinary people in their ordinary life and by scientists in their theories and experiments. He was right, too, in maintaining that it had not in fact been derived from the experience of ordinary life, and that it had not been based and never could be based on the results of scientific experiments, but was an absolute presupposition which underlay both everyday life and science.

The heritage of positivism is strong in us to-day, and throws all its weight into preventing us from grasping this second point. When we are off our guard, we find ourselves involuntarily thinking 'Surely Kant was wrong about that. Surely the principle which used to be called the "conservation of matter", not to mention its nineteenth-century assistant and successor the "conservation of energy", must be either one which human beings have learnt in the course of their daily life, as they learn that fire hurts them or that bread nourishes them; and, having learnt it, hand down the lesson from one generation to another; or else one which every one of us learns independently for himself so early in childhood that in later life he cannot remember ever not having known it; or else one which scientists have established, as they do establish things, by hypothesis and experiment.' And it costs us some labour to exorcize this ghost, first by considering each alternative in turn and satisfying ourselves that, on the question of fact, none of them is well founded; and secondly by considering them all together from the point of view of logic, and satisfying ourselves that any supposed experience or experiment from which our conviction might be thought to derive could never have either originated or confirmed it unless the same conviction had been firmly seated in our minds from the start in the shape of an absolute presupposition.

All the same, it is not a presupposition innate in the human mind. It belongs to the mental furniture of a certain age; and not a very long age. In the eighteenth century, when historical memory was short, the beginning of that age was no less completely forgotten than its end was unexpected. But it did in fact begin with the Renaissance, in that curious mixture of theology and physics which most people to-day hardly know to have existed except in Spinoza's formula *Natura sive Deus* which summed it all up at a much later date; for Spinoza, like Leibniz, was a scholar as well as a philosopher, and linked his philosophy up consciously and deliberately with philosophies of the past. Physicists of the Renaissance, deifying the material universe, translated the unity and eternity and changelessness of God into the attributes of a single cosmic 'substance', enduring through time without possibility of diminution or increment, and in every part of itself preserving its identity through what to our senses appeared to be change, but was in fact (since our senses cannot give knowledge about the world) no change at all. The 'religion of nature', so to call it, which Renaissance thinkers formulated in this theological physics lies deep among the foundations of the so-called 'classical' physics, and is the source from which many of its characteristic presuppositions, like this one about conservation, are derived.

What has a beginning has an ending; and a person who has realized that this idea about the 'conservation of substance' dates back only to the Renaissance will hardly expect it to remain a principle of human thought for ever. I should hesitate to say from my own slender first-hand knowledge of modern physics that the life of this conviction as a principle of natural science has already reached its term; but I have less hesitation about saying the same thing on the authority of Professor A. N. Whitehead, than whom I suppose there is nobody now alive more trustworthy as a liaison officer between the physicists and the philosophers.

According to Whitehead, the difference between the so-called classical physics and the physics of to-day is chiefly this: that the 'classical physics' rests on the presupposition of an absolute distinction between what things are and what they do or what happens to them, whereas in modern physics it is presupposed that this distinction is as meaningless there as the corresponding distinctions are universally admitted to be in the sciences of life and of mind.

According to the 'classical' physicist, there is the world of nature, consisting of bodies, and there is what happens in the world of nature, consisting of events in which bodies play their parts. Whatever may be the events in which a body is concerned, it always remains the same body. Suppose that for a moment no event at all were happening in which a given body were concerned, it would still be the same body. Or put it this way: every event takes time; and consequently within a given instant, where an instant means not a short space of time, as it does in photography, but a mathematical instant which includes no time at all, nothing is happening. At that instant, according to the classical physics, there are no events, but there are still bodies; and as 'nature' is the total assembly of bodies, there is 'nature', all present and complete.

According to modern physics, Whitehead explains, there is no distinction between the events that happen and the bodies to which they happen. Being and doing, where doing includes undergoing, are not distinguishable. The modern physicist cannot say: 'If this event were not happening to this body, this body would not of course be doing what it now is doing, but it would still be what it now is.' Or put it this way: at a given instant, where there are no events, there are no bodies. There is no nature at an instant. Nature is not body as distinct from event; it is body, no doubt, but body itself is only a complex of events; and since events take time, it takes time for nature to exist.[1]

[1] The most concise statement of this point is given in *Nature and Life* (1934), pp. 44–8.

The principle of Kant's First Analogy is here flatly contradicted. And it is contradicted on unexceptionable metaphysical grounds. It is contradicted on a point of historical fact by a man who knows how modern physicists do their thinking and tells us that they do not there presuppose the conservation of substance but its opposite.

(b) The second type of necessary connexion is between two perceptible things which are regarded as possible appearances of two different things one following the other in time. In so far as this is thought to be not merely a sequence but a necessary sequence, that thought is expressed by saying that the second thing not merely follows the first but follows it necessarily, or must follow it. The necessity of the connexion is what people express according to Kant by calling the first the cause of the second. Whenever you assert one thing to be the cause of another, as when you say 'This headache must be due to yesterday's tropical sunshine on my bare head', you are doing two different things.

(i) You are presupposing what no experience could teach and what no experiment could prove, that this headache has a cause; and not only that this headache has a cause but that all headaches have causes; and not only that all headaches have causes but that all events have causes, where 'all events' means not only the events which have been perceived and whose causes have been identified, but every event which in any possible circumstances might be perceived, and where 'having a cause' means being connected by way of necessary succession with some previous perceptible event.

(ii) You are asserting, further, that so far as analogies from experience enable you to decide what the previous event was with which this headache is necessarily connected, that event was the impact of yesterday's sunshine on your unprotected head.

For the present, I take Kant's word that this is an accurate account of what causation meant to him in his own practice as a physicist. I will make no further comment. There is too much that I want to say about the subject of causation for me to say it in part of a single chapter. I shall therefore make it the subject of a third *specimen philosophandi*, to which I shall proceed when I have finished with Kant.[1]

(*c*) Kant's third type of necessary connexion is between two perceptible things which are regarded as possible appearances of two different things existing simultaneously. In so far as this simultaneity is thought to be not merely a simultaneity but a necessary simultaneity, that thought is expressed by saying that each is necessary to the simultaneous existence of the other, or that what each is doing is a necessary

---

[1] I anticipate here only so far as to say that, precisely as Whitehead has denied the principle of the First Analogy on what I have called unexceptionable metaphysical grounds, viz., that modern physicists do not make that presupposition, so his brilliant colleague Russell has on precisely the same grounds denied the principle of the Second Analogy: 'In advanced sciences such as gravitational astronomy the word "cause" never occurs' ('On the Notion of Cause', *Mysticism and Logic* (1918), p. 180; quoted above, p. 69).

condition of what the other is doing. The necessity of this simultaneous coexistence is called by Kant 'mutual action', which is generally rendered in English translations as 'reciprocity'.

There is, of course, a sound historical reason why reciprocity should play so prominent a part in Kant's list of the absolute presuppositions of natural science. That reason is Newton's theory of gravitation. It was Newton who had made 'reciprocity' a cardinal principle in physics. The key with which Newton unlocked the ancient problem of celestial motions was the hypothesis that every body attracts every other body with a force varying directly as the product of their masses and inversely as the square of their distance. When Newton said this he was (i) presupposing that there is such a thing as necessary coexistence, or reciprocal action; which after all was not a new doctrine, for it had long been agreed that every body keeps every other body out of the space which it is said, for that reason, to 'occupy', and this 'impenetrability' is one kind of reciprocal action; (ii) further asserting that, so far as analogies from experience, in point of fact the analogy of the magnet, helped him to decide what sorts of reciprocal action there were or might be in nature, the assumption which would explain the astronomical facts about which he was thinking, as reported by the astronomers, was that one thing which every body does to every other is to attract it in the above way.

For us this part of Kant's metaphysics has only what is sometimes called an 'historical interest'; by which is meant an interest for persons who like to know about things that once existed but exist no longer. For Kant, the Newtonian conception of force was still an integral part of a physicist's equipment. For us, that conception is obsolete. It is not only that Newton's formula about varying inversely as the square of the distance is nowadays known to hold good, like Boyle's law, not universally but only within certain limits. It is worse than that. The whole conception of force, *vis* (a conception of very recent origin; for the term was introduced into the vocabulary of physics, and expounded as the name of a new idea, only by Kepler), has been abolished.

Thus, Sir Arthur Eddington in his Gifford Lectures[1] reminded his hearers of a curious passage in which Hegel protested against the Newtonian doctrine that the heavenly bodies are kept in their orbits by the operation of 'forces', that is to say, by being pushed and pulled about like stupid children at drill; the truth is, says Hegel, that the supposed forces which control them are altogether imaginary, and that the heavenly bodies are under no constraint

---

[1] *The Nature of the Physical World* (1928, p. 147). The discovery by a very distinguished scientist that there are grains of sense in Hegel's *Naturphilosophie*, and that he feels himself obliged to apologize for having made the discovery, is a sign of the times. How far was the habitual and monotonous execration of Hegel by nineteenth-century natural scientists due to the fact that he violently disliked the physics of his own day, and demanded the substitution for it of a physics which, it turns out, was to be in effect the physics that we have now? Sir Arthur's remark gives ground for hoping that some day, perhaps, somebody will try to answer this question.

whatever, but move with a freedom like that ascribed
by the ancients to 'the blessed gods'. Eddington
remarks that this might seem 'particularly foolish
even for a philosopher'; but that as a matter of fact
it is precisely the idea which a modern physicist is
trying to express when, for the conception of forces
compelling bodies to take one path when if they
moved freely they would have taken another, he substitutes the conception of a space in which there are certain ratios between the lengths of measuring-rods and
the 'radius of curvature of the world' (op. cit., p. 149),
so that 'the earth can play truant to any extent, but
our measurements will still report it in the place
assigned to it by the Nautical Almanac' (p. 150).
The Third Analogy has gone the way of the First
and Second.

Note on p. 270.—Newton distinguishes (*a*) certain movements
of heavenly bodies; (*b*) the *vis gravitatis* which causes these movements; (*c*) the reason why gravity works as it does (*ratio harum
gravitationis proprietatum*). He claims both (*a*) and (*b*) as facts;
but disclaims all opinion about (*c*) because, as he says, 'I have
hitherto not been able to deduce it from the phenomena, and I
do not make hypotheses' (*Scholium Generale; Principia* ad fin.).
This, he is careful to explain, is a strict rule *in hac philosophia*,
i.e. in physics. But he has drawn the line between fact and
hypothesis in the wrong place. He thinks that (*b*) is logically
implied in (*a*) ('deduced from the phenomena'). It is not. It is
an hypothesis devised to explain the phenomena. The disclaimer
of hypotheses is, of course, positivism. Newton, like all positivists,
mistakes his own hypotheses for statements of fact.

XXVIII

POSTULATES OF EMPIRICAL THOUGHT

KANT'S fourth and last set of principles are to the effect that the 'categories of modality', namely the notions of possibility, actuality, and necessity,[1] are applicable to the perceptible or natural world.

He does not mean that among the things in the world of nature there are some which are possible, others which are actual, and others again which are necessary. The Kantian categories are not pigeon-holes into which the items of the perceptible world are sorted out. When we are said to 'apply' these categories to the perceptible world it is not meant that we stand before a given fact in nature with a bundle of categories in our hands, as if they were labels, and wonder which we had better 'apply'. To think scientifically about any such fact, according to Kant, is to 'apply' to it all the categories.

Kant therefore did not think as Leibniz did that the 'actual world' is one among a number of 'possible worlds'. He thought any such notion nonsensical, because the categories were for him simply ways of thinking about the perceptible world, and a Leibnitian 'possible world' that is not also 'actual' is certainly not perceptible. Nor is it, properly speaking, possible.

---

[1] In this chapter I shall deal only with the distinction between possibility and actuality, and especially with the 'principle of possibility'. I have said in the preceding chapter all that I think need here be said about necessity.

If it were possible, why does it not exist? Presumably because there is a sufficient reason against its existing. But if there is a sufficient reason against a thing's existing, that thing is not possible, it is impossible. Whatever is really possible is actual. Whatever is actual is necessary. In the world of nature the actual, the possible, and the necessary are one and the same.

It is only in the activity of scientific research that they are distinct. The distinction is a methodological distinction, a distinction between three stages in that research. When a scientist describes something as actual he means that it has been observed. When he describes it as necessary he means that its connexions with other things have been discovered. When he describes it as possible he means that it is being looked for; that is, that the question whether it is actual is a question that is being asked. This means, I need hardly say, not that the question is being verbally asked but that it is being logically asked, asked because it arises inevitably at the stage which has now been reached in the development of a certain process of scientific thought. If the reader will remind himself of the 'Note' to prop. 1, Chapter V, he will see that this definition of possibility does not involve the consequence that to call a thing actual is to deny by implication that it is possible. For the question does not cease to be asked when the answer is forthcoming. It is still a question; but now it is an answered question.

Thus, to take an example from the kind of science about which Kant was always chiefly thinking, though it is an example which occured after his death: when Adams and Leverrier in the 1840's searched for a planet whose orbit lay outside that of Uranus, the fact that they were doing so might have been expressed by their saying 'It is possible that such a planet exists'. If they had used those words they would have meant by them not simply that they were searching this or that part of the heavens with their telescopes, but that they had reasons for doing so; reasons which in fact arose out of observed irregularities in the orbit of Uranus.

The fact expressed by a statement in the 'problematic' form, such as 'There may be a planet outside Uranus', is therefore the fact of scientific research, the asking of a question together with the comment that this is not a random or unscientific question but a question which 'arises', a question which for logical reasons has to be asked. As a 'postulate of empirical thought', therefore, the principle of possibility, that there are possible objects of perception which as yet have not been perceived, is an absolute presupposition of all science in so far as science implies the organized and systematic asking of questions. If the doctrine that this is what science implies is called the Baconian doctrine, with reference to the Baconian phrase about the scientist 'putting nature to the question', the historical aspect of what Kant is here saying might be brought out if we said that he is here affirming the fundamental metaphysical truth about Baconian science, that is, about all modern science from Bacon's time onwards.

It might be said that when Bacon insisted on the scientist's questioning activity he was doing no more than merely emphasizing one of the things that scientist's had always done, even if philosophers had hitherto failed to notice it. But this would be, if not exactly untrue, at least misleading. Different kinds of scientific thought are possible according as the centre of gravity in a particular piece of research lies in observing or in questioning.[1] It is possible for an inquirer to approach his subject in either of two frames of mind. He may approach it with what is called an open mind, anxious merely to find out what he can, and not begin 'theorizing' until sheer familiarity with the facts has begun to breed 'theories' in his head. Or he may approach it with a definite 'theory' already formed, anxious not just to find out whatever he can, but to settle whether his 'theory' is right or wrong.

These are different scientific attitudes, and they lead to the creation of different types of science. The second is a more sophisticated or mature attitude than the first; it could never come into existence except after long experience of the first, whether personal or vicarious; when it does come into existence it very quickly raises science to a level of efficiency which previously would have seemed quite

[1] I say this with the more confidence because it is matter of personal experience to me that in historical and archaeological research, in which I claim some degree of expertness, the difference between the two attitudes is sufficiently clear to divide researchers into two camps. There has been a kind of war between these two camps, in which I have taken part.

impossible. Bacon was not talking about something scientists had always done. He was talking about something they had only recently begun to do; something that future historians would pitch upon as the characteristic feature distinguishing the methods of 'modern science' from those of the medieval and ancient science out of which it had grown.

Essential though it is to all science from Bacon's time to the present day, for it is not one of those features in respect of which I have described Kant's metaphysics as obsolete, the principle of possibility must obviously prove a stumbling-block to any form of positivism. I have already suggested that what is wrong with positivism is not the importance it attaches to natural science, but its errors as to what natural science is like. Among these errors I have called attention to its medieval conception of the way in which facts are known, namely by observation.

According to the positivists, facts are things which present themselves to our senses. According to modern science, from Bacon onwards, facts are things which give us answers to our questions. The difference may seem a merely verbal one. Why should not something that presents itself to our senses give us the answer to a question? But it is not a verbal difference; it is a crucial difference on a matter of fact with regard to the procedure of scientific research. The positivist is describing the typical procedure of pre-Baconian science, the kind of science in which the first stage is to observe facts and the second stage is to ask what, if anything, they prove. The kind of science which Bacon described and all 'modern scientists' have practised is the kind of science in which the first stage is to ask a question and the second stage is to get it answered.

Positivistic logic, because it does not recognize the existence of the questioning activity, cannot recognize the principle of possibility. To a 'logical positivist' it is simply an outrage to say 'there may be things that have never been perceived'. It is 'metaphysics', for it is not either a statement of observed fact nor analysable into such statements. It is unmeaning, because it cannot be verified. As soon as anything has been perceived for the first time, it is no longer unperceived, so the discovery that it exists goes no way towards proving that anything either exists or can exist unperceived.

Logicians of this kind, once they are convinced that the principle of possibility is indispensable to modern science, might condescend to play 'heads I win' with it, by attempting to 'analyse' it according to their own rules. All such attempts must fail, because the rules are so framed as to make science, at any rate science of a post-medieval type, impossible; but it may be worth our while to think how a few of them might proceed.

1. It might be suggested that the proposition 'there may be a planet outside Uranus' is equivalent to 'I do not know whether there is such a planet or not'. But it cannot be equivalent to this, because it is compatible with the contradictory of this. A thing

does not become impossible by being true. Indeed, cases occur in which our knowledge that something is actual is regarded as an indispensable condition of our knowing it to be possible; for example, all those cases about which it is said that you never know what you can do until you try. This would be nonsense, if to say that a thing is possible were a way of saying that you did not know whether it was actual or not.

2. It might be suggested that affirming the proposition 'there may be a planet outside Uranus' is equivalent to what is called 'entertaining' the proposition 'there is a planet outside Uranus'. But this is no better. To 'entertain a proposition' is defined as simply to apprehend its meaning. In that sense an astronomer may 'entertain the proposition' that the moon is made of green cheese. It would be easy to show that he really does 'entertain' it, by showing that he can do what he could not do unless he apprehended its meaning, viz. draw inferences which would follow from it if it were true; such as, that the lunar mice would have a glorious time, or that the people in the country east of the sun and west of the moon would shut their windows when the wind was in the east. But no astronomer thinks it possible that the moon is made of green cheese. Any historian, again, can 'entertain the proposition' that Napoleon won the battle of Waterloo; but no historian thinks it possible that the received account of the battle is wrong on one point of detail, viz. who won it.

3. It might be suggested that 'there may be a planet outside Uranus' is equivalent to something

like this: 'If you turn your telescope in a certain direction on a certain kind of occasion you will see a luminous disk not shown on the star-maps'. That would be verifiable, and a 'logical positivist' could play 'heads I win' with it quite happily. But the equivalence is illusory. The proposition that can be verified by seeing Neptune is not the proposition that there may be such a planet but the proposition that there is such a planet.

In short, I can think of no way by which statements of possibility can be rendered acceptable to positivists; and I think this is because they belong to an element in science which positivism ignores and by implication denies. It would not be surprising to find that 'logical positivists', on discovering that modern natural science can take not a single step without making statements of that kind, decided to let such statements pass as covered by the diplomatic immunity of the privileged class who make them. But if they did, it would be mere logical snobbery, and its beneficiaries ought to be warned that the benefits they receive from it are held on a precarious tenure.

According to the rigour of the game the votaries of 'logical positivism', beginning with a declaration of the bankruptcy of metaphysics, should go on to announce the bankruptcy of science. At present, this step is only not taken because the 'logical positivists' entertain a superstitious reverence for a vaguely defined body of men supposed to practise an altogether misunderstood thing called natural science. This situation would cease to exist in a moment if the desire of 'logical positivists' to think logically could ever become strong enough to overpower their superstitions. It is a curious situation, and not without interest as illustrating the way in which modern irrationalism, wishing to destroy the spirit of scientific inquiry, but wishing at the same time to go on enjoying the technical benefits conferred by modern natural science, converts the desire for these benefits into a motive for refusing to draw the logical conclusion from its own premises.

Intelligible when thus regarded as a symptom of the irrationalist epidemic, the situation becomes highly paradoxical when regarded as an event in the history of logic. From this point of view, one must say that a slight increase in the clarity of their own thought would convert the 'logical positivists' into enemies not only of metaphysics but of the natural science they now claim to befriend: in short, of clear thinking as such, whether in themselves or in others; and bring them out as declared partisans of superstition against science. At present, if they profess themselves enemies of superstition and friends of clear thinking, they do so only because in their own minds the inclination towards superstition is stronger than the inclination towards clear thinking.

But this paradox need not disconcert us. We are not dealing with an event in the history of logic. We are dealing with the ravages of a disease that is attacking the European intellect. If the thoughts of a diseased intellect prove to be paradoxes, there is nothing paradoxical in that.

C
CAUSATION

XXIX

THREE SENSES OF THE WORD 'CAUSE'

CONFORMABLY to the historical nature of meta-physics, any discussion of a metaphysical difficulty must be historically conducted. One major difficulty, or group of difficulties, now exercising students of metaphysics is connected with the idea of causation. I do not hope in the present part of my essay to offer a complete solution for this difficulty or group of difficulties; all I propose to do is to show what I mean by saying that it ought to be discussed historically.

I shall confine myself to making two main points.

1. That the term 'cause', as actually used in modern English and other languages, is ambiguous. It has three senses; possibly more; but at any rate three.

Sense I. Here that which is 'caused' is the free and deliberate act of a conscious and responsible agent, and 'causing' him to do it means affording him a motive for doing it.

Sense II. Here that which is 'caused' is an event in nature, and its 'cause' is an event or state of things by producing or preventing which we can produce or prevent that whose cause it is said to be.

Sense III. Here that which is 'caused' is an event or state of things, and its 'cause' is another event or state of things standing to it in a one-one relation of causal priority: i.e. a relation of such a kind that (*a*) if the cause happens or exists the effect also must happen or exist, even if no further conditions are fulfilled, (*b*) the effect cannot happen or exist unless the cause happens or exists, (*c*) in some sense which remains to be defined, the cause is prior to the effect; for without such priority there would be no telling which is which. If C and E were connected merely by a one-one relation such as is described in the sentences (*a*) and (*b*) above, there would be no reason why C should be called the cause of E, and E the effect of C, rather than vice versa. But whether causal priority is temporal priority, or a special case of temporal priority, or priority of some other kind, is another question.

Sense I may be called the *historical* sense of the word 'cause', because it refers to a type of case in which both C and E are human activities such as form the subject-matter of history. When historians talk about causes, this is the sense in which they are using the word, unless they are aping the methods and vocabulary of natural science.

Sense II refers to a type of case in which natural events are considered from a human point of view, as events grouped in pairs where one member in each pair, C, is immediately under human control, whereas the other, E, is not immediately under human control but can be indirectly controlled by man because of the relation in which it stands to C. This is the sense which the word 'cause' has in the *practical sciences of nature*, i.e. the sciences of nature whose primary aim is not to achieve theoretical knowledge about nature but to enable man to enlarge his control of nature. This is the sense in which the word 'cause' is used, for example, in engineering or medicine.

Sense III refers to a type of case in which an attempt is made to consider natural events not practically, as things to be produced or prevented by human agency, but theoretically, as things that happen independently of human will but not independently of each other: causation being the name by which this dependence is designated. This is the sense which the word has traditionally borne in physics and chemistry and, in general, the *theoretical sciences of nature*.

The difficulties to which I referred at the beginning of this chapter are all connected with sense III. The other two senses are relatively straightforward and easy to understand. They give rise to no perplexities. The only perplexities that ever occur in connexion with them are such as arise from a confusion of sense I with sense II, or from a confusion of either with sense III. But sense III, as I shall show, raises difficult problems quite by itself, and apart from any confusion with other senses. These problems are due to internal conflict. The various elements which go to make up the definition of sense III are mutually incompatible. This incompatibility, at the lowest estimate, constitutes what I called in Chapter VII a 'strain' in the current modern idea of causation, and therefore in the whole structure of modern natural science in so far as modern natural science is based on that idea.

I have called I, II, and III different 'senses' of the

word 'cause'. A technical objection might be lodged against this expression on any of three grounds, if no more.

(*a*) 'What you have distinguished are not three senses of the word "cause", but three types of case to any one of which that word is appropriate, the sense in which it is used being constant.' But, as I shall try to show, if you ask what exactly you mean by the word on each type of occasion you will get three different answers.

(*b*) 'What you have distinguished is three kinds of causation.' But the three definitions of causation referred to in the foregoing paragraph are not related to each other as species of any common genus; nor is there any fourth definition, the definition of cause in general, of which the three 'kinds' of causation are species.

(*c*) 'One of your three so-called senses of the word "cause" is the only proper sense; the other two represent metaphorical usages of the word.' In order to show how baseless this objection is, it would be necessary to show that the distinction between 'proper' and 'metaphorical' senses of words is illusory. The contradictory of 'proper' is not 'metaphorical' but 'improper'. A proper usage of a word is one which as a matter of historical fact occurs in the language to which the word belongs. The contradictory of 'metaphorical' is 'literal'; and if the distinction between literal and metaphorical usages is a genuine distinction, which in one sense it is, both kinds of usage are equally proper. There is another sense in which all

language is metaphorical; and in that sense the objection to certain linguistic usages on the ground that
they are metaphorical is an objection to language as
such, and proceeds from an aspiration towards what
Charles Lamb called the uncommunicating muteness
of fishes. But this topic belongs to the theory of
language, that is, to the science of aesthetic, with
which this essay is not concerned.[1]

At the same time I do not wish to imply that the
distinction between I, II, and III is an example of
what Aristotle calls 'accidental equivocation'.[2] It is
not mere equivocation, for there is a continuity between the three things distinguished, though this
continuity is not of the kind suggested in any of the
three objections I have quoted. And the differences
between them are not accidental; they are the product of an historical process; and to the historian
historical processes are not accidental, because his
business is to understand them, and calling an event
accidental means that it is not capable of being understood. This brings me to my second main point.

2. That the relation between these three senses of
the word 'cause' is an historical relation: No. I being
the earliest of the three, No. II a development from
it, and No. III a development from that.

---

[1] The main questions involved, as I see them, are discussed in
my *Principles of Art*, especially Chapter XI.

[2] *Eth. Nic.* 1096^b 26–7: (although the various goodnesses of
honour, wisdom, and pleasure are not identical in definition but
differ *qua* goodnesses) 'the case does not resemble one of accidental equivocation', οὐκ ἔοικε τοῖς γε ἀπὸ τύχης ὁμωνύμοις.

XXX

CAUSATION IN HISTORY

In sense I of the word 'cause' that which is caused is the free and deliberate act of a conscious and responsible agent, and 'causing' him to do it means affording him a motive for doing it. For 'causing' we may substitute 'making', 'inducing', 'persuading', 'urging', 'forcing', 'compelling', according to differences in the kind of motive in question.

This is a current and familiar sense of the word (together with its cognates, correlatives, and equivalents) in English, and of the corresponding words in other modern languages. A headline in the *Morning Post* in 1936 ran, 'Mr. Baldwin's speech causes adjournment of House'. This did not mean that Mr. Baldwin's speech compelled the Speaker to adjourn the House whether or no that event conformed with his own ideas and intentions; it meant that on hearing Mr. Baldwin's speech the Speaker freely made up his mind to adjourn. In the same sense we say that a solicitor's letter causes a man to pay a debt or that bad weather causes him to return from an expedition.

I have heard it suggested that this is a secondary sense of the word 'cause', presupposing and derived from what I call sense III. The relation here described as 'presupposing' or 'being derived from' might, I take it, be understood either (1) as an historical relation, where '*b* presupposes *a*' means that a state of things *a* has given rise by an historical process into a state of things *b*, as a state of the English language in which 'cat' means an animal with claws gives rise by an historical process to a state in which it also means a kind of whip that lacerates the flesh of its victim; or (2) as a logical relation, where '*b* presupposes *a*' means that a state of things *a* exists contemporaneously with a state of things *b*, and *a* is an indispensable condition of *b*; as a state of the English language in which 'cat' still means an animal exists contemporaneously with a state in which it means a whip, and is an indispensable condition of it.

1. Sense I is not historically derived from sense III. On the contrary, when we trace the historical changes in the meaning of the word 'cause' in English and other modern languages, together with the Latin *causa* and the Greek αἰτία, we find that sense I is not only an established modern sense, it is also of great antiquity. In English it goes back, as the quotations in the *Oxford English Dictionary* show, to the Middle Ages. In Latin it is the commonest of all the senses distinguished by Lewis and Short, and also the oldest. In Greek, as the articles αἰτία, αἴτιος in Liddell and Scott show, the word which in Latin is translated *causa* meant originally 'guilt', 'blame', or 'accusation', and when first it began to mean 'cause', which it sometimes does in fifth-century literature, it was used in sense I, for the cause of a war or the like. In fact, the historical relation between these senses is the opposite of what has been suggested. Sense I is the original sense, and senses II and III have been derived from it by a process I shall trace in the sequel.

2. Sense I does not logically presuppose sense III. On the contrary, as I shall show in the following chapters, both sense II and sense III logically presuppose sense I; and any attempt to use the word in sense II or III without the anthropomorphic implications belonging to sense I must result either in a misuse of the word cause (that is, its use in a sense not consistent with the facts of established usage), or in a redefinition of it so as to make it mean what in established usage it does not mean: two alternatives which differ only in that established usage is defied with or without a formal declaration of war.

A cause in sense I is made up of two elements, a *causa quod* or efficient cause and a *causa ut* or final cause. The *causa quod* is a situation or state of things existing; the *causa ut* is a purpose or state of things to be brought about. Neither of these could be a cause if the other were absent. A man who tells his stockbroker to sell a certain holding may be caused to act thus by a rumour about the financial position of that company; but this rumour would not cause him to sell out unless he wanted to avoid being involved in the affairs of an unsound business. And *per contra* a man's desire to avoid being involved in the affairs of an unsound business would not cause him to sell his shares in a certain company unless he knew or believed that it was unsound.

The *causa quod* is not a mere situation or state of things, it is a situation or state of things known or believed by the agent in question to exist. If a prospective litigant briefs a certain barrister because of his exceptional ability, the *causa quod* of his doing so is not this ability simply as such, it is this ability as something known to the litigant or believed in by him.

The *causa ut* is not a mere desire or wish, it is an intention. The *causa ut* of a man's acting in a certain way is not his wanting to act in that way, but his meaning to act in that way. There may be cases where mere desire leads to action without the intermediate phase of intention; but such action is not deliberate, and therefore has no cause in sense I of the word.

Causes in sense I of the word may come into operation through the act of a second conscious and responsible agent, in so far as he (1) either puts the first in a certain situation in such a way that the first now believes or knows himself to be in that situation, or alternatively informs or persuades the first that he is in a certain situation; or (2) persuades the first to form a certain intention. In either of these two cases, the second agent is said to cause the first to do a certain act, or to 'make him do it'.

The act so caused is still an act; it could not be done (and therefore could not be caused) unless the agent did it of his own free will. If A causes B to do an act β, β is B's act and not A's; B is a free agent in doing it, and is responsible for it. If β is a murder, which A persuaded B to commit by pointing out certain facts or urging certain expediencies, B is the murderer. There is no contradiction between the proposition that the act β was caused by A, and the proposition that B was a free agent in respect of β, and is thus responsible for it. On the contrary, the first proposition implies the second.

Nevertheless, in this case A is said to 'share the responsibility' for the act β. This does not imply that a responsibility is a divisible thing, which would be absurd; it means that, whereas B is responsible for the act β, A is responsible for his own act, a, viz. the act of pointing out certain facts to B or urging upon him certain expediencies, whereby he induces him to commit the act β. When a child accused of a misdeed rounds on its accuser, saying, 'You made me do it', he is not excusing himself, he is implicating his accuser as an accessory. This is what Adam was doing when he said, 'The woman whom thou gavest to be with me, she gave me of the tree, and I did eat'.

A man is said to act 'on his own responsibility' or 'on his sole responsibility' when (1) his knowledge or belief about the situation is not dependent on information or persuasion from any one else, and (2) his intentions or purposes are similarly independent. In this case (the case in which a man is ordinarily said to exhibit 'initiative') his action is not uncaused. It still has both a *causa quod* and a *causa ut*. But because he has done for himself, unaided, the double work of envisaging the situation and forming the intention, which in the alternative case another man (who is therefore said to cause his action) has done for him, he can now be said to cause his own action as well as to do it. If he invariably acted in that way the total complex of his activities could be called self-causing (*causa sui*); an expression which refers to absence of persuasion or inducement on the part of another, and is hence quite intelligible and significant, although it has been denounced as non-sensical by people who have not taken the trouble to consider what the word 'cause' means.

XXXI

CAUSATION IN PRACTICAL NATURAL SCIENCE

In sense I of the word 'cause' that which is caused is a human action (including under that name actions of other, non-human, agents, if there are any, which act in the same conscious, deliberate, and responsible way which is supposed to be characteristic of human beings). That which causes may, as we have seen, come into operation through the activity of a second human agent.

In sense II that which is caused is an event in nature; but the word 'cause' still expresses an idea relative to human conduct, because that which causes is something under human control, and this control serves as means whereby human beings can control that which is caused. In this sense, the cause of an event in nature is the handle, so to speak, by which human beings can manipulate it. If we human beings want to produce or prevent such a thing, and cannot produce or prevent it immediately (as we can produce or prevent certain movements of our own bodies), we set about looking for its 'cause'. The question 'What is the cause of an event y?' means in this case 'How can we produce or prevent y at will?'

This sense of the word may be defined as follows. *A cause is an event or state of things which it is in our power to produce or prevent, and by producing or preventing which we can produce or prevent that whose cause it is said to be.* When I speak of 'producing' something I refer to such occasions as when one turns a switch and thus produces the state of things described by the proposition 'the switch is now at the ON position'. By preventing something I mean producing something incompatible with it, e.g. turning the switch to the OFF position.

Turning a switch to one or other position by finger-pressure is an instance of producing a certain state of things (the ON or OFF position of the switch) immediately, for it is nothing but a certain complex of bodily movements all immediately produced. These movements are not our means of turning the switch, they are the turning of the switch. Subject to certain indispensable conditions, the turning of the switch is our 'means' of producing a further state of things, viz. incandescence or its absence in a certain filament. What is immediately produced (the position of the switch) is the 'cause' in sense II of what is thus mediately produced.

The search for causes in sense II is natural science in that sense of the phrase in which natural science is what Aristotle calls a 'practical science', valued not for its truth pure and simple but for its utility, for the 'power over nature' which it gives us: Baconian science, where 'knowledge is power' and where 'nature is conquered by obeying her'. The field of a 'practical science' is the contingent, or in Aristotle's terminology 'what admits of being otherwise'. The light, for example, is on, but it admits of being off; i.e. I find by experiment that I am able to extinguish it by turning the switch to the OFF position. To discover that things are contingent is to discover that we can produce and prevent them.

Before the above definition of sense II is accepted, a preliminary question must be answered. I will put the question by distinguishing between two ideas, the idea of a 'practical' science of nature and the idea of an 'applied' science of nature, and asking to which of these ideas sense II belongs. By a 'practical' science of nature I mean one whose relation to practice is more intimate than that of means to end: one whose practical utility is not an ulterior end for whose sake it is valued, but its essence. By an 'applied' science of nature I mean one whose essence *qua* science is not practical utility but theoretical truth, but one which, in addition to being true, is useful as providing the solution for practical problems by being 'applied' to them. The Aristotelian and Baconian formulae might be understood as covering either of these two cases; but my present inquiry demands that they should be distinguished.

Sense II of the word 'cause' is bound up with the idea of a 'practical' science. An 'applied' science, being *qua* science not practical but theoretical, uses the word cause in sense III: a sense in which it is only an 'accident' (in the vocabulary of traditional logic) that knowing a cause enables some one to produce the effect, and in which, therefore, the statement '*x* causes *y*' would be in no way invalidated by the statement that *x* is a thing of such a kind as cannot be produced or prevented by human beings. I am not here denying that there is such a sense. What I am doing is to assert that there is another sense, recognizable in actual and long-established usage, in which it is not accidental but essential to the idea of causation that knowing the cause should enable some one to produce the effect, and in which the statement 'x causes y' would be flatly contradicted by the statement that x is a thing of such a kind as cannot be produced or prevented by human beings.

This usage, representing sense II of the word 'cause', can be recognized by two criteria: the thing described as a cause is always conceived as something in the world of nature or physical world, and it is always something conceived as capable of being produced or prevented by human agency. Here are some examples. The cause of malaria is the bite of a mosquito; the cause of a boat's sinking is her being overloaded; the cause of books going mouldy is their being in a damp room; the cause of a man's sweating is a dose of aspirin; the cause of a furnace going out in the night is that the draught-door was insufficiently open; the cause of seedlings dying is that nobody watered them.

In any one of the above cases, for example the first, the question whether the effect can be produced or prevented by producing or preventing the cause is not a further question which arises for persons practically interested when the proposition that (for example) malaria is due to mosquito-bites has been established; it is a question which has already been answered in the affirmative by the establishment of that proposition. This affirmative answer is in fact what the proposition means. In other words: medicine (the science to which the proposition belongs) is not a theoretical science which may on occasion be applied to the solution of practical problems, it is a practical science. The causal propositions which it establishes are not propositions which may or may not be found applicable in practice, but whose truth is independent of such applicability; they are propositions whose applicability is their meaning.

Consider a (hypothetical) negative instance. A great deal of time and money is being spent on 'cancer research', that is, on the attempt to discover 'the cause of cancer'. I submit that the word 'cause' is here used in sense II; that is to say, discovering the cause of cancer means discovering something which it is in the power of human beings to produce or prevent, by producing or preventing which they can produce or prevent cancer. Suppose some one claimed to have discovered the cause of cancer, but added that his discovery would be of no practical use because the cause he had discovered was not a thing that could be produced or prevented at will. Such a person would be ridiculed by his colleagues in the medical profession. His 'discovery' would be denounced as a sham. He would not be allowed to have done what he claimed to have done. It would be pointed out that he was not using the word 'cause' in the established sense which it bears in a medical context. To use my own terminology, it would be pointed out that he was thinking of medicine as an

applied science, whereas it is a practical science; and
using the word cause in sense III, whereas in medicine
it bears sense II.

This usage of the word is not exclusively modern.
It can be traced back through Middle English usages
to familiar Latin usages of the word *causa*, and thence
to the Greek αἰτία and its equivalent πρόφασις in, for
example, the Hippocratic writings of the fifth century
before Christ.

A cause in sense II is never able by itself to produce
the corresponding effect. The switch, as I said, only
works the light subject to certain indispensable conditions. Among these are the existence of an appropriate current and its maintenance by insulation and
contacts. These are called *conditiones sine quibus non.*
Their existence, over and above the cause, constitutes
one of the differences between sense II and sense III
of the word 'cause'. As we shall see in the next
chapter, a cause in sense III requires no such accom-
paniment. A cause in sense II is conditional, a cause
in sense III is unconditional. This distinction was
correctly understood by John Stuart Mill, whose
formal definition of the term 'cause' is a definition of
sense III, but who recognizes that ordinarily when
people speak of a cause they are using the word in
sense II. A cause, he tells us, is the invariable unconditional antecedent of its effect. This antecedent,
he thinks, is always complex, and any one of the
elements that go to make it up is called a condition.
But what people ordinarily call a cause is one of these
conditions, arbitrarily selected, and dignified by a

mere abuse of language with a name that properly belongs to the whole set.[1]

Mill deserves great credit for seeing that the word 'cause' was used in these two different ways. But his account of the relation between a cause in sense II and the conditions that accompany it is not quite satisfactory. Closer inspection would have shown him that the 'selection' of one condition to be dignified by the name of cause is by no means arbitrary. It is made according to a principle. The 'condition' which I call the cause (in sense II) of an event in which I take a practical interest is the condition I am able to produce or prevent at will. Thus, if my car fails to climb a steep hill, and I wonder why, I shall not consider my problem solved by a passer-by who tells me that the top of a hill is farther away from the earth's centre than its bottom, and that consequently more power is needed to take a car uphill than to take her along the level. All this is quite true; what the passer-by has described is one of the conditions which together form the 'real cause' (Mill's phrase; what I call the cause in sense III) of my car's stopping; and

[1] 'Since then, mankind are accustomed with acknowledged propriety so far as the ordinances of language are concerned, to give the name of cause to almost any one of the conditions of a phenomenon, or any portion of the whole number, *arbitrarily selected*, without excepting even those conditions which are purely negative, and in themselves incapable of causing anything; it will probably be admitted without longer discussion, that no one of the conditions has more claim to that title than another, and that *the real cause of the phenomenon is the assemblage of all its conditions.*' (J. S. Mill, *System of Logic*, Book III, chap. v, § 3; ed. 1, vol. i, p. 403, my italics.)

as he has 'arbitrarily selected' one of these and called it the cause, he has satisfied Mill's definition of what the word ordinarily means. But suppose an A.A. man comes along, opens the bonnet, holds up a loose high-tension lead, and says: 'Look here, sir, you're running on three cylinders'. My problem is now solved. I know the cause of the stoppage. It is *the* cause, just because it has not been 'arbitrarily selected'; it has been correctly identified as the thing that I can put right, after which the car will go properly. If I had been a person who could flatten out hills by stamping on them the passer-by would have been right to call my attention to the hill as the cause of the stoppage; not because the hill was a hill but because I was able to flatten it out.

To be precise, the 'condition' which is thus 'selected' is in fact not 'selected' at all; for selection implies that the person selecting has before him a finite number of things from among which he takes his choice. But this does not happen. In the first place the conditions of any given event are quite possibly infinite in number, so that no one could thus marshal them for selection even if he tried. In the second place no one ever tries to enumerate them completely. Why should he? If I find that I can get a result by certain means I may be sure that I should not be getting it unless a great many conditions were fulfilled; but so long as I get it I do not mind what these conditions are. If owing to a change in one of them I fail to get it, I still do not want to know what they all are; I only want to know what the one is that has changed.

From this a principle follows which I shall call 'the relativity of causes'. Suppose that the conditions of an event y include three things, a, β, γ; and suppose that there are three persons A, B, C, of whom A is able to produce or prevent a and only a; B is able to produce or prevent β and only β; and C is able to produce or prevent γ and only γ. Then if each of them asks 'What was the cause of y?' each will have to give a different answer. For A, a is the cause; for B, β; and for C, γ. The principle may be stated by saying that *for any given person the cause in sense II of a given thing is that one of its conditions which he is able to produce or prevent.*

For example, a car skids while cornering at a certain point, strikes the kerb, and turns turtle. From the car-driver's point of view the cause of the accident was cornering too fast, and the lesson is that one must drive more carefully. From the county surveyor's point of view the cause was a defect in the surface or camber of the road, and the lesson is that greater care must be taken to make roads skid-proof. From the motor-manufacturer's point of view the cause was defective design in the car, and the lesson is that one must place the centre of gravity lower.

If the three parties concerned take these three lessons respectively to heart accidents will become rarer. A knowledge of the causes of accidents will be gained in such a sense that knowledge is power: causes are causes in sense II, and knowledge of the cause of a thing we wish to prevent is (not merely brings, but is) knowledge how to prevent it. As in

the science of medicine so in the study of 'accidents',
where 'accident' means something people wish to
prevent, the word 'cause' is used in sense II.

As in medicine, therefore, so in the study of 'accidents' the use of the word in any other sense, or its
use by some one who fails to grasp the implications
of this sense, leads to confusion. If the driver, the
surveyor, and the manufacturer agreed in thinking
they knew the cause of the accident I have described,
but differed as to what it was, and if each thought that
it was a thing one of the others could produce or
prevent, but not himself, the result would be that
none of them would do anything towards preventing
such accidents in future, and their so-called knowledge of the cause of such accidents would be a
'knowledge' that was not, and did not even bring,
power. But since in the present context the word
'cause' is used in sense II, the reason why their
'knowledge' of the 'cause' of such accidents does not
enable them to prevent such accidents is that it is
not knowledge of their cause. What each of them
mistakes for such knowledge is the following nonsense proposition: 'the cause of accidents like this is
something which somebody else is able to produce
or prevent, but I am not.' Nonsense, because 'cause'
means 'cause in sense II', and owing to the relativity
of causes 'the cause of this accident' means 'that one
of its conditions which I am able to produce or
prevent'. Hence the folly of blaming other people in
respect of an event in which we and they are together
involved. Every one knows that such blame is foolish;

but without such an analysis of the idea of causation as I am here giving it is not easy to say why.

In medicine the principle of the relativity of causes means that, since any significant statement about the cause of a disease is a statement about the way in which that disease can be treated, two persons who can treat the same disease in two different ways will make different statements as to its cause. Suppose that one medical man can cure a certain disease by administering drugs, and another by 'psychological' treatment. For the first the 'cause' of the disease will be definable in terms of bio-chemistry; for the second in terms of psychology. If the disease itself is defined in terms of bio-chemistry, or in terms that admit of explanation or analysis in bio-chemical language, the definition of its cause in terms of psychology may be thought to imply an 'interactionist' theory of the relation between body and mind; and may be thought objectionable in so far as such theories are open to objection. But this would be a mistake. Definition of its cause in terms of psychology implies no theory as to the relation between body and mind. It simply records the fact that cases of the disease have been successfully treated by psychological methods, together with the hope that psychological methods may prove beneficial in future cases. To speak of this as 'evidence for an interactionist theory' would be to talk nonsense.

A corollary of the relativity principle is that *for a person who is not able to produce or prevent any of its conditions a given event has no cause in sense II at all*, and any statement he makes as to its cause in this sense of the word will be a nonsense statement. Thus the managing director of a large insurance company once told me that his wide experience of motor accidents had convinced him that the cause of all accidents was people driving too fast. This was a nonsense statement; but one could expect nothing better from a man whose practical concern with these affairs was limited to paying for them. In sense II of the word 'cause' only a person who is concerned with producing or preventing a certain kind of event can form an opinion about its cause. For a mere spectator there are no causes. When Hume tried to explain how the mere act of spectation could in time generate the idea of a cause, where 'cause' meant the cause of empirical science, that is, the cause in sense II, he was trying to explain how something happens which in fact does not happen.

If sciences are constructed consisting of causal propositions in sense II of the word 'cause', they will of course be in essence codifications of the various ways in which the people who construct them can bend nature to their purposes, and of the means by which in each case this can be done. Their constituent propositions will be (*a*) experimental, (*b*) general.

(*a*) In calling them experimental I mean that they will be established by means of experiment. No amount of observation will serve to establish such a proposition; for any such proposition is a declaration of ability to produce or prevent a certain state of things by the use of certain means; and no one knows what he can do, or how he can do it, until he tries. By observing and thinking he may form the opinion that he can probably do a given thing that resembles one he has done in the past; he may, that is, form an opinion as to its cause; but he cannot acquire knowledge.

(b) Because the proposition 'x causes y', in sense II of the word 'cause', is a constituent part of a practical science, it is essentially something that can be applied to cases arising in practice; that is to say, the terms x and y are not individuals but universals, and the proposition itself, rightly understood, reads 'any instance of x is a thing whose production or prevention is means respectively of producing or preventing some instance of y'. It would be nonsense, in this sense of the word 'cause', to inquire after the cause of any individual thing as such. It is a peculiarity of sense II that every causal proposition is a general proposition or 'propositional function'. In sense I every causal proposition is an individual proposition. In sense III causal propositions might equally well be either individual or general.

If the above analysis of the cause-effect relation (in sense II) into a means-end relation is correct, why do people describe this means-end relation in cause-effect terminology? People do not choose words at random; they choose them because they think them appropriate. If they apply cause-effect terminology to things whose relation is really that of means and end the reason must be that they want to apply to those things some idea which is conveyed by the cause-effect terminology and not by the means-end terminology. What is this idea? The answer is not doubtful. The cause-effect terminology conveys an idea not only of one thing's leading to another but of one thing's forcing another to happen or exist; an idea of power or compulsion or constraint.

From what impression, as Hume asks, is this idea derived? I answer, from impressions received in our social life, in the practical relations of man to man; specifically, from the impression of causing (in sense I) some other man to do something when, by argument or command or threat or the like, we place him in a situation in which he can only carry out his intentions by doing that thing; and conversely, from the impression of being caused to do something.

Why, then, did people think it appropriate to apply this idea to the case of actions in which we achieve our ends by means, not of other human beings, but of things in nature?

Sense II of the word 'cause' is especially a Greek sense; in modern times it is especially associated with the survival or revival of Greek ideas in the earlier Renaissance thinkers; and both the Greeks and the earlier Renaissance thinkers held quite seriously an animistic theory of nature. They thought of what we call the material or physical world as a living organism or complex of living organisms, each with its own sensations and desires and intentions and thoughts. In Plato's *Timaeus*, and in the Renaissance Platonists whose part in the formation of modern natural science was so decisive, the constant use of language with animistic implications is neither an accident nor a metaphor; these expressions are meant to be taken literally and to imply what they seem to imply, namely that the way in which men use what we nowadays call inorganic nature as means to our ends is not in principle different from the way in which we use other men. We use other men by assuming them to be free agents with wills of their own, and influencing them in such a way that they shall decide to do what is in conformity with our plans. This is 'causing' them so to act in sense I of the word 'cause'. If 'inorganic nature' is alive in much the same way as human beings, we must use it according to much the same principles; and therefore we can apply to this use of it the same word 'cause', as implying that there are certain ways in which natural things behave if left to themselves, but that man, being more powerful than they, is able to thwart their inclination to behave in these ways and make them behave not as they like but as he likes.

To sum up. Sense II of the word 'cause' rests on two different ideas about the relation between man and nature.

1. The anthropocentric idea that man looks at nature from his own point of view; not the point of view of a thinker, anxious to find out the truth about nature as it is in itself, but the point of view of a practical agent, anxious to find out how he can manipulate nature for the achieving of his own ends.

2. The anthropomorphic idea that man's manipulation of nature resembles one man's manipulation

of another man, because natural things are alive in much the same way in which men are alive, and have therefore to be similarly handled.

The first idea is admittedly part of what civilized and educated European men nowadays think about their relations with nature. The second idea is part of what they notoriously did think down to (say) four centuries ago. How they began to get rid of this idea, and how completely they have even now got rid of it, are questions I shall not raise. My point is that even to-day, when they use the word 'cause' in sense II, they are talking as if they had not yet entirely got rid of it. For if the vocabulary of practical natural science were overhauled with a view to eliminating all traces of anthropomorphism, language about causes in sense II would disappear and language about means and ends would take its place.

Fifty years ago, anthropologists were content to note the fact that 'survivals' occur. Since then, they have seen that the occurrence of such things constitutes a problem, and a difficult one. 'Students have made some progress in ascertaining what causes folklore to decay, but what causes the surviving elements to survive? What vacuum does the survival fill? . . . These questions . . . remain a problem for the future.'[1] What causes the survival of language which taken literally implies the survival of supposedly obsolete thought-forms is, I submit, the fact that these thought-forms are not so dead as they are supposed to be. It is certainly true that modern

[1] Charlotte S. Burne, *Folklore*, vol. xxii (1911), p. 37.

natural science has tried very hard to expel anthropomorphic elements from its conception of nature.
Among natural scientists to-day it is orthodox to take
the will for the deed. For the historical metaphysician
it is a question how far this anti-anthropomorphic
movement has been successful. The continued use
of the word 'cause' in sense II is prima-facie evidence
that its success has not been complete.

XXXII

CAUSATION IN THEORETICAL NATURAL SCIENCE

SENSE III of the word 'cause' represents an attempt to apply it not to a 'practical' but to a 'theoretical' science of nature. I shall first explain the characteristics which would belong to this sense if the attempt were successful, and then consider certain difficulties which in the long run prove fatal to it.

In the contingent world to which sense II belongs a cause is contingent (*a*) in its existence, as depending for its existence on human volition, (*b*) in its operation, as depending for the production of its effect on *conditiones sine quibus non*. In the necessary world to which sense III belongs a cause is necessary (*a*) in its existence, as existing whether or no human beings want it to exist, (*b*) in its operation, as producing its effect no matter what else exists or does not exist. There are no *conditiones sine quibus non*. The cause leads to its effect by itself, or 'unconditionally'; in other words the relation between cause and effect is a one-one relation. There can be no relativity of causes, and no diversity of effects due to fulfilment or non-fulfilment of conditions.

I propose to distinguish the one-many and many-one[1] character of the cause-effect relation in sense II

---

[1] One-many, because a cause in sense II leads to its effect only when the *conditiones sine quibus non* are fulfilled. Many-one, because of the relativity of causes (see p. 304).

from its one-one character in sense III by calling these senses *loose* and *tight* respectively. A loose cause requires some third thing other than itself and its effect to bind the two together, namely a group of *conditiones sine quibus non*; a tight cause is one whose connexion with its effect is independent of such adventitious aids.

In order to illustrate the implications of sense III, I will refer to the contradiction between the traditional denial of *actio in distans* (which, I suppose, would hold as against action across a lapse of time no less than across a distance in space) and the assumption, commonly made nowadays, that a cause precedes its effect in time. I shall argue that *actio in distans* is perfectly intelligible in sense II but nonsense in sense III.

If I set fire to one end of a time-fuse, and five minutes later the charge at its other end explodes, there is said to be a causal connexion between the first and second events, and a time-interval of five minutes between them. But this interval is occupied by the burning of the fuse at a determinate rate of feet per minute; and this process is a *conditio sine qua non* of the causal efficacy ascribed to the first event. That is to say, the connexion between the lighting of the fuse and the detonation of the charge is causal in the loose sense, not the tight one. If in the proposition '*x* causes the explosion' we wish to use the word 'cause' in the tight sense, *x* must be so defined as to include in itself every such *conditio sine qua non*. It must include the burning of the whole fuse; not its burning until 'just before' that process reaches the detonator, for then there would still be an interval to be bridged, but its burning until the detonator is reached. Only then is the cause in sense III complete; and when it is complete it produces its effect, not afterwards (however soon afterwards) but then. Cause in sense III is simultaneous with effect.

Similarly, it is coincident with its effect in space. The cause of the explosion is where the explosion is. For suppose x causes y, and suppose that x is in a position p_1 and y in a position p_2, the distance from p_1 to p_2 being δ. If 'cause' is used in sense II, δ may be any distance, so long as it is bridged by a series of events which are *conditiones sine quibus non* of x causing y. But if 'cause' is used in sense III, δ must $= 0$. For if it did not, p_2 would be any position on the surface of a sphere whose centre was p_1 and whose radius would $= \delta$; so the relation between p_1 and p_2 would be a one-many relation. But the relation between x and y, where x causes y in sense III, is a one-one relation. Therefore, where δ does not $= 0$, x cannot cause y in sense III.

The denial of *actio in distans*, spatial or temporal, where the 'agent' is a cause in sense III, is therefore not a 'prejudice'[1] but is logically involved in the definition of sense III.

The main difficulty about sense III is to explain what is meant by saying that a cause 'produces' or 'necessitates' its effect. When similar language is used of senses I and II we know what it means. In sense I

---

[1] As Russell calls it: *Mysticism and Logic*, cit., p. 192.

it means that x affords somebody a motive for doing y; in sense II, that x is somebody's means of bringing y about. But what (since it cannot mean either of these) does it mean in sense III?

There are two well-known answers to this question, which may be called the rationalist and empiricist answers respectively.

(i) The rationalist answer runs: 'necessitation means implication'. A cause, on this view, is a 'ground', and its relation to its effect is the relation of ground to consequent, a logical relation. When some one says that x necessitates y he means on this view that x implies y, and is claiming the same kind of insight into y which one has (for example) into the length of one side of a triangle given the lengths of the other two sides and the included angle. Whatever view one takes as to the nature of implication, one must admit that in such a case the length of the third side can be ascertained without measuring it and even without seeing it, e.g. when it lies on the other side of a hill. The implication theory, therefore, implies that 'if the cause is given the effect follows', not only in the sense that whenever the cause actually exists the effect actually follows, but that from the thought of the cause the thought of the effect follows logically. That is to say, any one who wishes to discover the effect of a given thing x can discover the answer by simply thinking out the logical implications of x. Nothing in the nature of observation or experiment is needed.

This is in itself a tenable position in the sense that, if any one wants to construct a system of science in which the search for causes means a search for grounds, there is nothing to prevent him from trying. This was in fact what Descartes tried to do. His projected 'universal science' was to be a system of grounds and consequents. And if, as is sometimes said, modern physics represents a return in some degree to the Cartesian project, it would seem that the attempt is being made once more. But the rationalist theory of causation, however valuable it may be as the manifesto of a particular scientific enterprise, cannot be regarded as an 'analysis' of the causal propositions asserted by natural science as it has existed for the last few centuries. If it were accepted, these propositions would have to be abandoned as untrue. For no one believes that they can be established by sheer 'thinking', that is, by finding the so-called effects to be logically implied in the so-called causes. It is just because this is impossible that the questions what causes a given effect and what effect a given cause produces have to be answered by observation and experiment. Hence the result of establishing a science of the Cartesian type would be not an analysis of propositions of the type 'x causes y' into propositions of the type 'x implies y' but the disuse of causal propositions in that kind of science and the use of implicational propositions instead; while in the sciences of observation and experiment causal propositions not analysable into implicational propositions would still be used; the meaning of 'necessity' in these causal propositions being still doubtful.

This situation would not be illuminated by alleging that the sciences in which causal propositions occur are 'backward' or 'immature sciences'. Such a statement would imply that the idea of causation is a half-baked idea which when properly thought out will turn into the different idea of implication. This I take to be the Hegelian theory of the dialectic of concepts, and if any one wishes to maintain it I do not want to forbid him; but I must observe that it does not excuse him from answering the question what the half-baked idea is *an sich*, that is, before its expected transformation has happened.

(ii) I turn to the empiricist answer: 'necessitation means observed uniformity of conjunction'. Like the former answer this one cannot be taken literally; for no one, I think, will pretend that the proposition 'x necessitates y' means merely 'all the observed x's have been observed to be conjoined with y's', and does not also mean 'x's observed in the future will also be conjoined with y's'. In fact the question (so urgent for, e.g., Hume and Mill) how we proceed from the mere experience of conjunction to the assertion of causal connexion resolves itself into the question how we pass from the first of these to the second. For Hume and Mill the proposition 'all the observed x's have been observed to be conjoined with y's' is not what we mean by saying 'x necessitates y', it is only the empirical evidence on the strength of which we assert the very different proposition 'x necessitates y'. Thus, if any one says 'necessitation means observed uniformity of conjunction', it must be sup-

posed either that he is talking without thinking; or
that he is carelessly expressing what, expressed more
accurately, would run: 'necessitation is something
we assert on the strength of observed uniformity of
conjunction', without telling us what he thinks necessitation to be; or, thirdly, that he is expressing still
more carelessly what should run: 'in order to assert
a necessitation we must pass from the first of the
above propositions to the second; now I cannot see
how this is possible; therefore I submit that we ought
never to assert necessitations, but on the occasions
when we do assert them we ought to be asserting
something quite different, namely observed conjunction'. Necessitation being again left undefined.

(iii) A third answer to our question has been given
by Earl Russell, in a paper[1] of very great importance,
to which I have already referred; but I want here and
now to express my great admiration for it and my
great indebtedness to it. He says: '*necessary* is a pre-
dicate of a propositional function meaning that it is
true for all possible values of its argument or arguments'. This I will call the 'functional' answer. In
so far as it amounts to saying that causation in sense
III implies a one-one relation between cause and
effect, I entirely agree. But I find myself, very re-
luctantly, unable to accept all of what I take Earl
Russell to mean. I will give two examples.

(a) How, on the functional theory, could any one
ever know a causal proposition to be true, or even
know that the facts in his possession tended to justify

[1] 'On the Notion of Cause', referred to on p. 69, above.

a belief in it? Only, so far as I can see, if there is a relation of implication between x and y. For 'all *possible* values' of x may be an infinite number; and, even if they are not, it may not be practicable to examine them individually. If a, b, c are the sides of any triangle, we know that $a+b-c$ will always be a positive quantity, because that is implied in the definition of a triangle. Thus the functional theory presupposes the rationalistic or implicational theory, which I have already given reasons for rejecting.

(β) I do not know whether Earl Russell, in the sentence quoted above, wished to be understood as meaning that the word 'necessary' has no other meaning than that which he there ascribes to it. If so, he was mistaken. It has another meaning, which is in fact its original meaning. Just as the original sense of the word 'cause' is what I have called the historical sense, according to which that which is caused is the act of a conscious and responsible agent, so the original sense of the word 'necessary' is an historical sense, according to which it is necessary for a person to act in a certain way: deciding so to act and acting therefore freely and responsibly, yet (in a sense which in no wise derogates from his responsibility) 'necessitated' to act in that way by certain 'causes', in sense I of the word 'cause'.

Even if Earl Russell does not wish to deny that the word 'necessary' has this historical sense, I cannot think that his failure to mention it is well advised. This original sense of the word 'necessary' is just as much the foundation on which the other senses of the word 'necessary' have been built, as the corresponding sense of the word 'cause' (sense I, the 'historical' sense) is the foundation on which have been built the other senses of the word 'cause'. Between the respective histories of these two words there is not only parallelism, there is interconnexion. It is therefore very natural that Earl Russell should appeal to the word 'necessary' in his attempt to clear up the meaning of the word 'cause'. But the metaphysical problems connected with the idea of causation are historical problems, not to be solved except by historical treatment; and if the history of the word 'necessary' has run on parallel lines to the history of the word 'cause', the appeal from the latter to the former is scientifically barren, because it takes us not from one problem to the solution of that problem, but from one unsolved problem to another unsolved problem of the same kind.

Most people think that when we use the word 'causation' in sense III we mean to express by it something different from logical implication, and something more than uniformity of conjunction, whether observed only, or observed in the past and also expected in the future; and that this 'something different' and 'something more' is in the nature of compulsion. On the historical issue of what has actually been meant when words have actually been used, this is correct.

Earl Russell (op. cit., p. 190) argues that people cannot mean this because (as he very truly says) 'where desire does not come in, there can be no question of compulsion'. All the same, as I shall now try to show, they do mean this. Causation in sense III is an anthropomorphic idea. Natural scientists have tried to use it as a weapon for attacking anthropomorphic conceptions of nature; but it has been a treacherous weapon. It has led them unawares to reaffirm the view they were attacking. And that may be why, in Earl Russell's own words, 'physics has ceased to look for causes' (op. cit., p. 180).

We found the idea of compulsion present in sense II of the word 'cause'. From what impression, we then asked, is this idea derived? We now find it present in sense III, and we must ask the same question, and answer it in the same way. The idea of compulsion, as applied to events in nature, is derived from our experience of occasions on which we have compelled others to act in certain ways by placing them in situations (or calling their attention to the fact that they are in situations) of such a kind that only by so acting can they realize the intentions we know or rightly assume them to entertain: and conversely, occasions in which we have ourselves been thus compelled. Compulsion is an idea derived from our social experience, and applied in what is called a 'metaphorical' way not only to our relations with things in nature (sense II of the word 'cause') but also to the relations which these things have among themselves (sense III). Causal propositions in sense III are descriptions of relations between natural events in anthropomorphic terms.

The reason why we are in the habit of using these

anthropomorphic terms is, of course, that they are traditional. Inquiry into the history of the tradition shows that it grew up in connexion with the same animistic theory of nature to which I referred in discussing sense II of the word 'cause', but that in this case the predominant factor was a theology of Neoplatonic inspiration.

If a man can be said to cause certain events in nature by adopting certain means to bringing them about, and if God is conceived semi-anthropomorphically[1] as having faculties like those of the human mind but greatly magnified, it will follow that God also will be regarded as bringing about certain things in nature by the adoption of certain means.

Now comes a step in the argument which, if we tried to reconstruct it without historical knowledge, we should probably reconstruct wrongly. If x is a thing in nature produced by God as a means of producing y, we might fancy x to be a purely passive instrument in God's hand, having no power of its own, but 'inert', as Berkeley in the true spirit of post-Galilean physics insists that matter must be. And in

[1] I distinguish an anthropomorphic conception of God (cf. p. 185) from a semi-anthropomorphic. An anthropomorphic God would be simply what Matthew Arnold called a 'magnified non-natural man'. His attributes would be merely the attributes of man, enlarged. For example, he would be liable to anger, but his anger would be a more formidable thing than man's. A semi-anthropomorphic God would be the result of criticizing this childish idea in the light of the reflection that, if God is really greater than man, he cannot have those attributes which in man are due to man's littleness; e.g. anger, which comes of being thwarted.

that case God alone would possess that compulsive force which is expressed by the word 'cause'; that word would not be given as a name to x, and God would be the sole cause.

Actually, God is for medieval thinkers not the sole cause but the first cause. This does not mean the first term in a series of efficient causes (a barbarous misinterpretation of the phrase), but a cause of a peculiar kind, as distinct from 'secondary causes'. The *Liber de Causis*, a Neoplatonic Arabic work of the ninth century, whose influence on medieval cosmology was at this point decisive, lays it down that God in creating certain instruments for the realization of certain ends confers upon these instruments a power in certain ways like his own, though inferior to it.

Thus endowed with a kind of minor and derivative godhead, these instruments accordingly acquire the character of causes, and constitute that division of nature which, according to John the Scot, 'both is created and creates'. Their causality is thus a special kind of causality existing wholly within nature, whereby one thing in nature produces or necessitates another thing in nature. The words 'produces' and 'necessitates' are here used literally and deliberately to convey a sense of volition and compulsion; for the anthropomorphic account of natural things is taken as literally true; the activity of these secondary causes is a scaled-down version of God's and God's is a scaled-up version of man's.

This idea of God is only semi-anthropomorphic,

because it implies the ascription to God of a power not belonging to man, the power of creating instruments of His will which are themselves possessed of will.

This was the atmosphere in which our modern conception of nature took shape. For in the sixteenth and seventeenth centuries, when the animistic conception of nature was replaced among scientists and philosophers by a mechanistic one, the word 'cause' was not a novelty; it was a long-established term, and its meaning was rooted in these Neoplatonic notions.

Thus when we come to Newton, and read (e.g.) the *Scholium* appended to his Definitions, we find him using as a matter of course a whole vocabulary which, taken literally, ascribes to 'causes' in nature a kind of power which properly belongs to one human being inducing another to act as he wishes him to act. Causes are said, in the twelfth paragraph of that *Scholium*, to be 'forces impressed upon bodies for the generation of motion. True motion is neither generated nor altered, but by some force impressed upon the body moved.' The cause, for Newton, is not that which impresses the force, it is the force itself.

Here and throughout his treatment of the subject it is perfectly clear that for him the idea of causation is the idea of force, compulsion, constraint, exercised by something powerful over another thing which if not under this constraint would behave differently; this hypothetical different behaviour being called by contrast 'free' behaviour. This constraint of one thing in nature by another is the secondary causation of medieval cosmology.

Taken *au pied de la lettre*, Newton is implying that a billiard-ball struck by another and set in motion would have liked to be left in peace; it is reluctant to move, and this reluctance, which is called inertia, has to be overcome by an effort on the part of the ball that strikes it. This effort costs the striker something, namely part of its own momentum, which it pays over to the sluggard ball as an inducement to move. I am not suggesting that this reduction of physics to social psychology is the doctrine Newton set out to teach; all I say is that he expounded it, no doubt as a metaphor beneath which the truths of physics are concealed.

I have already reminded the reader that in Newton there is no law of universal causation. He not only does not assert that every event must have a cause, he explicitly denies it; and this in two ways.

(i) In the case of a body moving freely (even though its motion be what he calls 'true' motion as distinct from relative motion), there is uncaused motion; for caused means constrained, and free means unconstrained. If a body moves freely from p_1 to p_2 and thence to p_3, the 'event' which is its moving from p_2 to p_3 is in no sense caused by the preceding 'event' of its moving from p_1 to p_2; for it is not caused at all. Newton's doctrine is that any movement which happens according to the laws of motion is an uncaused event; the laws of motion are in fact the laws of free or causeless motion.

(ii) He asserts that there is such a thing as relative motion; but, as he puts it, 'relative motion may be generated or altered without any force impressed upon the body'. If, therefore, it were possible to show either that all motion is 'free', that is to say, takes place according to laws having the same logical character as the Newtonian laws of motion; or that all motion is 'relative'; then on Newton's own principles it would follow that no motion is caused, and the cat would be out of the bag. It would have become plain that there is no truth concealed beneath the animistic metaphor; and that 'the idea of causation' is simply a relic of animism foisted upon a science to which it is irrelevant.

This is what modern physics has done. Developing the Newtonian doctrine in the simplest and most logical way, it has eliminated the notion of cause altogether. In place of that notion, we get a new and highly complex development of the Newtonian 'laws of motion'. Of the two Newtonian classes of events, (*a*) those that happen according to law (*b*) those that happen as the effects of causes, class (*a*) has expanded to such an extent as to swallow up (*b*). At the same time, the survival of the term 'cause' in certain sciences other than physics, such as medicine, is not a symptom of their 'backwardness', because in them the word 'cause' is not used in the same sense. They are practical sciences, and they accordingly use the word in sense II.

XXXIII

CAUSATION IN KANTIAN PHILOSOPHY

THE situation in post-Newtonian philosophy has been very different. Kant,[1] whose gigantic effort at a synthesis of all existing philosophies here, unless I am mistaken, overreached itself, swept into one bag the Baconian tradition, with its insistence on causes in sense II, the Cartesian identification of causes (in sense III) with grounds, the Leibnitian law of sufficient reason, and the Humian conception of the cause as an event prior in time to its effect; and, neglecting the one thing in Newton which modern physics has found most valuable, namely the doctrine that what happens according to a law happens without a cause, devised a doctrine which was very soon accepted as orthodox. The central points are three.

(a) *That every event has a cause,*

(b) *That the cause of an event is a previous event,*

(c) *That (a) and (b) are known to us a priori.*

These are, of course, metaphysical propositions: i.e. taken by themselves they express not propositions but suppositions; to be understood as propositions, they must be understood as prefaced by the metaphysical rubric. I shall comment on (a) and (b).

(a) On this statement I have two questions to ask: what did Kant mean by it and why did he believe it?

[1] What I have here to say about causation in Kant is not meant to cover every sense the word has in Kant's writings, but only the sense it has in the first *Critique* in connexion with natural science.

1. What did he mean by it? First, he meant to traverse the Newtonian distinction between events due to the operation of causes and events due to the operation of laws. Secondly, he meant the word 'cause' to be understood in sense III. His language in the *Critique of Pure Reason* leaves no doubt on this point. He calls the cause an event upon which the effect must follow in conformity with a rule (A 194, B 239). This 'rule' implies a one-one relation.

2. Why did he believe it? Not because it was a commonplace. As I have pointed out, it directly traversed Newton; and in a general way Kant accepted Newton as his master in physical science. Nor was it derived from either the Leibnitian or the Humian side of his philosophical education. It is not in Leibniz. The Leibnitian Law of Sufficient Reason is not that everything has a cause, it is that everything has a ground. The demonstration that causes, as the word is understood in natural science, are not the same as grounds, is an essential part of that Humian argument to whose acceptance by himself Kant is referring where he speaks of Hume as rousing him from his dogmatic slumber. Nor is it in Wolff, who holds that the cause of an effect is that from which the effect can be logically deduced, i.e. its ground. It is not in Hume, who is clearly following Newton when he says: "'tis a general maxim in philosophy, that whatever *begins to exist*, must have a cause of existence', and asks 'for what reason we pronounce it necessary, that every thing *whose existence has a*

beginning should also have a cause' (*Treatise*, part iii, § iii *ad init.*, § ii *ad fin.*; *Works*, Edinburgh, 1826, vol. i, pp. 110, 109; I have italicized the words that emphasize Hume's agreement with Newton at the point in which Kant differs from him). Locke takes the same line in the fourth section of his chapter 'Of Power', though with some hesitation: he does not actually deny that every event in nature is an instance of 'power' (causation), but says that 'the Impulse Bodies are observ'd to make one upon another' is at any rate a much clearer case of it than a continuation of the motion thus initiated in the second body, which is 'little more an Action, than the Continuation of the Alteration of its Figure by the same Blow, is an Action'.

The transition from the Newtonian doctrine that every 'change' has a cause (where 'change' means an event not accounted for by the laws of motion), to the Kantian doctrine that every 'event' has a cause, might no doubt be understood as a correction of wording rather than as an alteration of doctrine: for if that which causes be called, as it was by Newton, a force, and if inertia be called a force (*vis inertiae*), it follows that an event which can be accounted for by the First Law of Motion, such as the passing of a certain point at a certain time by a body moving with uniform velocity in a straight line, where the continuance of the movement is ascribed to inertia, is being accounted for by a cause, the *vis inertiae*: and by similar argument it can be shown that every event in nature was implicitly regarded by Newton as having a cause, although Newton himself did not recognize the implication. And this, I imagine, is the reason why Kant's statement, at first sight revolutionary, was so readily adopted by his contemporaries and successors, and has excited so little remark among commentators and historians.

For it is a fact that histories of philosophy and commentaries on Kant, so far as I have consulted them, throw no light on the question why Kant abandoned the Newtonian doctrine on this point and substituted the statement I am now discussing. Whether he derived this statement from the works of any predecessor, and if so who the predecessor was, I do not know.

(b) The second Kantian statement, that the cause of an event is a previous event, is Humian: for Hume's discussion is wholly based on the presupposition that a cause and its effect are two 'objects', constantly conjoined by way of temporal succession. Now the cause of an event can be a previous event only when 'cause' is used in sense II. If 'cause' is used in sense III, as it is in Kant's first statement, there can be (as I have shown) no difference of time between the cause and its effect: for sense III implies a one-one relation between cause and effect, and events between which there is a one-one relation must be simultaneous (above, pp. 314–15).

The two suppositions which together constitute Kant's definition of the term 'cause' are not consupponible: or at any rate not consupponible except under a pressure which must produce a somewhat

violent strain in the resulting structure. For in these
two statements the word 'cause' is used in two different senses. In (*a*) it is used in sense II; in (*b*) it is
used in sense III. The combination of the two is an
attempt at philosophical syncretism; an unsuccessful
attempt, because they are not propositions about the
same thing. The relevance of each to the other is an
illusory relevance, a merely verbal relevance which
is not a real relevance because they use the word
'cause' in two different senses.

It does not follow that Kant was mistaken in thinking both statements to be true. He was trying to
state what people (himself included) meant when they
spoke of causes. They meant to express a certain
absolute presupposition which they habitually made
in the course of their thinking about nature: the presupposition which is called the idea of causation.
This presupposition was itself a constellation of presuppositions; and among the elements that went to
compose it, if Kant is right, were these: that a cause
and its effect are related by a necessary connexion,
and that a cause and its effect are related by way of
temporal sequence. The logical incompatibility of
these two suppositions does not prove that they were
not concurrently made; it only proves that, if they
were concurrently made, the structure of the constellation that included them both was subject to
severe strain, and that the entire fabric of the science
based upon them was in a dangerously unstable
condition.

The general acceptance of Kant's analysis in the

nineteenth century is strong, though of course not necessarily conclusive, evidence that it was correct. If so, it follows that during what I will call the Kantian period, roughly speaking from Kant to Einstein, the fabric of natural science, spectacular though its progress was, rested on an insecure foundation. Whether the hatred of metaphysics fashionable among natural scientists in this period was due to a sense of this insecurity (diseased organisms often hate the remedy) I shall not ask. What I shall do is to say wherein this insecurity consisted, so far as it arose out of the idea of causation.

It consisted in two metaphysical dilemmas, which I shall call the anthropocentric dilemma and the anthropomorphic dilemma. The first of these was brought to light by the philosophical movement of the late nineteenth century, and its existence is consequently a notorious fact. The second lies deeper in the structure of nineteenth-century thought, and though often suspected it has not been generally recognized.

1. *The anthropocentric dilemma.* The alternatives are:

1 (*a*). The natural scientist is trying to construct an anthropocentric science of nature, a practical science of the Baconian or experimental type. His materials are such facts as this, that on a certain occasion a certain person has obtained certain results by manipulating natural things in a certain way. Causes in such a science are causes in sense II. To know nature as the natural scientist tries to know nature means

knowing how to bend nature to one's purposes. He does not wish to know what nature is in itself. He wishes to know what he can do with it. His attitude towards nature is primarily a practical attitude; it is only theoretical in the secondary sense that it entails knowing what results his attempts at practice have yielded. Whatever superstructure is built on this strictly historical knowledge is a superstructure of more or less well-founded conjecture as to what results may be expected on more or less similar occasions in the future. Any attempt to replace this conjectural superstructure by a superstructure of known or proved certainties involves a surreptitious transition from 1(a) to 1(b).

1(b). The natural scientist is trying to construct a science of nature as it is in itself, a theoretical science of nature. To such a theoretical science experimental results may afford clues, but no more. The ideal aimed at is a knowledge of what the natural world is in itself as distinct from a knowledge of what man has done (and therefore may hope to do) by manipulating the natural world.

The orthodox or accepted view of natural science during the Kantian period was 1(b). But the issue as between the two alternatives was not clearly envisaged; and in the latter part of the century 1(b) tended to lose its hold on men's minds, and to be replaced by 1(a).

2. *The anthropomorphic dilemma.* The question here is whether the natural scientist in his detailed study of the world of nature presupposes that this

world is animated by something like human mind, or at any rate human psyche, or whether he makes no such presupposition. It is not a pseudo-metaphysical question. It is not a question as to whether the world of nature is in fact thus animated or not. It is a question as to the presuppositions which in fact underlie the natural scientist's approach to that world. The alternatives are:

2(*a*). The natural scientist is trying to construct a science of nature in terms of analogies drawn from the conscious life of man. It is only through such analogies that nature becomes intelligible to man; a science of nature which renounced their use would accordingly be no science at all. When Darwin in the *Origin of Species* announces 'the highly important fact that an organ originally constructed for one purpose may be converted into one for a widely different purpose' (Ch. VI), his use of frankly teleological language need bring no blush to the cheek of his disciples. Thus described, the facts of animal anatomy become intelligible. Described without appeal to the analogy with the human activities of constructing and adapting, means and ends, they would be unintelligible.

2(*b*). The natural scientist, in so far as he uses these analogies, is obscuring his own thought by saying what he does not mean. A well-devised vocabulary for use in natural science would avoid them. The natural scientist does not really believe that nature devises and adapts, invents means to bring about her ends; he thinks that this is a purely human type of behaviour, and that his business is to describe everything he can in terms of physical and chemical processes in which it has no place.

The orthodox view of natural science during the Kantian period was 2(b). But once more the issue was not clearly defined. The natural science of the period regarded itself as a non-anthropomorphic natural science, and in attacking anthropomorphism pinned its faith to causation in sense III as its favourite weapon. It failed to realize that within this sense of the word there lay concealed an element of anthropomorphism, concealed because to discover it would have required the exercise of metaphysical analysis, and metaphysics was barred: and that the so-called 'materialism' which was the favourite metaphysical doctrine of these anti-metaphysicians was in consequence only in name a repudiation of anthropomorphism; really it was anthropomorphic at the core.

The war-cries 'Back to Kant' and 'No more metaphysics' were the mottoes of a reactionary and obscurantist anti-metaphysics whose purpose was to prevent these two problems from being faced and solved. Even where those war-cries were not heard the same purpose has been visibly at work. While physicists have been escaping from the *damnosa haereditas* of the Kantian confusion by the heroic measure of reconstructing their own science in such a way that the idea of causation no longer figures in it at all, philosophers, especially those of the reactionary and obscurantist schools which put forward the

programmes of 'realism' and 'logical positivism',
show their desire to perpetuate whatever confusions
there were in nineteenth-century science by reiterating
the contradiction that vitiated the nineteenth-century
idea of causation.

XXXIV

EPILOGUE

WHAT is our present situation?

The obscurantist movement mentioned in the preceding paragraph is not yet spent. Its hall-mark is the acceptance of the two incompatibles quoted from Kant as (*a*) and (*b*) at the beginning of the last chapter: that every event has a cause, and that the cause of an event is a previous event. I will give a few examples.

Cook Wilson (*Statement and Inference*, 1926: a posthumous publication containing professorial lectures delivered in Oxford over many years from a chair occupied since 1889; vol. ii, pp. 516–17) promises that 'causality will ultimately be found to mean that the events belonging to an object, or a system of objects, have a definite order, that is, therefore, a necessary order . . . *we* apprehend this necessity as belonging to the order of events'. An order here means a temporal order.

Professor H. A. Prichard, in a book about Kant which does not by any means profess a slavish adherence to Kant's doctrines (*Kant's Theory of Knowledge* (1909), p. 300), nevertheless agrees with Kant that 'it is of the very nature of a physical event to be an element in a process of change . . . this process being through and through necessary in the sense that any event . . . is the outcome of certain preceding events'.

He differs from Kant only on the point which at the beginning of the last chapter I labelled (*c*). Where Kant says that the principle of causation is a matter of synthetic *a priori* knowledge, and where Cook Wilson says that we 'apprehend' it 'much as we do the events, though we do not apprehend it in the way of experiencing it' (loc. cit.), Prichard says that it is what Kant called analytic ('to attain this insight, *we* have only to reflect upon what we really mean by a physical event', loc. cit.) and observes that this is exactly the view which Kant rejects as 'dogmatic'. It is the less surprising that certain other writers have doubted whether this self-contradictory principle is in reality a matter of knowledge at all.

Mr. J. M. Keynes (*A Treatise on Probability* (1929), p. 263) is among these. '*We* believe', says he, 'that every object in time has a "necessary" connection with some set of objects at a previous time.' But he mentions this belief with a conspicuous absence of fervour. He will not admit that we 'know' the Law of Causation, either on evidence, or as an analytic proposition, or as a 'necessity' which we 'apprehend'. All he will admit is that '*we* believe' it.

Mr. John Wisdom (*Problems of Mind and Matter* (1934), pp. 110 seqq.) is another believer. He says that there is something called 'the Law of Causation', to the effect that 'everything which happens is due to something else which caused it to happen', or as he alternatively puts it, 'due to something else which happened before'. He seems aware that Laodiceans like Mr. Keynes exist; but he shouts them down, exclaiming that we all know there is such a law, though he admits that it cannot be demonstrated or otherwise justified. But, he protests, demonstration is unnecessary. 'I do not know *how* we know that things are as they are because they were as they were. But *we* do know it.'

According to Mr. A. J. Ayer (*Language Truth and Logic* (1936), p. 57) '*we* adopt' the view 'that every assertion of a particular causal connection involves the assertion of a causal law, and that every general proposition of the form "C causes E" is equivalent to a proposition of the form "whenever C, then E", where the symbol "whenever" must be taken to refer, not to a finite number of actual instances of C, but to the infinite number of possible instances'. Here the one-one relation is plain; and his subsequent discussion makes it equally plain that C and E stand for events happening in that order.

All these writers, it will be seen, attach themselves to some group or society of persons to whom they refer as 'we'. I have ventured to italicize the word in my quotations. What is this group or society? It is the group or society of persons who accept the Kantian definition of the term 'cause'. They are not, and do not include, contemporary natural scientists: for these, or at any rate those among them who are physicists, have abandoned the term. Nor do they include such philosophers as have, like Whitehead and Russell, understood and accepted the work which these physicists are doing.

They are a group of neo-Kantians whose reverence

for the master has induced them to accept not indeed all his doctrines but this particular doctrine. I say this because, the doctrine being a self-contradictory one, it can hardly have commended itself to them by its inherent reasonableness; nor can they have had for accepting it the same reason which I suppose Kant to have had, namely the fact that, self-contradictory or not, it was actually presupposed by contemporary physicists. It has somehow got itself fixed in their minds; presumably from their study of Kant. To quote the bitter words of Earl Russell: 'The law of causality, I believe, like much that passes muster among philosophers, is a relic of a bygone age, surviving, like the monarchy, only because it is erroneously supposed to do no harm' (op. cit., p. 180).

The harm it does, or the harm of which it is symptomatic, is that they are a group of reactionary thinkers, wedded to the errors of the past, enemies of modern science, and obstructors of all progress whether in metaphysics or in science, natural or historical.

The sciences, both natural and historical, are at present in a flourishing condition. By means of heroic efforts they have succeeded in disentangling themselves from the fallacies of method that vitiated much of their apparent progress in the nineteenth century. Their prospects of advance along the lines upon which they have now established themselves are incalculable. Internally, they have nothing to fear. The only dangers that now beset them are external. These external dangers reduce themselves on analysis to one: the irrationalist movement of which something was said in Chapter XIII.

This movement may impede the advancement of science (and the advancement of science and the existence of science, I repeat, are not two things but one) in two different ways. Politically, by creating in the body politic a demand that scientific thinking should be put down by force. There are places where this is already happening. Academically, by creating in the specialized organs through which society endeavours to further science and learning a feeling of hostility to that furtherance. This feeling of hostility to science as such may be 'rationalized' through an obscurantist philosophy which by sophistical arguments pretends to prove that the advances which are actually being made are in fact no advances. Sophistical, because reactionary: based on the assumption that the superseded views are true, and thence proceeding to argue that the views which have superseded them must be false because they do not agree with the views they have superseded. The partisans of such an obscurantist philosophy are traitors to their academic calling. Within the body of persons ostensibly devoted to the advancement of science and learning they are working, unconsciously perhaps but still working, to obstruct that advancement and weaken the resistance with which that body is bound in honour to confront the onslaughts of irrationalism.

I attribute no such conscious motives to the writers I have quoted. Fighting on the side of irrationalism they certainly are; but not, I will believe, from malice

towards reason. What has led them blindly into the
ranks of that army has been a misunderstanding as
to the nature of the issues they have discussed.
These issues are metaphysical. If so many philosophers have turned traitor to their calling, it is
because they have failed to distinguish metaphysics
from pseudo-metaphysics. The conversion of metaphysical questions into pseudo-metaphysical questions, as I explained in Chapter VIII, necessarily
turns metaphysicians into anti-metaphysicians of the
reactionary type. Since metaphysics is an indispensable condition of science an enemy to metaphysics is an enemy to science, and a reactionary
anti-metaphysician is an enemy to whatever in science
is progressive. Trying with a clumsy hand to put
back the clock of scientific progress, he stops it.

This is my reason for offering to the public what
might seem essentially an academic essay, suitable
only for readers who are already, like myself, committed to an interest in metaphysics. The fate of
European science and European civilization is at
stake. The gravity of the peril lies especially in the
fact that so few recognize any peril to exist. When
Rome was in danger, it was the cackling of the sacred
geese that saved the Capitol. I am only a professorial
goose, consecrated with a cap and gown and fed at a
college table; but cackling is my job, and cackle I will.

INDEX